Workbook II

ATHENAZE

An Introduction to Ancient Greek

SECOND EDITION

Gilbert Lawall

James F. Johnson

Cynthia King

New York   Oxford
OXFORD UNIVERSITY PRESS
2004

Oxford University Press

Oxford   New York
Auckland Bangkok Buenos Aires Cape Town Chennai
Dar es Salaam Delhi Hong Kong Istanbul Karachi Kolkata
Kuala Lumpur Madrid Melbourne Mexico City Mumbai
Nairobi São Paulo Shanghai Taipei Tokyo Toronto

Published by Oxford University Press, Inc.
198 Madison Avenue, New York, New York, 10016
www.oup.com

ISBN: 0–19–514955–6

Printing number: 9 8 7 6 5 4 3 2 1

Printed in the United States of America
on acid-free paper

PREFACE

The authors are grateful to the following for proofreading the manuscript for this book: Elizabeth Baer of the Berkshire Country Day School, Lenox, Massachusetts; Maurice Balme of York, England; and Kolbeinn Sæmundsson of the Menntaskólinn í Reykjavík, Iceland.

Gilbert Lawall
James Johnson
Cynthia King

CONTENTS

INTRODUCTION

To Students Using This Workbook:

This Workbook accompanies Book II of *Athenaze: An Introduction to Ancient Greek*, Second Edition. It provides exercises covering all the grammar sections, all the vocabulary lists, and all the lists of principal parts in the chapters of the textbook. It also provides periodic cumulative vocabulary lists arranged by parts of speech, covering chapters 17–20, 21–24, 25–28, and 29–30. Also included, at the end, is supplementary grammatical material, most of it designed for review and consolidation and some of it containing material not covered in the textbook. The topics here may be studied anytime and in any order, but some of the related exercises are marked for use after certain chapters of the textbook.

In order to help build your reading skills, we include in each chapter of the Workbook unadapted passages from *The Tablet of Cebes,* a text dating probably from the first century A.D., which has a charming "live" description of a picture on a tablet (*tabula* in Latin, πίναξ in Greek) dedicated in a sanctuary of Kronos many years before the unspecified date of the dialogue. An old man present in the sanctuary offers to explain the picture to some out-of-town visitors, one of whom is the narrator of the piece. The picture is an allegory of Life and shows the difficult path an individual must take to reach True Education and Happiness and leave behind Vices and False Education. In its basic form the allegory is reminiscent of the tale told by Socrates' contemporary, the sophist Prodicus of Ceos, of the choice that Heracles had to make between Virtue and Vice (see Xenophon, *Memorabilia* 2.1.21–34). *The Tablet of Cebes* was attributed in antiquity to Cebes of Thebes, who was a friend of Socrates. Most now believe, however, that this Cebes could not have been the author of the work as we have it, which refers to the followers of Aristotle and contains features of the Koine Greek used in New Testament times. It may, in fact, be that Cebes is not to be thought of as the author of the work at all but rather as the author of the allegorical tale represented on the tablet, the work itself being anonymous; it is the tablet that is Cebes' and not the work as we have it. Scholars have noted elements of various philosophical, religious, and mystical traditions in the allegory as it develops in the description of the pictures on the tablet and have seen the description as representative of the syncretistic cultural world of the first century A.D. There was something in the work for people of nearly all persuasions, and at the same time it possesses a certain enigmatic quality: what is "True Education" and what is "Happiness"? For these very reasons it was widely read in late antiquity, the Renaissance, and early modern times and still retains remarkable appeal and relevance to all those contemplating the paths available for them to follow in the life that lies before them.

As Greek readings in this workbook we offer thirty-two of the forty-three chapters into which the *Tablet* is divided in modern editions. The remainder of the surviving Greek text of the *Tablet* (Chapters XXXIII–XLI) is given in English translation at the very end of this workbook. We do not include the last two chapters of the *Tablet*, which are preserved only in an Arabic paraphrase of the original Greek and in a Latin translation of the Arabic paraphrase.

Those wishing more information on *The Tablet of Cebes* will find much of interest in a thorough restudy of the text by John T. Fitzgerald and L. Michael White, *The Tabula of Cebes,* Society of Biblical Literature, Texts and Translations 24, Graeco-Roman Religion Series 7: Scholars Press, 1983.

All words in the reading passages that have not occurred in chapter vocabulary lists prior to the reading are glossed on the facing pages. These glosses include words that have been used in the stories in the textbook and are glossed there because they have not occurred in vocabulary lists. Even for subsequent chapters of the *Tablet* in this book we continue to gloss words that have not occurred in the vocabulary lists in *Athenaze*, even though they have been glossed earlier in the Cebes passages. You will therefore be familiar with many of the words that are glossed in the readings in this book. Our aim has been to include as much help as needed to enable rapid comprehension and translation of the readings. We recommend that you read through the glosses on the facing pages before reading the Greek passage itself. Remember that if you find words in the readings that are not glossed and for which you do not recall the meanings, you can find the words in the Greek to English Vocabulary at the end of the textbook.

Answers for all the exercises and translations of all the readings are given in the Answer Key at the back of this book, so that you can check all your answers and translations. You can write your answers in the slots provided in each exercise, and you can write translations of the readings on separate sheets of paper. Some of you will prefer, however, to write answers to the exercises on separate sheets of paper rather than in the workbook itself. This will allow you to use the exercises more than once. We would, in fact, recommend that you use these exercises several times—first after completing the work in the textbook for each half of a chapter, then as review prior to quizzes on chapters or groups of chapters, then as review prior to tests such as midterms, and finally as review prior to the final examination. If you do not write in the book, you will find yourself freshly challenged each time you use these exercises for review.

When using the cumulative vocabulary lists, we recommend that you cut a small notch in a piece of paper and cover the column of English equivalents and test your knowledge of the Greek word before moving your notched paper down to reveal the English. Do this in reverse to test your knowledge of the vocabulary from English to Greek.

We hope that you will find the material in this book useful and the readings from *The Tablet of Cebes* interesting. Always be honest with yourself; do not use the Answer Key until you have completed the exercises. Don't cheat on yourself; use the Answer Key to check yourself; use it as a learning tool; use it to your benefit!

17
Η ΕΠΙΔΑΥΡΟΣ (α)

Exercise 17a

*Translate the English phrases with the correct form (aorist or future passive)
of the Greek verbs supplied. If there is more than one spelling of a form, you
need give only one:*

1. λαμβάνω: he/she/it was taken _____
   λαμβάνω: he/she/it will be taken _____
2. λαμβάνω: we were taken _____
   λαμβάνω: we will be taken _____
3. λαμβάνω: they were taken _____
   λαμβάνω: they will be taken _____
4. φιλέω: you (sing.) were loved _____
   φιλέω: you (sing.) will be loved _____
5. φιλέω: we were loved _____
   φιλέω: we will be loved _____
6. φιλέω: you (pl.) were loved _____
   φιλέω: you (pl.) will be loved _____
7. τῑμάω: they were honored _____
   τῑμάω: they will be honored _____
8. τῑμάω: he/she was honored _____
   τῑμάω: he/she will be honored _____
9. τῑμάω: I was honored _____
   τῑμάω: I will be honored _____
10. δηλόω: I was shown _____
    δηλόω: I will be shown _____
11. δηλόω: you (sing.) were shown _____
    δηλόω: you (sing.) will be shown _____
12. δηλόω: to be shown _____
    δηλόω: to be about to be shown _____

1

Exercise 17β

*Complete the following sentences with an aorist passive participle of the verb
supplied. Make it agree with the underlined word or phrase:*

1. <u>ἡ ναῦς</u> _____ διὰ τῶν κυμάτων ταχέως ἔπλει. (λύω)

2. <u>ἡ γυνὴ</u> ὑπὸ τοῦ ἀνδρὸς _____ ὀλβίᾱ (*happy*) ἐστίν. (φιλέω)

3. <u>τὸ ἀργύριον τὸ εἰς τὸν οἶκον</u> _____ οὐ πάρεστιν. (λαμβάνω)

4. <u>οἱ ἄνδρες οἱ ἐν τῇ πόλει</u> _____ οἴκαδε ἐπανῆλθον. (τῑμάω)

5. ἡδέως δεχόμεθα <u>τὸ ἀληθὲς τὸ ἡμῖν</u> _____. (δηλόω)

Exercise 17γ

*Transform the following verbs to the aorist passive and future passive, keep-
ing the same person and number. If there is more than one spelling of a
form, you need give only one:*

		Aorist Passive	Future Passive
1.	πέμπει	_____	_____
2.	φυλάττεις	_____	_____
3.	ψεύδομεν	_____	_____
4.	πεῖθε	_____	
5.	γιγνώσκουσι(ν)	_____	_____
6.	κελεύετε (indic.)	_____	_____
7.	βάλλω	_____	_____
8.	ἐλαύνω	_____	_____
9.	εὑρίσκεις	_____	_____
10.	ὁρῶσιν	_____	_____

Exercise 17δ

Give an English equivalent of:

1. ἀφικνέομαι _____
2. κάθημαι _____
3. πρότερον _____
4. ἕπομαι _____
5. τυγχάνω
   καθήμενος _____

6. γιγνώσκω _____
7. ποῖ; _____
8. ἐμαυτὴν αἴρω _____
9. σύν _____

Exercise 17ε

Give the Greek equivalent of:

1. I indeed   _____
2. I am distant   _____
3. God willing   _____
4. I bind   _____
5. whether . . . or _____

6. I lift   _____
7. I know   _____
8. I sail   _____
9. I hit upon   _____

Exercise 17ζ*

Give the remaining principal parts of:

1. αἴρω   _____
                  _____
                  _____
                  _____

2. ἀπέχω   _____
                  _____

3. ἀφικνέομαι   _____
                  _____
                  _____

4. γιγνώσκω   _____
                  _____
                  _____
                  _____
                  _____

5. δέω   _____
                  _____
                  _____
                  _____
                  _____

6. ἕπομαι   _____
                  _____

7. πλέω   _____
                  _____
                  _____

8. τυγχάνω   _____
                  _____

9. λύω   _____
                  _____

10. δακρύω   _____
                  _____
                  _____

11. παύω   _____
                  _____

* This and similar exercises draw on the verbs in the vocabulary lists in the textbook and on the lists of verbs with their principal parts following the reading passages in the textbook.

Note:

Since you are about in the middle of your study of Greek grammar, you will encounter some forms in these reading passages that have not yet been formally presented in the chapters of your textbook. Some of these will, however, be familiar to you from the overview of the Greek verb in the Introduction to Book II. In any case, we always gloss forms that you have not yet studied and provide an immediate translation. Then we give references to the chapter, grammar section, and page number where these forms are presented. You are not expected to track down each of these references; the translations provided will suffice. For the curious and for later review, however, we do provide the references. Our purpose is to make these passages as accessible as possible as you progress in your learning of Greek grammar.

Κέβης, Κέβητος, ὁ, *Cebes*.
πίναξ, πίνακος, ὁ, *votive tablet; picture*.

1   περιπατέω, *I walk about*.
    Κρόνος, Κρόνου, ὁ, *Cronus* (king of the Titans, ruler during the golden age, and father of Zeus; associated with χρόνος, *time;* identified by the Romans with their god Saturn).
    ἱερῷ: here, *sanctuary*.
2   ἀνάθημα, ἀναθήματος, τό [ἀνατίθημι, *I set up, erect*], *object that one sets up in a temple, votive offering, temple offering* (dedicated in thanks for a victory or for deliverance from some illness or misfortune; for τίθημι, see Ch. 18, Gr. 2, pp. 29–31, and Ch. 30δ PP, p. 270).
    ἀνάκειμαι [used as passive of ἀνατίθημι], *I am set up; I am dedicated* (see κεῖμαι, Ch. 16, Gr. 2, p. 277).
    ἔμπροσθεν, prep. + gen., *in front of*.
    νεώς, νεώ, ὁ, *temple* (this word is in the Attic 2nd declension, as is λαγώς, λαγώ, ὁ, *hare;* see *Athenaze* II, p. 278).
3   γραφή, γραφῆς, ἡ, *inscription; painting, picture*.
    ξένος, ξένη, ξένον, *foreign; strange*.
    ἴδιος, ἰδίᾱ, ἴδιον, *peculiar*.
    ἠδυνάμεθα: imperfect of δύναμαι, here with double augment; for the usual forms, see Ch. 16, Gr. 2, pp. 276–277.
    συμβάλλω [συν- + βάλλω], *I gather together; I conjecture; I figure out*.
      συμβαλεῖν: aorist (not future) infinitive, introducing an indirect question.
    τίνες καί ποτε ἦσαν: καί emphasizes ποτε; translate *what in the world they were*.
4   τὸ γεγραμμένον: *the thing painted, the representation* (subject, since it has the definite article).
      γεγραμμένον: perfect passive participle from γράφω; see Ch. 27, Gr. 1, pp. 183–184; the perfect system is previewed in the Introduction to *Athenaze* II; note the charts on pp. xvi and xvii.
    στρατόπεδον, στρατοπέδου, τό, *military camp*.
5   περίβολος, περιβόλου, ὁ, *enclosure*.
    αὐτῷ: = ἑαυτῷ.
    ἕτερος, ἑτέρᾱ, ἕτερον, *one* or *the other* (of two); *other, another*.
    μείζω: = μείζονα (see Ch. 24, Gr. 5, p. 135).

Exercise 17η

Translate into English on a separate sheet of paper:

ΚΕΒΗΤΟΣ ΠΙΝΑΞ

the votive tablet of Cebes

I.

ἐτυγχάνομεν περιπατοῦντες ἐν τῷ τοῦ Κρόνου ἱερῷ, ἐν ᾧ πολλὰ μὲν καὶ ἄλλα 1
ἀναθήματα ἐθεωροῦμεν· ἀνέκειτο δὲ καὶ πίναξ τις ἔμπροσθεν τοῦ νεώ, ἐν ᾧ ἦν 2
γραφὴ ξένη τις καὶ μύθους ἔχουσα ἰδίους, οὓς οὐκ ἠδυνάμεθα συμβαλεῖν τίνες καί 3
ποτε ἦσαν. οὔτε γὰρ πόλις ἐδόκει ἡμῖν εἶναι τὸ γεγραμμένον οὔτε στρατόπεδον, 4
ἀλλὰ περίβολος ἦν ἐν αὐτῷ ἔχων ἑτέρους περιβόλους δύο, τὸν μὲν μείζω, τὸν δὲ 5
ἐλάττω. ἦν δὲ καὶ πύλη ἐπὶ τοῦ πρώτου περιβόλου. πρὸς δὲ τῇ πύλῃ ὄχλος ἐδόκει 6
ἡμῖν πολὺς ἐφεστάναι, καὶ ἔνδον δὲ ἐν τῷ περιβόλῳ πλῆθός τι γυναικῶν ἑωρᾶτο. 7
ἐπὶ δὲ τοῦ πυλῶνος γέρων τις ἑστὼς ἔμφασιν ἐποίει ὡς προστάττων τι τῷ εἰσιόντι 8
ὄχλῳ. 9

---

6   **ἐλάττω:** = ἐλάττονα (see Ch. 24, Gr. 5, p. 135).
   ἐπί, prep. + gen., *in*.
   ὄχλος, ὄχλου, ὁ, *crowd*.
7   **ἐφεστάναι:** *to stand at/near* (2nd perfect active infinitive from ἐφίσταμαι [ἐπί- + ἵσταμαι], *I stand at/near;* for ἵσταμαι, see Ch. 19, Gr. 3, p. 50; the perfect tense of this verb has a present sense).
   καὶ ... δὲ: *and also*.
   ἔνδον, adv., *within, inside*.
   ἑωρᾶτο: *was seen* (imperfect passive of ὁράω, *I see*, with double augment). There is no prepositional phrase expressing the agent, but *by us* is to be understood.
8   **πυλών, πυλῶνος, ὁ,** *gateway*.
   ἑστώς: *standing* (2nd perfect active participle, nominative singular masculine, of ἵσταμαι, *I stand;* for the declension of the perfect active participle, see Ch. 28, Gr. 2, p. 208; again, the perfect tense of this verb has a present sense).
   ἔμφασις, ἐμφάσεως, ἡ, *appearance, impression*.
   ὡς: *as [if]*.
   προστάττω, *I command, give an order*.
   τι: *something*, object of προστάττων.
   εἰσιόντι: dative singular participle (see εἰσέρχομαι; Ch. 10, Gr. 6, pp. 168–169).

I

We happened to be walking around in Cronus' sanctuary in which we were looking at many other votive offerings, and someone had set up a certain offering in front of the temple. On it was a certain strange inscription, strange and having peculiar stories which we were not able to figure out what in the world they were. For the representation seemed to us to be neither the city nor the military camp, but it was an enclosure having within itself two enclosures, one bigger the other smaller. And there was a gate in the first enclosure. And near the gate there seemed to us a crowd and also within the enclosure a number of women was seen. In the gateway an old man was standing. It made the impression as if commanding the entering crowd.

(β)

Exercise 17θ

Translate the English phrases with the correct form (aorist or future passive)
of the Greek verbs supplied (N.B. ἐγγράφω [ἐν- + γράφω], I enroll X):

1. ἐγγράφω: we were enrolled   _____
    ἐγγράφω: we will be enrolled   _____
2. ἐγγράφω: they were enrolled   _____
    ἐγγράφω: they will be enrolled   _____
3. ἐγγράφω: be enrolled! (sing.)   _____
4. διαφθείρω: it was destroyed   _____
    διαφθείρω: it will be destroyed   _____
5. διαφθείρω: to be destroyed   _____
    διαφθείρω: to be about to be destroyed _____
6. διαφθείρω: I was destroyed   _____
    διαφθείρω: I will be destroyed   _____
7. διαφθείρω: you (pl.) were destroyed _____
    διαφθείρω: you (pl.) will be destroyed _____

Exercise 17ι

Give the aorist of the following verbs, keeping the same person and number:

1. δύναμαι   _____   5. βούλει   _____
2. χαίρουσι(ν)   _____   6. ἐπιστάμενος   _____
3. ὀργίζεται   _____   7. ἐπίστασθαι   _____
4. πορεύεσθε (indic.) _____ 8. διαλεγόμεθα   _____

                                                        or _____

Exercise 17κ

Give an English equivalent of:

1. θάρρει   _____   6. πως   _____
2. ὁ ἱκέτης   _____   7. φρονέω   _____
3. ὅσιος   _____   8. ὁ ὑπηρέτης   _____
4. τὸ τέμενος   _____   9. ἐπιτρέπω   _____
5. οὐ διὰ πολλοῦ   _____

Exercise 17λ

Give the Greek equivalent of:

1. custom _____   6. according to _____
2. clean _____   7. it is necessary _____
3. late _____   8. I am confident _____
4. I heal _____   9. holy _____
5. soul _____   or _____

Exercise 17μ

Give the remaining principal parts of:

1. ἀκέομαι _____   4. κελεύω _____
                                              _____
2. ἐπιτρέπω _____   _____
                _____   _____
                _____
                _____   5. πορεύομαι _____
                _____   _____
3. πιστεύω _____   _____
                _____
                _____
                _____
                _____

1   ἀπορούντων . . . ἡμῶν . . . πρὸς ἀλλήλους: *while we were at a loss to one*
     another = *while we were puzzling among ourselves* (for the genitive absolute,
     see Ch. 19, Gr. 1, pp. 38–39).
     μῡθολογίᾱ, μῡθολογίᾱς, ἡ, *story-telling; story's meaning.*

2   πρεσβύτης, πρεσβύτου, ὁ, *old man.*
     παρεστώς: *standing nearby* (2nd perfect active participle, nominative singular
     masculine, of παρίσταμαι, *I stand nearby;* the perfect tense of this verb has a
     present sense).
     δεινὸν: in addition to *terrible,* this adjective may mean *strange.*

3   γραφή, γραφῆς, ἡ, *inscription; painting, picture.*
     ἐπιχώριοι, ἐπιχωρίων, οἱ, *natives.*
     οἴδᾱσι: = ἴσᾱσι, *(they) know* (introducing an indirect question; 3rd person plural of
     οἶδα, *I know;* see Ch. 28, Gr. 9, pp. 219–220).

4   δύναται: by itself the verb δύναμαι can mean *I mean / signify,* as well as *I am*
     able.
     πολῑτικός, πολῑτική, πολῑτικόν, *pertaining to the city, local.*
     ἀνάθημα, ἀναθήματος, τό, *object that one sets up in a temple, votive offering,*
     temple offering.
     πάλαι, adv., *long ago.*

5   ἔμφρων, ἔμφρον, *in possession of one's wits; sensible; intelligent.*
     δεινὸς: here, *skilled.*
     περί, prep. + acc., *with regard to.*
     σοφίᾱ, σοφίᾱς, ἡ, *wisdom.*
     Πῡθαγόρειος, Πῡθαγορείᾱ, Πῡθαγόρειον, *Pythagorean.*

6   Παρμενίδειος, Παρμενιδείᾱ, Παρμενίδειον, *Parmenidean* (Pythagoras,
     late sixth century B.C., and Parmenides, first half of the fifth century B.C., were
     pre-Socratic philosophers).
     ἐζηλωκὼς: *having pursued, pursuing* (perfect active participle, nominative
     singular masculine, of ζηλόω, *I emulate, copy; I pursue eagerly;* translate the
     perfect participle here as present).

7   ἀνέθηκε: *set up* (aorist active indicative, 3rd singular, of ἀνατίθημι, *I set up, erect;*
     see Ch. 18, Gr. 2, p. 30).

8   πότερον: merely introducing a question; do not translate.
     ἔφην: *I said* (imperfect of φημί).
     αὐτὸν: intensive in the predicate position (see Ch. 5, Gr. 9, pp. 68–69).
     γινώσκεις: after the time of Aristotle the word γιγνώσκω was spelled γινώσκω.
     ἑωρακώς: *having seen* (perfect active participle, nominative singular masculine, of
     ὁράω; note the double augment; see Ch. 29 α PP, p. 232).

9   καὶ ἐθαύμασα: *[Yes,] and I. . . .*
     πολυχρόνιος, πολυχρόνιον, *full of much time; very old.*
     νέος, νέᾱ, νέον, *young.*

10   σπουδαῖος, σπουδαίᾱ, σπουδαῖον, *serious, weighty.*
     διελέγετο: *he was discussing.*

11   ἠκηκόειν: *I had heard; I heard* = ἠκηκόη (pluperfect, 1st person singular, of
     ἀκούω; for the so-called Attic reduplication, see Ch. 29 β PP, p. 235; for the
     regular formation of the pluperfect active, see Ch. 28, Gr. 6, p. 210; Hellenistic
     Greek uses -ει- throughout the paradigm in place of the η/ ει/ ε shown there).
     διεξέρχομαι [δια- + ἐκ- + ἔρχομαι], *I go through; I explain.*
     διεξιόντος: genitive singular masculine participle (see Ch. 10, Gr. 6, pp. 168–
     169) agreeing with αὐτοῦ, the object of ἠκηκόειν.

Exercise 17v

Translate into English on a separate sheet of paper:

ΚΕΒΗΤΟΣ ΠΙΝΑΞ

II.

ἀπορούντων οὖν ἡμῶν περὶ τῆς μυθολογίᾱς πρὸς ἀλλήλους πολὺν χρόνον,   1
πρεσβύτης τις παρεστώς, "οὐδὲν δεινὸν πάσχετε, ὦ ξένοι," ἔφη, "ἀποροῦντες περὶ   2
τῆς γραφῆς ταύτης. οὐδὲ γὰρ τῶν ἐπιχωρίων πολλοὶ οἴδᾱσι τί ποτε αὕτη ἡ   3
μῡθολογίᾱ δύναται· οὐδὲ γάρ ἐστι πολῑτικὸν ἀνάθημα· ἀλλὰ ξένος τις πάλαι ποτὲ   4
ἀφίκετο δεῦρο, ἀνὴρ ἔμφρων καὶ δεινὸς περὶ σοφίᾱν, λόγῳ τε καὶ ἔργῳ Πῡθαγόρειόν   5
τινα καὶ Παρμενίδειον ἐζηλωκὼς βίον, ὃς τό τε ἱερὸν τοῦτο καὶ τὴν γραφὴν   6
ἀνέθηκε τῷ Κρόνῳ."   7

Ξένος "πότερον οὖν," ἔφην ἐγώ, "καὶ αὐτὸν τὸν ἄνδρα γινώσκεις ἑωρᾱκώς;"   8

Πρεσβύτης "καὶ ἐθαύμασά γε," ἔφη, "αὐτὸν πολυχρονιώτατον νεώτερος ὤν.   9
πολλὰ γὰρ καὶ σπουδαῖα διελέγετο. τότε δὴ καὶ περὶ ταύτης τῆς μῡθολογίᾱς   10
πολλάκις αὐτοῦ ἠκηκόειν διεξιόντος."   11

The tablet of Cebes II.   for a long time

So while we were puzzling among ourselves what was the story's meaning, a certain old man standing nearby said "You suffer nothing strange, strangers, being at a loss to this inscription. For not many of the natives know what this story's meaning signifies; for none of the votive offering is local: but long ago a certain stranger arrived here once an intelligent man and skilled with regards to wisdom having pursued both in word and indeed the pythagorian and parmenidean life. who dedicated to Kronos both the temple and the picture.

Stranger: I said "So do you know the man himself having seen him?"

Old man: and he said "yes and I admired him since he was an old man and being very young myself. For he was discussing many serious things. And at that very time I heard him explaining to go about this story telling many times."

18
Ο ΑΣΚΛΗΠΙΟΣ (α)

Exercise 18α

Translate the English phrases with the correct active form of δίδωμι:

1. you (sing.) give _____
2. they were giving _____
3. you (pl.) were giving _____
4. he/she gave _____
5. they will give _____
6. you (pl.) gave _____
7. I was giving _____
8. they give _____
9. to be giving _____
10. you (sing.) will give _____
11. give! (sing., present) _____
12. (ἡ γυνὴ) giving _____
13. (ὁ ἄνθρωπος) having given _____
14. give! (pl., aorist) _____
15. to give (aorist) _____

Exercise 18β

Transform from active to middle voice, keeping the same person and number or case, gender, and number:

1. δώσω _____
2. δίδωσι(ν) _____
3. δόντι _____
4. διδόναι _____
5. ἔδωκας _____
6. δοῦναι _____
7. διδόντος _____
8. δίδως _____
9. ἔδωκα _____
10. ἐδίδου _____
11. ἐδίδοσαν _____
12. ἐδίδουν _____
13. δώσειν _____
14. ἐδίδομεν _____
15. δότε _____
16. δίδοτε (imper.) _____

Exercise 18γ

Fill in the correct aorist or future passive form of δίδωμι in the blank provided:

1. ὁ σῖτος τῷ ξένῳ ὑπὸ τῆς παρθένου χθὲς (*yesterday*) _____ .

2. ὁ οἶνος τῷ ξένῳ ὑπὸ τοῦ αὐτουργοῦ αὔριον _____ .

3. οἱ ἀστράγαλοι τῷ ἱερεῖ ὑπὸ τοῦ παιδὸς αὔριον _____ .

4. οἱ ἀστράγαλοι τῷ ἱερεῖ ὑπὸ τοῦ παιδὸς χθὲς _____ .

Exercise 18δ

Give an English equivalent of:

1. δῆλόν ἐστι(ν) _____
2. τίθημι _____
3. ἡ χάρις _____
4. σεμνός _____

5. ὑπέρ + acc. _____
6. περί + gen. _____
7. γελάω _____

Exercise 18ε

Give the Greek equivalent of:

1. I thank _____
2. kindly _____
3. I give _____
4. sleep _____

5. I move _____
6. clear _____
7. over _____

Exercise 18ζ

Give the remaining principal parts of:

1. γελάω _____
   _____

2. δίδωμι _____
   _____
   _____
   _____

3. τίθημι _____
   _____
   _____

4. φιλέω _____
   _____
   _____
   _____

5. δοκέω _____
   _____

6. καλέω _____
   _____
   _____
   _____

7. πλέω _____
   or _____
   _____

8. σκοπέω _____
   _____
   _____

Continued on next page

9. κῑνέω   _____
                                  _____
                                  _____
                                  _____
                                  _____

1   πρὸς Διός: *by Zeus!*
    τοίνυν [τοι + νυν], particle, *therefore, accordingly;* in dialogue, to introduce an
        answer, *well then.*
    εἰ μή: *if not, unless.*
    ἀσχολίᾱ, ἀσχολίᾱς, ἡ [ἀ- + σχολή, σχολῆς, ἡ, *leisure*], *lack of leisure;*
        business.
2   διηγέομαι, *I describe.*
        διήγησαι: aorist middle imperative, 2nd person singular.
    πάνυ, adv., *very, very much.*
    ἐπιθῡμέω + infin., *I desire* (to).
3   φθόνος, φθόνου, ὁ, *ill-will; envy; grudging.*
        οὐδεὶς φθόνος: supply ἐστί and translate *there is no problem.*
    τουτῑ̀: = τοῦτο plus a long *iota* (-ῑ, a deictic [cf. δείκνῡμι, *I show, point out*] suffix
        added for emphasis; the suffix gets the accent and causes the *omicron* to be
        elided because it is short; this long accented *iota* can be added to any form of a
        demonstrative pronoun to make it more emphatic).
4   ἐπικίνδῡνος, ἐπικίνδῡνον, *connected with danger, dangerous.*
    ἐξήγησις, ἐξηγήσεως, ἡ, *explanation.*
5   οἷος, οἵᾱ, οἷον, *such as.*
6   ὅτι: [*Just this,*] *that.* . . .
    προσέχω, *I direct; I apply.*
        προσέχω (+ τὸν νοῦν, stated or implied), *I pay attention to.*
    συνῑ́ημι, συνήσω, *I understand* (for the forms of the uncompounded verb, ῑ́ημι,
        see Ch. 20, Gr. 2, p. 64–66).
            προσέξετε . . . συνήσετε: in the if-clause; ἔσεσθε (7) in the main
                clause; for the future minatory condition, see Ch. 26, Gr. 1a, p. 163.
    φρόνιμος, φρόνιμον, *in one's right mind, wise, prudent.*
7   εὐδαίμων, εὔδαιμον [= with a good δαίμων, *spirit, fate, lot*], *fortunate, happy.*
    ἄφρων, ἄφρον, *mindless, foolish.*
    κακοδαίμων, κακόδαιμον: the opposite of εὐδαίμων.
    πικρός, πικρά, πικρόν, *bitter; embittered; spiteful; mean.*
    ἀμαθής, ἀμαθές, *stupid; ignorant.*
8   βιόω, βιώσομαι, *I live.*
    ἐοικώς, ἐοικυῖα, ἐοικός + dat., *like, similar* (to).
    Σφίγξ, Σφιγγός, ἡ, *Sphinx* (mythical Theban monster with a human head and
        the body of a lion; it destroyed those who could not answer its riddle; Oedipus,
        made famous by Sophocles and Freud, answered it).
9   αἴνιγμα, αἰνίγματος, τό, *riddle, enigma.*
    προβάλλω, *I throw before;* middle, *I propose.*
    συνῑ́ει, *understood* (imperfect, 3rd person singular, active, of συνῑ́ημι,
        I understand).
10 ἀπόλλῡμι, ἀπολῶ, sigmatic 1st aorist, ἀπώλεσα, thematic 2nd aorist middle,
        ἀπωλόμην, *I destroy; I kill;* middle, *I perish; I die.*
    ὑπὸ τῆς Σφιγγός: *at the hands of.* . . .

Exercise 18η

Translate into English on a separate sheet of paper:

ΚΕΒΗΤΟΣ ΠΙΝΑΞ

III.

    Ξένος "πρὸς Διὸς τοίνυν," ἔφην ἐγώ, "εἰ μή τίς σοι μεγάλη ἀσχολίᾱ τυγχάνει   1
οὖσα, διήγησαι ἡμῖν· πάνυ γὰρ ἐπιθῡμοῦμεν ἀκοῦσαι τί ποτέ ἐστιν ὁ μῦθος."   2

    Πρεσβύτης "οὐδεὶς φθόνος, ὦ ξένοι," ἔφη. "ἀλλὰ τουτὶ πρῶτον δεῖ ὑμᾶς   3
ἀκοῦσαι, ὅτι ἐπικίνδῡνόν τι ἔχει ἡ ἐξήγησις."   4

    Ξένος "οἷον τί;" ἔφην ἐγώ.   5

    Πρεσβύτης "ὅτι, εἰ μὲν προσέξετε," ἔφη, "καὶ συνήσετε τὰ λεγόμενα, φρόνιμοι   6
καὶ εὐδαίμονες ἔσεσθε, εἰ δὲ μή, ἄφρονες καὶ κακοδαίμονες καὶ πικροὶ καὶ ἀμαθεῖς   7
γενόμενοι κακῶς βιώσεσθε. ἔστι γὰρ ἡ ἐξήγησις ἐοικυῖα τῷ τῆς Σφιγγὸς   8
αἰνίγματι, ὃ ἐκείνη προεβάλλετο τοῖς ἀνθρώποις. εἰ μὲν οὖν αὐτὸ συνίει τις, ἐσῴ-   9
ζετο, εἰ δὲ μὴ συνῑ́ει, ἀπώλετο ὑπὸ τῆς Σφιγγός.   10

The πρεσβύτης concludes his remarks in the passage at the end of the chapter.

(β)

Exercise 18θ

Translate the English phrases with the correct active form of τίθημι:

1. we are putting   _____
2. they will put   _____
3. he/she is putting   _____
4. I placed   _____
5. we placed   _____
6. to be putting   _____
7. to be about to put   _____
8. they were putting   _____
9. they are putting   _____
10. I was putting   _____
11. to put (aorist)   _____
12. put! (pl., present)   _____
13. (ἡ γυνὴ) putting   _____
14. (ὁ ἄνθρωπος) having put   _____
15. put! (sing., aorist)   _____

Exercise 18ι

Transform from active to middle voice, keeping the same person and number or case, gender, and number:

1.	τίθει	_____	9.	τίθησι(ν)	_____
2.	ἐτίθει	_____	10.	ἐτίθην	_____
3.	θήσομεν	_____	11.	ἐτίθεις	_____
4.	τιθέναι	_____	12.	θέτε	_____
5.	τιθείσῃ	_____	13.	θείσης	_____
6.	ἔθηκε(ν)	_____	14.	θήσειν	_____
7.	τιθέᾱσι(ν)	_____	15.	ἐτίθετε	_____
8.	ἔθηκα	_____	16.	θεῖναι	_____

Exercise 18κ

Fill in the correct aorist or future passive form of τίθημι in the blank provided:

1. τὸ ἄροτρον ἐπὶ τὴν γῆν ὑπὸ τοῦ δούλου χθὲς (*yesterday*) _____ .

2. τὸ ἄροτρον ἐπὶ τὴν γῆν ὑπὸ τοῦ δούλου αὔριον _____ .

3. αἱ ὑδρίαι ὑπὸ τῶν γυναικῶν εἰς τὴν οἰκίᾱν αὔριον _____ .

4. οἱ ἀστράγαλοι ἐπὶ τὴν γῆν ὑπὸ τῶν παίδων χθὲς _____ .

Exercise 18λ

Give an English equivalent of:

1. ἐπιστρατεύω _____
2. μᾶλλον ἤ _____
3. μέντοι _____
4. τὸ πρᾶγμα _____
5. πάλαι εἰσί(ν) _____
6. ἀνατίθημι _____
7. ὁ ἐχθρός _____
8. πῶς ἔχει τὰ πράγματα; _____

9. ἡ θυσίᾱ _____
10. διά + acc. _____
11. ἁμαρτάνω _____
12. προστρέχω _____
13. οὔκουν _____
14. ἐπί + dat. _____
15. ὀρθῶς γιγνώσκω _____

Exercise 18μ

Give the Greek equivalent of:

1. money _____
2. dearer _____
3. I rule _____
4. I hand over _____
5. because of _____
6. long ago _____
7. because _____
8. What do you think? _____

9. hostile _____
10. I run _____
11. more _____
12. power _____
13. healthy _____
14. for (of price) _____
15. judgment _____

11   ὡσαύτως [ὡς + αὔτως, adv., *in this very manner*], adv., *similarly, in like manner.*
     ὡσαύτως . . . ἔχει: adverbs with ἔχω equal εἰμί, *I am*, plus adjective, thus, *it's the same thing.*
     ἐπί, prep. + gen., *in the case of.*
     ἐξήγησις, ἐξηγήσεως, ἡ, *explanation.*
     ἀφροσύνη, ἀφροσύνης, ἡ, *mindlessness; foolishness.*
     ἡ . . . ἀφροσύνη . . . Σφίγξ ἐστιν (12): in late Greek moralizing texts, the Sphinx was seen as a symbol of human foolishness or folly.
     τοῖς ἀνθρώποις: *for humankind.*
12   αἰνίττομαι [cf. τὸ αἴνιγμα, *riddle, enigma*], *I speak about* X *in riddles; I pose* X *as a riddle.*
          αἰνίττεται: the subject is ἡ . . . ἀφροσύνη (11); human foolishness or folly poses the following questions as riddles.
13   **ταῦτ'**: = ταῦτα.
     ἐάν (εἰ + ἄν) + subjunctive, *if.*
     μὴ συνῐῇ: *does not understand* (present active subjunctive, 3rd person singular of συνίημι, *I understand;* for the subjunctive of the uncompounded verb, see Ch. 21, Gr. 4, p. 86; for the subjunctive mood and its forms, see Ch. 21, Gr. 1–2, pp. 75–77; for ἐάν and the subjunctive in conditional clauses, see Ch. 26, Gr. 1a, p. 163; here the if-clause has a present subjunctive and is headed by ἐάν, and the main clause has a verb in the present indicative, ἀπόλλυται; this is a present general condition).
     ἀπόλλυται: middle, *he perishes.*
     ὑπ' αὐτῆς: i.e., ὑπὸ τῆς ἀφροσύνης.
14   εἰσάπαξ [εἰς + ἅπαξ, *once*], adv., *once; at once.*
     καταβιβρώσκω, καταβρώσομαι, κατέβρων, καταβέβρωκα, καταβέβρωμαι, κατεβρώθην, *I eat up.*
     κατὰ μῑκρὸν: *little by little.*
15   ὅλος, ὅλη, ὅλον, *whole; entire.*
     καταφθείρω, *I destroy.*
     καθάπερ, adv., *just as, as.*
     ἐπί, prep. + dat., *for.*
     τῑμωρίᾱ, τῑμωρίᾱς, ἡ, *vengeance; retribution.*
     παραδιδόμενοι: passive, *handed over.*
16   **γνῷ**: *learns, does learn* (aorist subjunctive active, 3rd person singular, of γιγνώσκω/γινώσκω; for the principal parts of γιγνώσκω, see Ch. 24α PP, p. 134; for its aorist subjunctive, see *Athenaze* II, p. 306.
          ἐὰν . . . γνῷ: the if-clause of another present general condition.
     ἀνάπαλιν, adv., *back again; on the contrary; instead.*
     μακάριος, μακαρίᾱ, μακάριον, *blessed, happy.*

Exercise 18v

Translate into English on a separate sheet of paper:

ΚΕΒΗΤΟΣ ΠΙΝΑΞ

III.

The πρεσβύτης concludes his remarks:

"ὡσαύτως δὲ καὶ ἐπὶ τῆς ἐξηγήσεως ἔχει ταύτης. ἡ γὰρ ἀφροσύνη τοῖς ἀνθρώποις   11
Σφίγξ ἐστιν. αἰνίττεται δὲ τάδε, τί ἀγαθόν, τί κακόν, τί οὔτε ἀγαθὸν οὔτε κακόν   12
ἐστιν ἐν τῷ βίῳ. ταῦτ' οὖν ἐὰν μέν τις μὴ συνῇ, ἀπόλλυται ὑπ' αὐτῆς, οὐκ   13
εἰσάπαξ, ὥσπερ ὁ ὑπὸ τῆς Σφιγγὸς καταβρωθεὶς ἀπέθνῃσκεν, ἀλλὰ κατὰ μῑκρὸν   14
ἐν ὅλῳ τῷ βίῳ καταφθείρεται καθάπερ οἱ ἐπὶ τῑμωρίᾳ παραδιδόμενοι. ἐὰν δέ τις   15
γνῷ, ἀνάπαλιν ἡ μὲν ἀφροσύνη ἀπόλλυται, αὐτὸς δὲ σῴζεται καὶ μακάριος καὶ   16
εὐδαίμων γίνεται ἐν παντὶ τῷ βίῳ. ὑμεῖς οὖν προσέχετε καὶ μὴ παρακούετε."   17

---

17   **εὐδαίμων, εὔδαιμον** [= with a good δαίμων, *spirit, fate, lot*], *fortunate, happy.*
γίνεται: = γίγνεται (after the time of Aristotle the word γίγνομαι was spelled
γίνομαι).
προσέχω, *I direct; I apply.*
προσέχω (+ τὸν νοῦν, stated or implied), *I pay attention to.*
παρακούω [παρα-, *amiss, wrong* + ἀκούω], *I hear wrongly/carelessly; I take no
heed of.*

Exercise 18ξ

Give the remaining principal parts of:

1. ἁμαρτάνω _____   6. θεάομαι _____
   _____   _____
   _____
   _____   7. χράομαι _____
   _____   _____

2. τρέχω _____
   _____   8. γελάω _____
   _____   _____

3. τῑμάω _____
   _____   _____
   _____   9. δηλόω _____
   _____   _____

4. πειράω _____
   _____   _____
   _____   10. τολμάω _____
   _____
   _____   _____

5. κρατέω _____
   _____   _____
   _____
   _____
   _____
   _____

19
Ο ΝΟΣΤΟΣ (α)

Exercise 19α

Complete the following genitive absolutes with the correct form of the word supplied and give a possible translation of each phrase:

1. τοῦ αὐτουργοῦ Ἀθήναζε _____ (βαίνων)

    _____

2. τῆς _____ (γυνή) παρούσης

    _____

3. ἡμέρᾱς _____ (γενομένη)

    _____

4. τῶν δούλων ἐκ τοῦ ἀγροῦ _____ (ἐκφεύγων)

    _____

5. _____ (ὁ) ἀνδρὸς εἰς τὴν οἰκίᾱν ἰόντος

    _____

6. τοῦ ἱερέως τὴν θυσίᾱν _____ (ποιησάμενος)

    _____

7. τῶν _____ (παῖς) παρόντων

    _____

8. τῆς νεὼς _____ (πλεύσᾱς)

    _____

Exercise 19β

Match the Greek verbs in column A with appropriate translations in column B and write the numbers of the Greek verbs in the spaces provided. Some of the verbs in column A will have more than one translation in column B:

A		B		
1.	ἵστημι	a.	_____	I set X up (aor.)
2.	ἵστην	b.	_____	I set X up (aor.) for myself
3.	στήσω	c.	_____	I am being set up
4.	ἔστησα	d.	_____	I stand
5.	ἔστην	e.	_____	I am standing
6.	ἕστηκα	f.	_____	I will set X up
7.	ἵσταμαι	g.	_____	I will set X up for myself
8.	ἱστάμην	h.	_____	I was being set up
9.	στήσομαι	i.	_____	I stopped
10.	ἐστησάμην	j.	_____	I was standing
11.	ἐστάθην	k.	_____	I will stand
12.	σταθήσομαι	l.	_____	I was setting X up
		m.	_____	I was setting X up for myself
		n.	_____	I stood (aor.)
		o.	_____	I will be set up
		p.	_____	I was set up
		q.	_____	I am setting X up
		r.	_____	I am setting X up for myself

Exercise 19γ

Give an English equivalent of:

1. ἔστην   _____   4. συλλέγω   _____

2. ἡ ἐλάᾱ   _____   5. ἕστηκα   _____

3. νοστέω   _____

Exercise 19δ

Give the Greek equivalent of:

1. return (home)   _____   4. I eat   _____

2. I make X stand   _____   5. I was set (up)   _____

3. plain   _____   6. I raise X   _____

Exercise 19ε

Give the remaining principal parts of:

1. ἐσθίω _____
_____
_____

2. ἵστημι _____
_____
_____
_____

3. συλλέγω _____
_____
_____
_____

4. βλάπτω _____
_____
_____
_____
or _____

5. λείπω _____
_____
_____

6. πέμπω _____
_____
_____
_____
_____

1   Ἡρακλῆς, Ἡρακλέους, ὁ, *Heracles.*
         Ἡράκλεις: vocative case.
     ὡς, adv., *how* (heading an exclamation).
     ἐπιθῡμίᾱ, ἐπιθῡμίᾱς, ἡ, *desire, longing.*
     ἐμβέβληκας: *you have put X into* (perfect active, 2nd person singular, of
         ἐμβάλλω, *I throw/put into;* for the form, see Ch. 28, Gr. 3c, p. 209; for the
         meaning of the perfect tense, see Ch. 28, Gr. 4, p. 209).

2   ταῦθ' (= ταῦτα) οὕτως ἔχει: another example of ἔχω plus adverb equalling εἰμί
     plus adjective; literally, *these things hold thus*, better English, *these things are
     so.*

3   ἔχοντα: picking up ταῦθ'; ἔχοντα plus οὕτως means *(these) things being so* and is
     the subject of ἔστιν (neuter plural subjects take singular verbs), and the whole
     clause is *(these) things being so are (so).* The accent on ἔστι means that it is not
     a linking verb; it means *exist*, thus, *the things being so exist = these things are
     so.*

4   φθάνω, *I anticipate; I do* something *before* someone else.
         οὐκ ἄν φθάνοις ... διηγούμενος: *you could not anticipate describing =
             you could not be too quick in describing;* almost = an imperative, *describe
             it!* (for the use of φθάνω with a supplementary participle, see Ch. 20, Gr. 3,
             p. 67; for the potential optative with ἄν, see Ch. 25, Gr. 2, p. 143).
     τοίνυν [τοι + νυν], particle, *therefore, accordingly; well then.*
     διηγέομαι, *I describe.*
     ὡς ἡμῶν προσεξόντων: *since we will....* , genitive absolute.
         προσέχω, *I direct; I apply.*
         προσέχω (+ τὸν νοῦν, stated or implied), *I pay attention to.*

5   παρέργως [παρα- + ἔργον = *a work alongside, a side-project*], adv., *carelessly.*
     ἐπείπερ, conj., *since indeed.*
     ἐπιτῑμιον, ἐπιτῑμίου, τό, *penalty.*
     τοιοῦτος, τοιαύτη, τοιοῦτο, *such, of such a sort.*
         τοιοῦτον: Attic Greek has this neuter nominative/accusative singular form
             alongside τοιοῦτο.

6   ἀναλαμβάνω, ἀναλήψομαι, ἀνέλαβον, *I take up.*
     ῥάβδος, ῥάβδου, ἡ, *rod, staff.*
     ἐκτείνω, ἐκτενῶ, ἐξέτεινα, ἐκτέτακα, ἐκτέταμαι, ἐξετάθην, *I stretch
         forth/out; I extend.*
     γραφή, γραφῆς, ἡ, *inscription; painting, picture.*

7   περίβολος, περιβόλου, ὁ, *enclosure.*

9   εἰδέναι: *to know* (infinitive of οἶδα, *I know;* see Ch. 28, Gr. 9, pp. 219–220).
     καλεῖται: passive.
     τόπος, τόπου, ὁ, *place.*

10   ὄχλος, ὄχλου, ὁ, *crowd.*
     παρά, prep. + acc., *beside, near, by.*
     ἐφεστὼς: *standing near* (2nd perfect active participle, nominative singular
         masculine, of ἐφίστημι, *I make X stand at/near;* the perfect tense of this verb,
         ἐφέστηκα, is intransitive and has a present sense, *I stand at/near*).

11   ἄνω, adv., *up (there).*
     ἑστηκὼς: *standing* (1st perfect active participle, nominative singular masculine, of
         ἵστημι, *I make X stand;* the perfect tense of this verb, ἕστηκα, is intransitive and
         has a present sense, *I stand*).
     χάρτης, χάρτου, ὁ, *papyrus roll, scroll.*

Exercise 19ζ

Translate into English on a separate sheet of paper:

ΚΕΒΗΤΟΣ ΠΙΝΑΞ

IV.

Ξένος "ὦ Ἡράκλεις, ὡς εἰς μεγάλην τινὰ ἐπιθῡμίᾱν ἐμβέβληκας ἡμᾶς, εἰ ⟨1⟩
ταῦθ' οὕτως ἔχει." ⟨2⟩

Πρεσβύτης "ἀλλ' ἔστιν," ἔφη, "οὕτως ἔχοντα." ⟨3⟩

Ξένος "οὐκ ἂν φθάνοις τοίνυν διηγούμενος, ὡς ἡμῶν προσεξόντων οὐ ⟨4⟩
παρέργως, ἐπείπερ καὶ τὸ ἐπιτίμιον τοιοῦτόν ἐστιν." ⟨5⟩

Πρεσβύτης ἀναλαβὼν οὖν ῥάβδον τινὰ καὶ ἐκτείνᾱς πρὸς τὴν γραφήν, ⟨6⟩
"ὁρᾶτε," ἔφη, "τὸν περίβολον τοῦτον;" ⟨7⟩

Ξένος "ὁρῶμεν." ⟨8⟩

Πρεσβύτης "τοῦτο πρῶτον δεῖ εἰδέναι ῡ̔μᾶς, ὅτι καλεῖται οὗτος ὁ τόπος Βίος. ⟨9⟩
καὶ ὁ ὄχλος ὁ πολὺς ὁ παρὰ τὴν πύλην ἐφεστὼς οἱ μέλλοντες εἰσπορεύεσθαι εἰς τὸν ⟨10⟩
Βίον οὗτοί εἰσιν. ὁ δὲ γέρων ὁ ἄνω ἑστηκὼς ἔχων χάρτην τινὰ ἐν τῇ χειρὶ καὶ τῇ ⟨11⟩
ἑτέρᾳ ὥσπερ δεικνύων τι, οὗτος Δαίμων καλεῖται· προστάττει δὲ τοῖς ⟨12⟩
εἰσπορευομένοις τί δεῖ αὐτοὺς ποιεῖν, ὡς ἂν εἰσέλθωσιν εἰς τὸν Βίον· δεικνύει δὲ ⟨13⟩
ποίᾱν ὁδὸν αὐτοὺς δεῖ βαδίζειν, εἰ μέλλουσι σῴζεσθαι ἐν τῷ Βίῳ." ⟨14⟩

12　**ἕτερος, ἑτέρᾱ, ἕτερον,** *one* or *the other* (of two); *other, another.*
　　δεικνύω [= δείκνῡμι], *I show.*
　　Δαίμων, Δαίμονος, ὁ, *Daemon = Divine Spirit, God.*
　　προστάττω, *I command, give an order.*
13　**ὡς ἂν εἰσέλθωσιν:** *whenever / as they enter* (an indefinite temporal clause; see
　　　Ch. 22, Gr. 2, p. 94; the verb is aorist subjunctive; translate as present).
14　**ποῖος, ποίᾱ, ποῖον,** *what sort / kind of.*

(β)

Exercise 19η

Translate the English phrases with the correct active forms of the verb ἵστημι:

1.   he/she sets X (up)   _____

2.   you (pl.) are setting X (up)   _____

3.   they were setting X (up)   _____

4.   I was setting X (up)   _____

5.   I stop X   _____

6.   they made X stand   _____

7.   to be setting X (up)   _____

8.   set X (up)! (sing., aorist)   _____

9.   you (sing.) were making X stand   _____

10. (οἱ ἄνθρωποι) setting X (up)   _____

11. he/she set X (up)   _____

12. I stood   _____

13. you (sing.) will stop X   _____

14. (ἡ γυνὴ) being about to stop X   _____

15. he/she stood   _____

16. (ὁ ἄνθρωπος) having stood
     (2nd aorist)   _____

17. to be about to set X (up)   _____

18. (ὁ ἄνθρωπος) having made X stand   _____

19. to stand (2nd aorist)   _____

20. (ἡ γυνὴ) having stood
     (2nd aorist)   _____

Exercise 19θ

Match the Greek verbs in column A with appropriate translations in column B and write the numbers of the Greek verbs in the spaces provided:

A   B

Part I

1. ἵσταται   a. _____ he/she/it was set up

2. στήσονται   b. _____ he/she sets X up for his/herself

3. ἐστάθην   c. _____ set X up for yourselves!

4. ἵστασθε   d. _____ to set X up for oneself

5. σταθήσεται   e. _____ I am being set up

6. ἵσταμαι   f. _____ I set X up for myself (aor.)

7. στήσασθαι   g. _____ I was set up

8. ἐστησάμην   h. _____ they will set X up for themselves

9. ἐστάθη   i. _____ they are setting X up for themselves

10. ἵστανται   j. _____ he/she/it will be set up

Part II

1. σταθήσῃ   a. _____ we were setting X up for ourselves

2. ἱστάμην   b. _____ you (sing.) are being set up

3. ἵστασθαι   c. _____ you (pl.) set X up for yourselves (aor.)

4. στησόμεθα   d. _____ (τὸ ἄγαλμα) being set up

5. ἵστασαι   e. _____ you (sing.) will be set up

6. στησάμενος   f. _____ we will set X up for ourselves

7. στήσεται   g. _____ (ὁ ἄνθρωπος) having set X up for himself

8. ἱστάμεθα   h. _____ I was setting X up for myself

9. ἐστήσασθε   i. _____ he/she/it will stand

10. ἱστάμενον   j. _____ to be setting X up for oneself

Exercise 19ι

Translate into English:

1. ἀφίστανται ἀπὸ τοῦ βασιλέως.

_____

2. κατέστησαν τὸν ἄνδρα στρατηγόν.

_____

3.   ἡ γυνὴ εἰς φόβον κατέστη.

_____

4.   εἰς φυγὴν κατέστημεν.

_____

5.   κατεστήσατε τὸν Θησέᾱ βασιλέᾱ.

_____

6.   ἀπέστημεν ἀπὸ τῶν δεσποτῶν.

_____

7.   τήμερον (*today*) ἱερεὺς τοῦ Διονῦσου κατέστην.

_____

8.   τίς τοὺς νόμους κατέστησεν;

_____

9.   κατεστήσαμεν τοὺς πολεμίους εἰς φυγήν.

_____

10.   τί κατεστήσατε τοῦτον στρατηγόν;

_____

Exercise 19κ

Give an English equivalent of:

1. ἀφίσταμαι   _____
2. ἔρημος   _____
3. ὁ φόβος   _____
4. σημαίνω   _____
5. εἰς ἀπορίᾱν
      κατέστη   _____

6. ἥδιστα   _____
7. ἐντυγχάνω   _____
8. δεινός   _____
9. ἡ ὕλη   _____

Exercise 19λ

Give the Greek equivalent of:

1. shepherd   _____
2. I appoint   _____
3. rough   _____
4. I advise   _____

5. I do not know   _____
6. deep   _____
7. I rest   _____
8. shoulder   _____

Exercise 19μ

Give the remaining principal parts of:

1. ἀναπαύομαι   _____

      _____

      _____

2. παραινέω   _____

      or _____

      _____

3. σημαίνω   _____

      _____

      _____

      _____

4. κόπτω   _____

      _____

      _____

      _____

      _____

5. τύπτω   _____

6. γράφω   _____

      _____

      _____

7. ἀφίσταμαι   _____

      _____

1   ποῖος, ποία, ποῖον, *what sort/kind of.*
2   παρά, prep. + acc., *beside, near, by.*
    θρόνος, θρόνου, ὁ, *throne.*
    κατά, prep. + acc., *at.*
3   τόπος, τόπου, ὁ, *place.*
    ὄχλος, ὄχλου, ὁ, *crowd.*
    ἐπί, prep. + gen., *on.*
    πλάττω, πλάσω, ἔπλασα, πέπλακα, πέπλασμαι, ἐπλάσθην, *I form, shape,*
        make up.
            πεπλασμένη: *made up* (so as to be deceptive), *counterfeit* (perfect
                    passive participle).
    ἦθος, ἤθους, τό, *character.*
    ἤθει: dative of respect.
4   πιθανός, πιθανή, πιθανόν [related to πείθω], *persuasive, alluring.*
    ποτήριον, ποτηρίου, τό, *cup.*
5   αὕτη: translate *this woman* or simply *she.* Likewise in later passages, αὗται may
        be translated *these women* or *they,* οὗτος *this man* or *he,* and οὗτοι *these men*
        or *they.*
6   ἀπάτη, ἀπάτης, ἡ, *trick; deceit; deception.*
7   πλανάω, πλανήσω, *I make X wander; I lead X astray; I deceive X.*
8   εἶτα, adv., *then, next.*
9   ποτίζω, *I make X* (acc.) *drink of Y* (dat.).
    δύναμις, δυνάμεως, ἡ, *power.*
10 ποτόν, ποτοῦ, τό, *drink.*
11 πλάνος, πλάνου, ὁ, *wandering; error.*
    ἄγνοια, ἀγνοίας, ἡ, *ignorance.*

Exercise 19v

Translate into English on a separate sheet of paper:

ΚΕΒΗΤΟΣ ΠΙΝΑΞ

V.

Ξένος "ποίαν οὖν ὁδὸν κελεύει βαδίζειν ἢ πῶς;" ἔφην ἐγώ.   1

Πρεσβύτης "ὁρᾷς οὖν," εἶπε, "παρὰ τὴν πύλην θρόνον τινὰ κείμενον κατὰ   2
τὸν τόπον, καθ᾽ ὃν εἰσπορεύεται ὁ ὄχλος, ἐφ᾽ οὗ κάθηται γυνὴ πεπλασμένη τῷ ἤθει   3
καὶ πιθανὴ φαινομένη, ἣ ἐν τῇ χειρὶ ἔχει ποτήριόν τι;"   4

Ξένος "ὁρῶ. ἀλλὰ τίς ἐστιν αὕτη;" ἔφην.   5

Πρεσβύτης "᾽Απάτη   καλεῖται," φησίν, "ἡ πάντας τοὺς ἀνθρώπους   6
πλανῶσα."   7

Ξένος "εἶτα τί πράττει αὕτη;"   8

Πρεσβύτης "τοὺς εἰσπορευομένους εἰς τὸν Βίον ποτίζει τῇ ἑαυτῆς δυνάμει."   9

Ξένος "τοῦτο δὲ τί ἐστι τὸ ποτόν;"   10

Πρεσβύτης "πλάνος," ἔφη, "καὶ ἄγνοια."   11

Ξένος "εἶτα τί;"   12

Πρεσβύτης "πιόντες τοῦτο πορεύονται εἰς τὸν Βίον."   13

Ξένος "πότερον οὖν πάντες πίνουσι τὸν πλάνον ἢ οὔ;"   14

20
Ο ΝΟΣΤΟΣ (γ)

Exercise 20 α

Translate the following English phrases with the correct active forms of the verb δείκνῡμι:

1. he/she shows   _____
2. you (pl.) are showing   _____
3. I was showing   _____
4. we are showing   _____
5. to be showing   _____
6. you (pl.) will show   _____
7. he/she was showing   _____
8. he/she showed   _____
9. show! (pl., aorist)   _____
10. we will show   _____

Exercise 20 β

Translate the following English phrases with the correct active forms of the verb ζεύγνῡμι:

1. you (sing.) yoked   _____
2. you (pl.) yoked   _____
3. you (sing.) will yoke   _____
4. yoke! (pl., present)   _____
5. you (pl.) were yoking   _____
6. they are yoking   _____
7. to be about to yoke   _____
8. (ὁ ἄνθρωπος) yoking   _____
9. (ὁ ἄνθρωπος) having yoked   _____
10. to yoke (aorist)   _____

Exercise 20γ

Match the Greek verbs in column A with appropriate translations in column B and write the numbers of the Greek verbs in the spaces provided:

A   B
1. ἐζεύχθην   a. _____   it is being yoked
2. ζεύγνυμαι   b. _____   they were being yoked
3. ζευχθέντες   c. _____   I was yoked
4. ἐζεύγνυτο   d. _____   we will be yoked
5. ζεύγνυται   e. _____   (ὁ βοῦς) being yoked
6. ζευγνύμενος   f. _____   to be yoked (present)
7. ἐζεύγνυντο   g. _____   I am being yoked
8. ζεύγνυσθαι   h. _____   (οἱ βόες) having been yoked
9. ζεύχθητι   i. _____   be yoked! (sing., aorist)
10. ζευχθησόμεθα   j. _____   it was being yoked

Exercise 20δ

Give an English equivalent of:

1. ἐξαίφνης   _____   5. ὁ τόπος   _____
2. τὸ μέγεθος   _____   6. κάτω   _____
3. ἐντός   _____   7. ἀρέσκει   _____
4. καθοράω   _____   8. ἀσφαλής   _____

Exercise 20ε

Give the Greek equivalent of:

1. I show   _____   5. doubtless   _____
2. above   _____   6. child   _____
3. blood   _____   7. lion   _____
4. made of stone   _____   8. the Furies   _____

1   ἥττων, ἧττον, *inferior; weaker; less.*
        πλεῖον . . . ἧττον: adverbial, *more . . . less.*
2   ἔνδον, prep. + gen., *within, inside.*
    ἕτερος, ἑτέρᾱ, ἕτερον, *one* or *the other* (of two); *other, another.*
    παντοδαπός, παντοδαπή, παντοδαπόν, *of all kinds, various.*
    μορφή, μορφῆς, ἡ, *form, shape.*
4   τοίνυν [τοι + νυν], particle, *therefore, accordingly; well then.*
    δόξα, δόξης, ἡ, *notion; opinion; good reputation; honor.*
        Δόξαι: here, *Opinions.*
    ἐπιθῡμίᾱ, ἐπιθῡμίᾱς, ἡ, *desire, longing.*
    ἡδονή, ἡδονῆς, ἡ, *pleasure, sense-gratification.*
    ὅταν [ὅτε + ἄν], conj. + subjunctive, *whenever.*
5   εἰσπορεύηται: present subjunctive in a present general temporal clause
        introduced by ὅταν (see Ch. 22, Gr. 2, pp. 94 and 95).
    ὄχλος, ὄχλου, ὁ, *crowd.*
    ἀναπηδάω, *I leap up.*
    πλέκω, *I weave, twine;* middle + πρός + acc., *I embrace.*
    ἕκαστος, ἑκάστη, ἕκαστον, *each.*
    εἶτα, adv., *then, next.*
6   ἀπάγω, *I lead away.*
        ἀπάγουσι: note that this text does not always have movable ν where you
            would expect it.
7   ποῦ: = ποῖ.
8   τὸ σῴζεσθαι . . . τὸ ἀπόλλυσθαι: *salvation . . . perdition* (articular infinitives;
        see Ch. 23, Gr. 5, p. 118).
    ἀπόλλῡμι, ἀπολῶ, sigmatic 1st aorist, ἀπώλεσα, thematic 2nd aorist middle,
        ἀπωλόμην, *I destroy; I kill;* middle, *I perish; I die.*
9   ἀπάτη, ἀπάτης, ἡ, *trick; deceit; deception.*
10 δαιμόνιος, δαιμονίᾱ, δαιμόνιον, *belonging to a* δαίμων; as direct address, *sir.*
    χαλεπὸν: here, *dangerous.*
    πόμα, πόματος, τό, *drink.*
11 ἐπαγγέλλω, *I proclaim, announce;* middle, *I promise* (unasked); *I offer* (of my own
        free will).
    ὡς: *that,* with the future participle ἄξουσαι; indirect statement, *that they will. . . .*
        (see Ch. 23, Gr. 2, p. 111).
    ἐπί, prep. + acc., *to.*
    βέλτιστος, βελτίστη, βέλτιστον, *best.*
12 εὐδαίμων, εὔδαιμον [= with a good δαίμων, *spirit, fate, lot*], *fortunate, happy.*
    λυσιτελής, λυσιτελές, *paying what is due; profitable, advantageous.*
    ἄγνοια, ἀγνοίᾱς, ἡ, *ignorance.*
13 πλάνος, πλάνου, ὁ, *wandering; error.*
    πεπώκᾱσι: *they have drunk* (perfect of πίνω).
    παρά, prep. + gen., *from.*
    ποῖος, ποίᾱ, ποῖον, *what sort/kind of; of what sort/kind.*
    ἀληθινός, ἀληθινή, ἀληθινόν, *true.*
14 πλανάω, πλανήσω, *I make X wander; I lead X astray; I deceive X;* passive,
        I wander, stray.
    εἰκῇ, adv., *without plan/purpose; at random; recklessly.*

Exercise 20 ζ

Translate into English on a separate sheet of paper:

ΚΕΒΗΤΟΣ ΠΙΝΑΞ

VI.

Πρεσβύτης "πάντες πίνουσιν," ἔφη, "ἀλλ' οἱ μὲν πλεῖον, οἱ δὲ ἧττον. ἔτι δὲ οὐχ   1
ὁρᾷς ἔνδον τῆς πύλης πλῆθός τι γυναικῶν ἑτέρων παντοδαπὰς μορφὰς ἐχουσῶν;"   2

Ξένος "ὁρῶ."   3

Πρεσβύτης "αὗται τοίνυν Δόξαι καὶ Ἐπιθῡμίαι καὶ Ἡδοναὶ καλοῦνται. ὅταν   4
οὖν εἰσπορεύηται ὁ ὄχλος, ἀναπηδῶσιν αὗται καὶ πλέκονται πρὸς ἕκαστον, εἶτα   5
ἀπάγουσι."   6

Ξένος "ποῦ δὲ ἀπάγουσιν αὐτούς;"   7

Πρεσβύτης "αἱ μὲν εἰς τὸ σῴζεσθαι," ἔφη, "αἱ δὲ εἰς τὸ ἀπόλλυσθαι διὰ τὴν   8
ἀπάτην."   9

Ξένος "ὦ δαιμόνιε, ὡς χαλεπὸν τὸ πόμα λέγεις."   10

Πρεσβύτης "καὶ πᾶσαί γε," ἔφη, "ἐπαγγέλλονται ὡς ἐπὶ τὰ βέλτιστα   11
ἄξουσαι καὶ εἰς βίον εὐδαίμονα καὶ λυσιτελῆ. οἱ δὲ διὰ τὴν ἄγνοιαν καὶ τὸν   12
πλάνον, ὃν πεπώκᾱσι παρὰ τῆς Ἀπάτης, οὐχ εὑρίσκουσι ποίᾱ ἐστὶν ἡ ἀληθινὴ ὁδὸς ἡ   13
ἐν τῷ Βίῳ, ἀλλὰ πλανῶνται εἰκῆ, ὥσπερ ὁρᾷς καὶ τοὺς πρότερον εἰσπορευομένους   14
ὡς περιάγονται ὅποι ἂν τύχῃ."   15

---

15   **ὡς**, conj., *that; how.*
περιάγω, *I lead around.*
  περιάγονται: passive.
ὅποι, adv., *to what place, where.*
  ὅποι ἂν τύχῃ: *to wherever it happens*, i.e., *at random* (present general clause
    with ἂν and the aorist subjunctive).

Exercise 20η

Give the remaining principal parts of:

1. ἀρέσκει   _____   5. ἄγω   _____

                                                                                _____

2. δείκνῡμι   _____   _____

                              _____   _____

                              _____

                              _____   6. πρᾱ́ττω   _____

                              _____   _____

3. καθοράω   _____   _____

                              _____   _____

4. φεύγω   _____   _____

                              _____

                              _____

(δ)

Exercise 20 θ

Translate the following English phrases with the correct active forms of the verb ἵημι:

1. they sent _____
2. they will send _____
3. you (pl.) sent _____
4. they were sending _____
5. I was sending _____
6. send! (pl., aorist) _____
7. he/she sends _____
8. you (sing.) will send _____
9. he/she will send _____
10. (οἱ ἄνθρωποι) sending _____
11. you (pl.) are sending _____
12. to be sending _____
13. to send (aorist) _____
14. we are sending _____
15. to be about to send _____

Exercise 20 ι

Translate the following English phrases with the correct forms of the verb ἵημι in the middle voice:

1. they were hastening _____
2. I am hastening _____
3. to be hastening _____
4. I was hastening _____
5. hurry! (pl., present) _____
6. (ἡ παῖς) hurrying _____
7. they hasten _____

Review the following vocabulary for the next exercise:

ἀφίημι [= ἀπο- + ἵημι], *I let go, release; I send; I throw*
ἐφίημι [= ἐπι- + ἵημι], *I throw;* + ἐπί + acc., *I throw at*
συνίημι + gen. of person, acc. of thing, *I understand*

Exercise 20 κ

Match the Greek verbs in column A with appropriate translations in column B and write the numbers of the Greek verbs in the spaces provided:

A   B
1. ἐφήσομεν   a. ____ it is being thrown (at)
2. ἐφίεται   b. ____ they understand
3. ἀφιείς   c. ____ I released
4. συνῑᾶσι(ν)   d. ____ we will throw (at)
5. συνῑέναι   e. ____ to understand
6. ἀφῆκα   f. ____ (ὁ ἄνθρωπος) releasing

Exercise 20 λ

Match the aorist middle forms of ἵημι *in column A with identifications in column B and write the numbers of the Greek verbs in the spaces provided:*

A   B
1. εἵμην   a. ____ plural imperative
2. οὗ   b. ____ 1st person singular indicative
3. εἷσθε   c. ____ infinitive
4. ἕσθαι   d. ____ 2nd person plural indicative
5. ἕσθε   e. ____ singular imperative
6. εἷτο   f. ____ 3rd person singular indicative

Exercise 20 μ

Translate into English:

1. οἱ ἄνδρες ἡμᾶς ἐλάνθανον καθεύδοντες.

    _____

2. ἔτυχον οἱ ἄνδρες καθεύδοντες.

    _____

3. ὁ δοῦλος φαίνεται πονεῖν.

    _____

4. οἱ δοῦλοι φαίνονται πονοῦντες.

    _____

5. ἐφθάσαμεν τοὺς φίλους οἴκαδε νοστήσαντες.

    _____

6.   ἔλαθον τὸν δεσπότην εἰς τὴν οἰκίᾶν εἰσελθών.

_____

7.   φθάνει σε ἡ παρθένος τὸ ὕδωρ κομίζουσα.

_____

8.   τυγχάνεις εἰς καιρὸν παροῦσα.

_____

Exercise 20 ν

Give an English equivalent of:

1. ἀφῑ́ημι   _____   6. οἰκτῑ́ρω   _____
2. ἔνιοι   _____   7. ἐφῑ́ημι   _____
3. λανθάνω   _____   8. ἐπί + gen.   _____
4. πολύ   _____   9. παρέρχομαι   _____
5. ἡ ὀργή   _____

Exercise 20 ξ

Give the Greek equivalent of:

1. I hide   _____   6. against   _____
2. today   _____   7. I understand   _____
3. I send   _____   8. I advance   _____
4. I eat (dinner)   _____   9. outside   _____
5. not (with infin.) _____

Exercise 20 ο

Give the remaining principal parts of:

1. ἵημι   _____   5. φυλάττω   _____
                _____   _____
                _____   _____
                _____   _____

2. κρύπτω   _____   6. δοκέω   _____
                _____   _____
                _____   _____

3. λανθάνω   _____   7. εὔχομαι   _____
                _____   _____
                _____   _____
4. διώκω   _____   8. οἰκτῑ́ρω   _____
         or _____   _____
                _____   _____
                _____
                _____

2   μαίνομαι, *I rage, am insane, am mad.*
    ἑστηκυῖα: *standing* (perfect participle, feminine nominative singular of ἵστημι).
    στρογγύλος, στρογγύλη, στρογγύλον, *round*.
4   κωφός, κωφή, κωφόν, *mute; deaf.*
6   περιπορεύομαι, *I go around.*
    παρ' ὧν: *from some.*
    ἁρπάζω, *I snatch away.*
7   ὑπάρχοντα, ὑπαρχόντων, τά, *goods, possessions.*
    ἕτερος, ἑτέρᾱ, ἕτερον, *one* or *the other* (of two); *other, another.*
    παρὰ ... τῶν αὐτῶν: *from the same people* (referring to ἑτέροις).
    πάλιν, adv., *back; again; in turn.*
    ἀφαιρέομαι, ἀφαιρήσομαι, ἀφειλόμην, *I take away* (for myself); *I rob.*
    παραχρῆμα, adv., *forthwith, right away.*
8   ἅ: supply ἐκεῖνα as antecedent (see Ch. 23, Gr. 6c, p. 119).
    δέδωκε: *she has given* (perfect of δίδωμι; for the principal parts, see Ch. 30δ PP,
        p. 270).
    εἰκῆ, adv., *without plan/purpose; at random; recklessly.*
    ἀβεβαίως [ἀ- + βέβαιος, βεβαίᾱ, βέβαιον], adv., *unreliably, with no security.*
    διό, conj. = δι' ὅ, *wherefore, for which reason, therefore.*
    σημεῖον, σημείου, τό, *sign, emblem.*
9   μηνύω, *I inform; I reveal, make known.*
    φύσις, φύσεως, ἡ, *nature; natural disposition.*
10 ποῖος, ποίᾱ, ποῖον, *what sort/kind of; of what sort/kind?*
11 ἐπί, prep. + gen., *on.*
    ἕστηκεν: *she stands* (perfect of ἵστημι).
12 εἶτα, adv., *then, next.*
13 βέβαιος, βεβαίᾱ, βέβαιον, *firm; secure.*
    παρά, prep. + gen., *from.*
    δόσις, δόσεως, ἡ, *gift.*
    ἔκπτωσις, ἐκπτώσεως, ἡ [cf. πίπτω], *falling off; disappointment.*
14 σκληρός, σκληρά, σκληρόν, *hard; harsh; bitter.*
    ὅταν τις ... πιστεύῃ: *whenever anyone trusts/believes* (present subjunctive in
        a present indefinite or general temporal clause; see Ch. 22, Gr. 2, pp. 94 and 95).

Exercise 20π

Translate into English on a separate sheet of paper:

ΚΕΒΗΤΟΣ ΠΙΝΑΞ

VII.

Ξένος "ὁρῶ τούτους," ἔφην. "ἡ δὲ γυνὴ ἐκείνη τίς ἐστιν ἡ ὥσπερ τυφλὴ καὶ   1
μαινομένη τις εἶναι δοκοῦσα καὶ ἐστηκυῖα ἐπὶ λίθου τινὸς στρογγύλου;"   2

Πρεσβύτης "καλεῖται μέν," ἔφη, "Τύχη· ἔστι δὲ οὐ μόνον τυφλὴ καὶ   3
μαινομένη, ἀλλὰ καὶ κωφή."   4

Ξένος "αὕτη οὖν τί ἔργον ἔχει;"   5

Πρεσβύτης "περιπορεύεται πανταχοῦ," ἔφη· "καὶ παρ' ὧν μὲν ἁρπάζει τὰ   6
ὑπάρχοντα καὶ ἑτέροις δίδωσι· παρὰ δὲ τῶν αὐτῶν πάλιν ἀφαιρεῖται παραχρῆμα   7
ἃ δέδωκε καὶ ἄλλοις δίδωσιν εἰκῇ καὶ ἀβεβαίως. διὸ καὶ τὸ σημεῖον καλῶς   8
μηνύει τὴν φύσιν αὐτῆς."   9

Ξένος "ποῖον τοῦτο;" ἔφην ἐγώ.   10

Πρεσβύτης "ὅτι ἐπὶ λίθου στρογγύλου ἔστηκεν."   11

Ξένος "εἶτα τί τοῦτο σημαίνει;"   12

Πρεσβύτης "οὐκ ἀσφαλὴς οὐδὲ βεβαία ἐστὶν ἡ παρ' αὐτῆς δόσις. ἐκπτώσεις   13
γὰρ μεγάλαι καὶ σκληραὶ γίνονται, ὅταν τις αὐτῇ πιστεύῃ."   14

VOCABULARY
CHAPTERS 17–20

VERBS

-ω Verbs

αἴρω, ἀρῶ, ἦρα,
ἦρκα, ἦρμαι,
ἤρθην   *I lift;* with reflexive
pronoun, *I get up*

ἁμαρτάνω,
ἁμαρτήσομαι,
ἥμαρτον,
ἡμάρτηκα,
ἡμάρτημαι,
ἡμαρτήθην   + gen., *I miss; I make
a mistake, am
mistaken*

ἀπέχω, ἀφέξω,
ἀπέσχον   *I am distant;* + gen.,
I am distant from;
middle + gen.,
I abstain from

ἀρέσκει, ἀρέσει,
ἤρεσε   impersonal + dat., *it
is pleasing*

γιγνώσκω,
γνώσομαι,
ἔγνων,
ἔγνωκα,
ἔγνωσμαι,
ἐγνώσθην   *I get to know, learn*
ἐντυγχάνω   + dat., *I meet*
ἐπιστρατεύω   + dat. or ἐπί + acc.,
*I march against,
attack*

ἐπιτρέπω,
ἐπιτρέψω,
ἐπέτρεψα,
ἐπιτέτροφα,
ἐπιτέτραμμαι,
ἐπετράπην   *I entrust* X (acc.) to
Y (dat.)

ἐσθίω, ἔδομαι,
ἔφαγον,
ἐδήδοκα   *I eat*
κρύπτω, κρύψω,
ἔκρυψα,
κέκρυμμαι,
ἐκρύφθην   *I hide*

λανθάνω, λήσω,
ἔλαθον, λέληθα   + acc. and/or
participle, *I escape
someone's notice
doing something =
I do something
without someone's
noticing; I escape
the notice of
someone*

οἰκτίρω, οἰκτιρῶ,
ᾤκτῑρα   *I pity*
προστρέχω   *I run toward*
σημαίνω, σημανῶ,
ἐσήμηνα,
σεσήμασμαι,
ἐσημάνθην   *I signal; I sign;
I show*

συλλέγω, συλλέξω,
συνέλεξα,
συνείλοχα,
συνείλεγμαι,
συνελέγην   *I collect, gather*
τρέχω,
δραμοῦμαι,
ἔδραμον,
δεδράμηκα   *I run*
τυγχάνω,
τεύξομαι,
ἔτυχον,
τετύχηκα   + gen., *I hit; I hit
upon; I get;* +
participle,
*I happen to be
doing X*

Deponent or Middle -ω Verbs

ἀναπαύομαι,
ἀναπαύσομαι,
ἀνεπαυσάμην,
ἀναπέπαυμαι   *I rest*
ἕπομαι, ἕψομαι,
ἑσπόμην   + dat., *I follow*
παρέρχομαι   *I go past; I pass in,
enter; I come
forward* (to speak)

προέρχομαι, *I go forward,*
advance

-άω Contract Verbs

γελάω,
γελάσομαι,
ἐγέλασα,
ἐγελάσθην *I laugh*
καθοράω,
κατόψομαι,
κατεῖδον *I look down on*
τολμάω *I dare*

-έω Contract Verbs

ἀγνοέω *I do not know*
δειπνέω *I eat (dinner)*
δέω, δήσω, ἔδησα,
δέδεκα, δέδεμαι,
ἐδέθην *I tie, bind*
θαρρέω *I am confident*
κῑνέω *I move*
κρατέω + gen., *I rule, have*
power over,
control; I prevail
νοστέω *I return home*
παραινέω,
παραινέσω or
παραινέσομαι,
παρῄνεσα,
παρῄνεκα,
παρῄνημαι,
παρῃνέθην + dat. and infin.,
I advise someone
to do something
πλέω, πλεύσομαι
or πλευσοῦμαι,
ἔπλευσα,
πέπλευκα *I sail*
φρονέω *I think; I am minded*

Deponent -έω Contract Verbs

ἀκέομαι, ἀκοῦμαι,
ἠκεσάμην *I heal*
ἀφικνέομαι,
ἀφίξομαι,
ἀφῑκόμην,
ἀφῖγμαι *I arrive;* + εἰς + acc.,
I arrive at

-μι Verbs

ἀνατίθημι *I set up; I dedicate*

ἀνίστημι when transitive,
I make X *stand up;*
I raise X; *when*
intransitive,
I stand up
ἀποδίδωμι *I give back, return;*
I pay; middle, *I sell*
ἀφίημι *I let go, release;*
I send; I throw
δείκνῡμι, δείξω,
ἔδειξα, δέδειχα,
δέδειγμαι,
ἐδείχθην *I show*
δίδωμι, δώσω,
ἔδωκα, δέδωκα,
δέδομαι,
ἐδόθην *I give*
ἐπιτίθημι *I put* X (acc.) *on*
Y (dat.)
ἐφίημι *I throw;* + ἐπί + acc.,
I throw at
ἵημι, ἥσω, ἧκα,
εἷκα, εἷμαι,
εἵθην *I let go, release;*
I send; I throw
ἵστημι, στήσω,
ἔστησα *I make* X *stand;*
I stop X; *I am*
setting X *(up)*
ἔστην *I stood*
ἕστηκα *I stand*
ἐστάθην *I was set (up)*
καθίστημι when transitive, *I set*
X *up; I appoint* X;
+ εἰς + acc., *I put*
X *into a certain*
state; when intran-
sitive, *I am ap-*
pointed; I am es-
tablished; + εἰς +
acc., *I get/fall into*
a certain state;
I become
παραδίδωμι *I hand over; I give*
συνίημι + gen. of person, acc.
of thing, *I under-*
stand
τίθημι, θήσω,
ἔθηκα, τέθηκα,
ἐτέθην *I put, place*

Deponent or Middle -μι Verbs

ἀποδίδομαι	*I sell*
ἀφίσταμαι, ἀποστήσομαι, ἀπέστην	*I stand away from; I revolt from*
ἵεμαι	*I hasten*

Athematic Verbs

κάθημαι	*I sit*

Irregular Verbs

οἶδα	*I know*
χρή	*it is necessary; ought, must*

NOUNS

1st Declension

γνώμη, -ης, ἡ	*opinion; judgment; intention*
ἐλάᾱ, -ᾱς, ἡ	*olive; olive tree*
θυσίᾱ, -ᾱς, ἡ	*sacrifice*
ἱκέτης, -ου, ὁ	*suppliant*
ὀργή, -ῆς, ἡ	*anger*
ὕλη, -ης, ἡ	*woods, forest*
ὑπηρέτης, -ου, ὁ	*servant; attendant*
ψῡχή, -ῆς, ἡ	*soul*

2nd Declension

ἐχθρός, -οῦ, ὁ	*enemy*
νόμος, -ου, ὁ	*law; custom*
νόστος, -ου, ὁ	*return* (home)
πεδίον, -ου, τό	*plain*
τέκνον, -ου, τό	*child*
τόπος, -ου, ὁ	*place*
ὕπνος, -ου, ὁ	*sleep*
φόβος, -ου, ὁ	*fear; panic*
ὦμος, -ου, ὁ	*shoulder*

3rd Declension

αἷμα, αἵματος, τό	*blood*
κράτος, κράτους, τό	*power*
λέων, λέοντος, ὁ	*lion*
μέγεθος, μεγέθους, τό	*size*
ποιμήν, ποιμένος, ὁ	*shepherd*
πρᾶγμα, πράγματος, τό	*matter; trouble*
τέμενος, τεμένους, τό	*sacred precinct*

χάρις, χάριτος, ἡ	*thanks; gratitude*
χρήματα, χρημάτων, τά	*things; goods; money*

PRONOUNS

ἔγωγε	*I indeed*

ADJECTIVES

1st/2nd Declension

δεινός, -ή, -όν	*terrible; clever, skilled; +* infin., *clever at, skilled at*
δῆλος, -η, -ον	*clear*
ἔνιοι, -αι, -α	*some*
ἐχθρός, -ά, -όν	*hateful; hostile*
ἱερός, -ά, -όν	*holy, sacred*
καθαρός, -ά, -όν	*clean, pure*
λίθινος, -η, -ον	*of stone, made of stone*
ὅσιος, -α, -ον	*holy, pious*
σεμνός, -ή, -όν	*holy; august*
φιλαίτερος, -ᾱ, -ον and φιλαίτατος or φίλτατος, -η, -ον	*dearer; dearest*

2nd Declension

ἔρημος, -ον	*deserted*

3rd Declension

ἀσφαλής, -ές	*safe*
εὐμενής, -ές	*kindly*
ὑγιής, -ές	*healthy*

3rd and 1st Declension

βαθύς, -εῖα, -ύ	*deep*
τρᾱχύς, -εῖα, -ύ	*rough*

PREPOSITIONS

διά	+ gen., *through;* + acc. *because of*
ἐντός	+ gen., *within, inside*
ἐπί	+ gen., *toward, in the direction of;* + dat., *at; of price, for;* + acc., *at; against; onto; upon*

ἔξω,	+ gen., *outside*
κατά	+ acc., *down;* distributive, *each, every; by; on; according to*
περί	+ gen., *about, concerning; around;* + acc., *around*
σύν	+ dat., *with*
ὑπέρ	+ gen., *on behalf of, for; above;* + acc., *over, above*

ADVERBS

ἄνω	*up; above*
ἐντός	*within, inside*
ἐξαίφνης	*suddenly*
ἔξω	*outside*
ἡδέως	*sweetly; pleasantly; gladly*
ἥδιστα	*most sweetly; most pleasantly; most gladly*
ἴσως	*perhaps*
κάτω	*down; below*
μᾶλλον	*more; rather*
μή	with infin., *not*
οὔκουν	*certainly not*
ὀψέ	*late; too late*
πάλαι	*long ago*
ποῖ;	*to where? whither?*
πολύ	*far, by far*
πρότερον	*formerly, before, earlier; first*
πως	*somehow; in any way*
τήμερον	*today*

CONJUNCTIONS

| διότι | *because* |
| πότερον . . . ἤ | *(whether . . .) or* |

PARTICLES

| δήπου | *doubtless, surely* |
| μέντοι | *certainly; however* |

EXPRESSIONS

δῆλόν ἐστι(ν)	*it is clear*
εἰς ἀπορίαν κατέστη	*he/she fell into perplexity, became perplexed*
θάρρει	*Cheer up! Don't be afraid!*
μᾶλλον ἤ	*rather than*
ὀρθῶς γιγνώσκω	*I am right*
οὐ διὰ πολλοῦ	*not much later, soon*
πάλαι εἰσί(ν)	*they have been for a long time now*
πῶς ἔχει τὰ πράγματα;	*How are things?*
σὺν θεοῖς	*God willing; with luck*
τίνα γνώμην ἔχεις;	*What do you think?*
χάριν ἀποδίδωμι	+ dat., *I give thanks to; I thank*

PROPER NAMES & ADJECTIVES

Ἀσκληπιεῖον, -ου, τό	*the sanctuary of Asclepius*
Ἐρινύες, Ἐρινυῶν, αἱ	*the Furies* (avenging spirits)
Μυκῆναι, -ῶν, αἱ	*Mycenae*

21
Η ΕΚΚΛΗΣΙΑ (α)

Exercise 21α

Transform the following present indicative forms into the equivalent forms of the subjunctive:

1. λύουσι(ν) _____
2. δηλοῖ: he/she shows _____
3. φιλοῦμεν _____
4. τῑμᾶτε _____
5. δηλοῦσι(ν) _____
6. φιλῶ _____
7. τῑμᾶται _____
8. λύομαι _____
9. φιλεῖσθε _____
10. λύεις _____
11. φιλούμεθα _____
12. δηλοῦμεν _____
13. φιλεῖ: he/she loves _____
14. τῑμᾷ: he/she honors _____
15. λύεται _____
16. δηλοῦσθε _____
17. λύομεν _____
18. δηλοῦμαι _____
19. φιλεῖτε _____
20. τῑμῶσι(ν) _____
21. λύετε _____
22. δηλοῦται _____
23. τῑμῶ _____
24. λύονται _____
25. φιλοῦνται _____

Exercise 21β

*Transform the following aorist indicative forms into the equivalent forms of
the subjunctive:*

1. ἤρατε _____
2. ἔβην _____
3. ἐλῡσάμεθα _____
4. ἐποιήσατο _____
5. ἐγράφητε _____
6. ἐλῡσατε _____
7. ἔβησαν _____
8. ἔγνωτε _____
9. ἐποίησας _____
10. ἐγένοντο _____
11. ἔμεινα _____
12. ἐγράφης _____
13. ἐμείναμεν _____
14. ἐγένετο _____
15. ἔλιπεν _____
16. ἐγενόμην _____
17. ἐποιήσαμεν _____
18. ἐβουλήθην _____
19. ἐμείναντο _____
20. ἐλύθης _____
21. ἐποιήθησαν _____
22. ἐγράφην _____
23. ἠράμεθα _____
24. ἐποιήσαντο _____
25. ἐλίπετε _____

Exercise 21γ

Label each of the following uses of the subjunctive with one of the grammatical descriptors listed below and then translate the sentence or clause:

Descriptors: (A) Hortatory Subjunctive, (B) Deliberative Question,
(C) Prohibition, (D) Purpose Clause, (E) Conditional Clause

____ 1. τί ποιῶ;   _____

____ 2. ἐὰν τοῦτο ποιῇς, . . .   _____

____ 3. μὴ εἰς τὸν ἀγρὸν εἰσβῇς.   _____

____ 4. οἴκαδε σπεύδωμεν.   _____

____ 5. . . . ἵνα τοὺς ἀνθρώπους σώσῃς.   _____

____ 6. μὴ τοῦτο ποιήσῃς.   _____

____ 7. τὸν Παρθενῶνα νῦν ἴδωμεν.   _____

____ 8. πότερον καθεύδωμεν ἢ οὔ;   _____

____ 9. . . . ὡς οἴκαδε βαίνωμεν.   _____

____ 10. ἐὰν πρὸ νυκτὸς ἀφικώμεθα, . . .   _____

Exercise 21δ

Give an English equivalent of:

1. θύω	_____	5. ψηφίζομαι	_____
2. μύριοι	_____	6. ἡ ἀρχή	_____
3. ἐάν	_____	7. ἕνεκα	_____
4. ὁ πρέσβυς	_____	8. ἀναγιγνώσκω	_____

Exercise 21ε

Give the Greek equivalent of:

1. assembly	_____	5. politician	_____
2. I make war	_____	6. young	_____
3. in order to	_____	7. I plan	_____
4. I speak in the Assembly	_____	8. I lie before	_____

Exercise 21ζ

Give the remaining principal parts of:

1. ἀναγιγνώσκω   _____

       _____

2. βουλεύω   _____

       _____

       _____

3. θύω   _____

       _____

       _____

       _____

       _____

4. πολεμέω   _____

       _____

       _____

       _____

       _____

5. πρόκειμαι   _____

6. ψηφίζομαι   _____

       _____

       _____

7. σπεύδω   _____

       _____

       _____

8. πείθω   _____

       _____

       _____

or _____

       _____

       _____

1   ὄχλος, ὄχλου, ὁ, *crowd*.
    ἑστηκώς: *standing* (1st perfect active participle, nominative singular masculine, of
        ἵστημι).
    βούλεται: this verb can mean *mean* as well as *want, wish*.
3   ἀπροβούλευτος, ἀπροβούλευτον [ἀ- + προ-, *before* + βουλεύω], *not planning
        ahead, improvident*.
    ἕκαστος, ἑκάστη, ἕκαστον, *each*.
    αἰτοῦσι... ἕκαστος: the distributive subject takes a plural verb.
4   ἃ: supply ἐκεῖνα as antecedent.
    ῥίπτω, *I throw*.
5   ὅμοιος, ὁμοία, ὅμοιον, *similar, like*.
    μορφή, μορφῆς, ἡ, *form, shape*.
6   ἀθῡμέω, *I am disheartened / discouraged; I despair*.
    ἐκτετακότες: *having stretched out* (perfect active participle, nominative plural
        masculine, of ἐκτείνω, ἐκτενῶ, ἐξέτεινα, ἐκτέτακα, ἐκτέταμαι,
        ἐξετάθην, *I stretch forth / out*).
7   οἱ εἰληφότες: *the ones who have taken* (perfect active participle, nominative
        plural masculine, of λαμβάνω; see Ch. 23β PP, p. 115).
8   παρά, prep. + gen., *from*.
9   κλαίω, *I cry, wail, lament*.
    παρ' ὧν: supply ἐκεῖνοι as antecedent.
    ἀφαιρέομαι, ἀφαιρήσομαι, ἀφειλόμην, *I take away* (for myself); *I rob*.
    ἃ: supply ἐκεῖνα as antecedent (and in line 11 below).
    δέδωκε: *she has given* (perfect of δίδωμι; for the principal parts, see Ch. 30δ PP,
        p. 270).
    πάλιν, adv., *back; again; in turn*.
11 τίνα: neuter plural.
12 ἀποβάλλοντες: note that the verb ἀποβάλλω can mean *lose* as well as *throw
        away*.
13 παρά, prep. + dat., *among*.
16 πλοῦτος, πλούτου, ὁ, *wealth, riches*.
    δηλονότι: = δῆλόν ἐστιν ὅτι, lit., *it is quite clear that;* (better English), *quite clearly,
        certainly*.
    δόξα, δόξης, ἡ, *notion; opinion; good reputation; honor*.
    εὐγένεια, εὐγενείᾱς, ἡ, *high birth, nobility*.
17 τυραννίς, τυραννίδος, ἡ, *monarchy, sovereignty, despotic rule*.
    βασιλείᾱ, βασιλείᾱς, ἡ, *kingdom*.
    τἆλλα: = τὰ ἄλλα.
    ὅσος, ὅση, ὅσον, *as great as; as much as;* pl., *as many as*.
    παραπλήσιος, παραπλήσιον + dat., *resembling, similar* (to).
19 ἐκποιέω, *I make complete, finish off*.
    ἐκποιήσει: used impersonally, *it will suffice*.
    διαλέγεσθαι: here, *to discuss, discourse*.
20 μῡθολογίᾱ, μῡθολογίᾱς, ἡ, *story-telling; story's meaning*.
    γῑνώμεθα: = γιγνώμεθα, *let us be* (subjunctive expressing an exhortation; see Ch.
        21, Gr. 3a, p. 78). Take the verb closely with περὶ, *concerned with.* . . .
21 ἔστω: *let it be!* (3rd person singular present imperative of εἰμί).

Exercise 21η

Translate into English on a separate sheet of paper:

ΚΕΒΗΤΟΣ ΠΙΝΑΞ

VIII.

Ξένος "ὁ δὲ πολὺς ὄχλος οὗτος ὁ περὶ αὐτὴν ἑστηκώς, τί βούλεται καὶ τίνες 1
καλοῦνται;" 2

Πρεσβύτης "καλοῦνται μὲν οὗτοι ἀπροβούλευτοι· αἰτοῦσι δὲ ἕκαστος αὐτῶν 3
ἃ ῥίπτει." 4

Ξένος "πῶς οὖν οὐχ ὁμοίαν ἔχουσι τὴν μορφήν, ἀλλ' οἱ μὲν αὐτῶν δοκοῦσι 5
χαίρειν, οἱ δὲ ἀθυμοῦσιν ἐκτετακότες τὰς χεῖρας;" 6

Πρεσβύτης "οἱ μὲν δοκοῦντες," ἔφη, "χαίρειν καὶ γελᾶν αὐτῶν οἱ εἰληφότες 7
τι παρ' αὐτῆς εἰσιν· οὗτοι δὲ καὶ Ἀγαθὴν Τύχην αὐτὴν καλοῦσιν. οἱ δὲ δοκοῦντες 8
κλαίειν εἰσὶ παρ' ὧν ἀφείλετο ἃ δέδωκε πρότερον αὐτοῖς. οὗτοι δὲ πάλιν αὐτὴν 9
Κακὴν Τύχην καλοῦσι." 10

Ξένος "τίνα οὖν ἐστιν ἃ δίδωσιν αὐτοῖς, ὅτι οὕτως οἱ μὲν λαμβάνοντες 11
χαίρουσιν, οἱ δὲ ἀποβάλλοντες κλαίουσι;" 12

Πρεσβύτης "ταῦτα," ἔφη, "ἃ παρὰ τοῖς πολλοῖς ἀνθρώποις δοκεῖ εἶναι 13
ἀγαθά." 14

Ξένος "ταῦτα οὖν τίνα ἐστί;" 15

Πρεσβύτης "πλοῦτος δηλονότι καὶ δόξα καὶ εὐγένεια καὶ τέκνα καὶ 16
τυραννίδες καὶ βασιλεῖαι καὶ τἆλλα ὅσα τούτοις παραπλήσια." 17

Ξένος "ταῦτα οὖν πῶς οὐκ ἔστιν ἀγαθά;" 18

Πρεσβύτης "περὶ μὲν τούτων," ἔφη, "καὶ αὖθις ἐκποιήσει διαλέγεσθαι, νῦν 19
δὲ περὶ τὴν μῡθολογίαν γῑνώμεθα." 20

Ξένος "ἔστω οὕτως." 21

(β)

Exercise 21θ

Translate the English phrases with the correct present active or passive subjunctive forms of the verbs supplied:

1. ἵημι: let us be sending   _____
2. ἵημι: am I to be sent?   _____
3. ἵημι: what <u>should we be sending</u>?   _____
4. δείκνῡμι: let us be showing!   _____
5. δείκνῡμι: if <u>he/she is being shown</u>   _____
6. πάρειμι: if <u>you</u> (pl.) <u>are here</u> _____
7. πάρειμι: so that <u>they may be here</u>   _____
8. δίδωμι: let us be giving!   _____
9. δίδωμι: are they to be given?   _____
10. εἶμι: if <u>you</u> (sing.) <u>are going</u> _____
11. εἶμι: should we be going?   _____
12. τίθημι:
        so that <u>he/she may be putting</u>   _____
13. τίθημι: if <u>we are being put</u>   _____
14. τίθημι: let us be putting!   _____
15. ἵστημι:
        so that <u>we may be setting</u> X <u>up</u> _____
16. ἵστημι:
        if <u>you</u> (pl.) <u>are being set up</u>   _____
17. ἵστημι: are they to be setting X up?   _____

Exercise 21ι

Translate the English phrases with the correct aorist active or passive subjunctive forms of the verbs supplied:

1. ἵημι: let us send!   _____
2. ἵημι: if <u>you (sing.) send</u>   _____
3. ἵημι: what <u>are they to send</u>?   _____
4. δείκνῡμι: if <u>he/she shows</u>   _____
5. δείκνῡμι: don't <u>show</u>! (pl.)   _____
6. δείκνῡμι: so that it <u>may be shown</u>   _____

7. δείκνῡμι: let us show!   _____

8. δίδωμι: don't <u>give</u>! (sing.)   _____

9. δίδωμι: let us give!   _____

10. δίδωμι: is he/she to give?   _____

11. τίθημι: so that <u>I may put</u>   _____

12. τίθημι: if <u>they put</u>   _____

13. τίθημι: don't <u>put</u>! (pl.)   _____

14. ἵστημι: so that <u>we may be set up</u> _____

15. ἵστημι: if <u>you</u> (pl.) <u>set</u> X <u>up</u> _____

16. ἵστημι: are we to set X up?   _____

Exercise 21κ

Match the Greek verbs in column A with appropriate translations in column B and write the numbers of the Greek verbs in the spaces provided:

A   B

1. στήσεσθε   a. ____ let us throw X for ourselves!

2. ἀποδῶται   b. ____ don't <u>set</u> X <u>up for yourselves</u>!

3. ἱστώμεθα   c. ____ so that <u>we may sell</u>

4. ὤμεθα   d. ____ let us be setting X up for ourselves

5. στῇς   e. ____ so that <u>you</u> (pl.) <u>may hasten</u>

6. ἱῶνται   f. ____ don't <u>stand</u>! (sing.)

7. ἀποδιδώμεθα   g. ____ if <u>he/she sells</u>

8. στήσωνται   h. ____ so that <u>they may hasten</u>

9. ἱῆσθε   i. ____ so that <u>they may set</u> X <u>up for themselves</u>

Exercise 21λ

Give an English equivalent of:

1. πληρόω   _____   7. ἐπιβουλεύω   _____

2. ὁ ἰδιώτης   _____   8. ἡ δύναμις   _____

3. ἑκάτερος   _____   9. ἀδύνατος   _____

4. ἡ χώρᾱ   _____   10. νομίζω   _____

5. πεζῇ   _____   11. τελευταῖος   _____

6. τοιοῦτος   _____   12. ἀνάγκη
                                         ἐστί(ν)   _____

1 ὡς ἄν + subjunctive, *when(ever)*.
   ἀνωτέρω, comparative adv., *higher up*.
2 περίβολος, περιβόλου, ὁ, *enclosure*.
   ἑστηκυίᾱς: *standing* (perfect participle, feminine accusative plural, of ἵστημι).
   κοσμέω, *I put in order; I adorn*.
      κεκοσμημένᾱς: *(having been) adorned* (perfect passive participle).
3 ἑταίρᾱ, ἑταίρᾱς, ἡ, *courtesan*.
   εἰώθᾱσι: *(they) are accustomed* (perfect of ἔθω, *I am accustomed;* the perfect tense
      of this verb has a present sense).
4 καὶ μάλα: *certainly; yes*.
5 τοίνυν [τοι + νυν], particle, *therefore, accordingly; well then*.
   ἀκρασίᾱ, ἀκρασίᾱς, ἡ [ἀ- + τὸ κράτος], *lack of power/control over one's
      passions; intemperance*.
   ἀσωτίᾱ, ἀσωτίᾱς, ἡ [ἀ- + σῴζω], *wastefulness, prodigality, profligacy*.
6 ἀπληστίᾱ, ἀπληστίᾱς, ἡ [ἀ- + πίμπλημι, πλήσω, *I fill*], *greediness,
      covetousness*.
   κολακείᾱ, κολακείᾱς, ἡ [κολακεύω, *I flatter*], *flattery*.
7 ὧδε, adv., *thus; here*.
   ἑστήκᾱσιν: *(they) stand* (perfect, 3rd person plural, of ἵστημι).
8 παρατηρέω, *I watch closely*.
   εἰληφότας: *the ones who have taken* (perfect active participle, accusative plural
      masculine, of λαμβάνω; see Ch. 23β PP, p. 115).
   παρά, prep. + gen., *from*.
9 εἶτα, adv., *then, next*.
10 ἀναπηδάω, *I leap up*.
   συμπλέκομαι + dat., *I embrace*.
   κολακεύω, *I flatter*.
11 ἀξιόω, *I think X worthy; I ask*.
   παρά, prep. + dat., *among, with*.
   αὐταῖς: = ἑαυταῖς.
   ἡδύς, ἡδεῖα, ἡδύ, *sweet, pleasant*.
   ἄπονος, ἄπονον, *free from toil, painless*.
12 κακοπάθεια, κακοπαθείᾱς, ἡ, *bad experience, distress, misery, hardship*.
13 ἡδυπάθεια, ἡδυπαθείᾱς, ἡ, *sweet experience; luxury*.
   μέχρι, prep. + gen., *up to, until*.
      μέχρι μέν τινος: *up to a certain point;* μέν by itself confers emphasis.
   διατριβή, διατριβῆς, ἡ, *way of spending time, pastime*.
   ἕως, conj., *until;* here + ἄν + subjunctive, *so long as, while*.
   γαργαλίζω, *I tickle, titillate*.
14 ὅταν, conj., *when(ever)*.
   ἀνανήφω, ἀνανήψω, ἀνένηψα, *I regain my senses; I become sober again*.
      ὅταν … ἀνανήψῃ: *whenever he regains his senses / sobers up* (aorist
         subjunctive in a present general temporal clause introduced by ὅταν; see
         Ch. 22, Gr. 2, pp. 94 and 95; translate as present).
   αἰσθάνομαι, *I perceive; I realize*.
15 κατεσθίω [κατα- + ἐσθίω], *I eat up, devour*.
   ὑβρίζω, *I maltreat, outrage, treat insultingly*.
   διό, conj. = δι᾽ ὅ, *wherefore, for which reason, therefore*.
   ἀναλίσκω, ἀναλώσω, ἀνήλωσα, *I use up, spend, squander*.
   ὅσος, ὅση, ὅσον, *as great as; as much as;* pl., *as many as*.

Exercise 21μ

Translate into English on a separate sheet of paper:

ΚΕΒΗΤΟΣ ΠΙΝΑΞ

IX.

Πρεσβύτης "ὁρᾷς οὖν, ὡς ἂν παρέλθῃς τὴν πύλην ταύτην, ἀνωτέρω ἄλλον 1
περίβολον καὶ γυναῖκας ἔξω τοῦ περιβόλου ἑστηκυίας, κεκοσμημένᾱς ὥσπερ 2
ἑταῖραι εἰώθᾱσι;" 3

Ξένος "καὶ μάλα." 4

Πρεσβύτης "αὗται τοίνυν ἡ μὲν Ἀκρασίᾱ καλεῖται, ἡ δὲ Ἀσωτίᾱ, ἡ δὲ 5
Ἀπληστίᾱ, ἡ δὲ Κολακείᾱ." 6

Ξένος "τί οὖν ὧδε ἑστήκᾱσιν αὗται;" 7

Πρεσβύτης "παρατηροῦσιν," ἔφη, "τοὺς εἰληφότας τι παρὰ τῆς Τύχης." 8

Ξένος "εἶτα τί;" 9

Πρεσβύτης "ἀναπηδῶσι καὶ συμπλέκονται αὐτοῖς καὶ κολακεύουσι καὶ 10
ἀξιοῦσι παρ' αὐταῖς μένειν λέγουσαι ὅτι βίον ἕξουσιν ἡδύν τε καὶ ἄπονον καὶ 11
κακοπάθειαν ἔχοντα οὐδεμίαν. ἐὰν οὖν τις πεισθῇ ὑπ' αὐτῶν εἰσελθεῖν εἰς τὴν 12
Ἡδυπάθειαν, μέχρι μέν τινος ἡδεῖα δοκεῖ εἶναι ἡ διατριβή, ἕως ἂν γαργαλίζῃ τὸν 13
ἄνθρωπον, εἶτ' οὐκέτι. ὅταν γὰρ ἀνανήψῃ, αἰσθάνεται ὅτι οὐκ ἤσθιεν, ἀλλ' ὑπ' 14
αὐτῆς κατησθίετο καὶ ὑβρίζετο. διὸ καὶ ὅταν ἀναλώσῃ πάντα ὅσα ἔλαβε παρὰ 15
τῆς Τύχης, ἀναγκάζεται ταύταις ταῖς γυναιξὶ δουλεύειν καὶ πάνθ' ὑπομένειν καὶ 16
ἀσχημονεῖν καὶ ποιεῖν ἕνεκεν τούτων πάντα ὅσα ἐστὶ βλαβερά, οἷον ἀποστερεῖν, 17
ἱεροσυλεῖν, ἐπιορκεῖν, προδιδόναι, ληΐζεσθαι καὶ πάνθ' ὅσα τούτοις παραπλήσια. 18
ὅταν οὖν πάντα αὐτοῖς ἐπιλίπῃ, παραδίδονται τῇ Τῑμωρίᾳ." 19

---

16 **δουλεύω** + dat., *I serve* X *as a slave, I am a slave* to X.
   ὑπομένω, *I submit to; I endure.*

17 **ἀσχημονέω,** *I behave in an unseemly / indecent manner.*
   ἕνεκεν [= ἕνεκα], prep. + gen., *for the sake of, on account of, because of.*
   βλαβερός, βλαβερά, βλαβερόν [βλάπτω], *harmful, injurious.*
   οἷον, adv., *such as.*
   ἀποστερέω, *I rob, steal.*

18 **ἱεροσυλέω,** *I rob temples.*
   ἐπιορκέω, *I swear falsely; I commit perjury.*
   προδίδωμι, *I give up; I betray.*
   ληΐζομαι, *I plunder.*
   παραπλήσιος, παραπλήσιον + dat., *resembling, similar* (to).

19 **ἐπιλείπω, ἐπιλείψω, ἐπέλιπον** + dat., *I fail* (someone); *I run out* (for someone).
   ὅταν ... ἐπιλίπῃ: aorist subjunctive, *whenever....*
   τῑμωρίᾱ, τῑμωρίᾱς, ἡ, *vengeance; retribution.*

Exercise 21ν

Give the Greek equivalent of:

1.	I begin	_____	7.	at (of time)	_____
2.	privately	_____	8.	I lead forward	_____
3.	army	_____	9.	lengthy	_____
4.	like	_____	10.	honor	_____
5.	manner	_____	11.	justice	_____
6.	capable	_____	12.	such as the following	_____

Exercise 21ξ

Give the remaining principal parts of:

1. ἄρχω   _____   5. θαυμάζω   _____
                          _____   _____
                          _____   _____
                          _____   _____

2. νομίζω   _____   _____
                          _____   6. φράζω   _____
                          _____   _____
                          _____   _____
                          _____   _____

3. πληρόω   _____   _____
                          _____   7. κομίζω   _____
                          _____   _____
                          _____   _____
                          _____   _____

4. ὀργίζομαι   _____   _____

                  or _____

                          _____
                          _____

22
Η ΑΝΑΣΤΑΣΙΣ (α)

Exercise 22 α

Write Greek equivalents for the underlined clauses or phrases below using the verbs supplied:

1. I'm afraid <u>that he will come</u>. (ἐλθεῖν)

2. There is always the danger <u>that it will not happen</u>. (γενέσθαι)

3. The farmer was afraid <u>that the enemy would come</u>. (ἐλθεῖν)

4. She was afraid <u>to see</u> this. (ἰδεῖν)

5. We fear <u>that she may listen to</u> him. (ἀκούειν)

6. The enemy did not fear <u>to invade</u> Attica. (εἰσβαλεῖν)

7. He was afraid <u>that it might not happen</u>. (γενέσθαι)

8. We were afraid <u>to be doing</u> this. (ποιεῖν)

Exercise 22 β

Write Greek equivalents for the underlined clauses below using the verbs supplied. Identify each underlined clause, using the first letter of one of the descriptors from the A list and one from the B list:

    A: <u>R</u>elative, <u>T</u>emporal, <u>C</u>onditional
    B: <u>D</u>efinite, <u>I</u>ndefinite

1.   <u>When he came</u> yesterday, there was trouble. (ἐλθεῖν) ___ ___

2.   <u>Whenever he comes</u>, there is trouble. (ἐλθεῖν) ___ ___

3.   <u>Whoever sees this thing</u> does not praise it. (ἰδεῖν) ___ ___

4.   The boy <u>who saw this thing</u> did not praise it. (ἰδεῖν) ___ ___

5.   Let's wait <u>until the messenger arrives</u>. (ἀφικέσθαι) ___ ___

6.   <u>When the messenger arrived</u>, we saw him. (ἀφικέσθαι) ___ ___

7.   The thing <u>that she is saying</u> is not clear to us. (λέγειν) ___ ___

8.   <u>Whatever she says</u> is not clear to us. (λέγειν) ___ ___

9.   <u>If you are doing this</u> now, we are pleased. (ποιεῖν) ___ ___

10. <u>If you ever do this</u>, it always pleases us. (ποιεῖν) ___ ___

11. <u>Whenever we return to Athens</u>, he tells us what has happened.

    (ἐπανελθεῖν) ___ ___

12. <u>When we returned to Athens</u> today, he told us what had happened.

    (ἐπανελθεῖν) ___ ___

13. <u>Whoever waits</u> here will be seen by the enemy. (μένειν) __ __

_____

14. <u>If you wait</u> here, you will be sorry! (μένειν) __ __

_____

Exercise 22 γ

Give an English equivalent of:

1. ἀνίσταμαι _____   5. πρίν _____

2. ἡ οἴκησις _____   6. λούω _____

3. ἐπειδή _____   7. ὅστις _____

4. πάντες ὅσοι _____   8. ἐπειδάν _____

Exercise 22 δ

Give the Greek equivalent of:

1. I invade _____   5. since _____

2. forced move _____   6. as great as _____

3. guard _____   7. I exist _____

4. I wash myself _____   8. I stand up
                                       against _____

Exercise 22 ε

Give the remaining principal parts of:

1. ἀνθίσταμαι _____   5. ἀγγέλλω _____
   _____   _____
   _____   _____

2. ἀνίσταμαι _____   _____
   _____   _____
   _____   6. βάλλω _____

3. λούω _____   _____
   _____   _____
   _____   _____

4. φαίνω _____   _____
   or _____   7. φαίνομαι _____
   _____   or _____
   _____   _____

1 ποῖος, ποίᾱ, ποῖον, *what sort/kind of; of what sort/kind?*
   αὕτη: i.e., ἡ Τῑμωρίᾱ (see ΚΕΒΗΤΟΣ ΠΙΝΑΞ IX:19, p. 53).

2 ὀπίσω, prep. + gen., *behind*.
   τι: *somewhat, a little*, with ὀπίσω.
   αὐτῶν: with ὀπίσω.
   θύριον, θυρίου, τό [diminutive of ἡ θύρᾱ], *little door*.

3 σκοτεινός, σκοτεινή, σκοτεινόν, *dark*.

4 καὶ μάλα: *certainly; yes*.

5 οὐκοῦν, adv., *then* (introducing a question that expects the answer "yes" and
      carries the thought forward from a previous assent).
   αἰσχρός, αἰσχρά, αἰσχρόν, *shameful; ugly*.
   ῥυπαρός, ῥυπαρά, ῥυπαρόν, *dirty, filthy*.
   ῥάκος, ῥάκους, τό, *ragged garment*.

6 ἠμφιεσμέναι: *clothed in* + acc. (perfect passive participle of ἀμφιέννῡμι [ἀμφι- +
      ἕννῡμι, *I put clothes on* X], *I put around/on; I clothe*; this verb is peculiar in
      augmenting its prefix; the principal parts are ἀμφιέννῡμι, ἀμφιέσω, ἠμφίεσα,
      ἠμφίεσμαι, ἠμφιέσθην).
   συνεῖναι: *to be together*.

8 αὗται τοίνυν: *Well then, these* (are as follows).
   μάστιξ, μάστιγος, ἡ, *whip, lash*.

9 τῑμωρίᾱ, τῑμωρίᾱς, ἡ, *vengeance; retribution*.
   γόνυ, γόνατος, τό, *knee*.
   λύπη, λύπης, ἡ [λῡπέω], *pain* (of body); *pain* (of mind); *grief*.
   θρίξ, τριχός, ἡ, *hair* (a single one); (usually in plural), *hair*.
   τίλλω, *I pull/pluck out*.

10 ὀδύνη, ὀδύνης, ἡ [ὀδυνάω, *I cause pain*], *pain* (of body); *pain* (of mind); *grief;
      distress*.

11 παρεστηκὼς: *standing near* (1st perfect active participle, nominative singular
      masculine, of παρίστημι).
   δυσειδής, δυσειδές [δυσ-, *un-, mis-, bad* + εἶδος, εἴδους, τό, *form, figure*],
      misshapen, deformed, ugly.
   λεπτός, λεπτή, λεπτόν, *thin, gaunt*.

12 γυμνός, γυμνή, γυμνόν, *naked*.

13 ὀδυρμός, ὀδυρμοῦ, ὁ [cf. ὀδύρομαι, *I grieve*], *lamentation*.
   ἀθῡμίᾱ, ἀθῡμίᾱς, ἡ, *lack of spirit; discouragement, dejection, despair*.
   ἀδελφή, ἀδελφῆς, ἡ, *sister*.

14 συμβιόω, *I live with*.
   τῑμωρέω, *I avenge*; passive, *I am visited with vengeance; I am punished*.
   εἶτα, adv., *then, next*.

15 πάλιν, adv., *back; again; in turn*.
   ἕτερος, ἑτέρᾱ, ἕτερον, *one* or *the other* (of two); *other, another*.
   ῥίπτω, *I throw*.
   κακοδαιμονίᾱ, κακοδαιμονίᾱς, ἡ, *evil fortune; unhappiness*.
   ὧδε, adv., *thus; here*.

Exercise 22ζ

Translate into English on a separate sheet of paper:

ΚΕΒΗΤΟΣ ΠΙΝΑΞ

X.

Ξένος "ποίᾱ δέ ἐστιν αὕτη;" 1

Πρεσβύτης "ὁρᾷς ὀπίσω τι," ἔφη, "αὐτῶν ἄνω ὥσπερ θύριον μικρὸν καὶ τόπον 2
στενόν τινα καὶ σκοτεινόν;" 3

Ξένος "καὶ μάλα." 4

Πρεσβύτης "οὐκοῦν καὶ γυναῖκες αἰσχραὶ καὶ ῥυπαραὶ καὶ ῥάκη 5
ἠμφιεσμέναι δοκοῦσι συνεῖναι;" 6

Ξένος "καὶ μάλα." 7

Πρεσβύτης "αὗται τοίνυν," ἔφη, "ἡ μὲν τὴν μάστιγα ἔχουσα καλεῖται 8
Τῑμωρίᾱ, ἡ δὲ τὴν κεφαλὴν ἐν τοῖς γόνασιν ἔχουσα Λύπη, ἡ δὲ τὰς τρίχας τίλλουσα 9
ἑαυτῆς Ὀδύνη." 10

Ξένος "ὁ δὲ ἄλλος οὗτος ὁ παρεστηκὼς αὐταῖς δυσειδής τις καὶ λεπτὸς καὶ 11
γυμνός, καὶ μετ' αὐτοῦ τις ἄλλη ὁμοίᾱ αὐτῷ αἰσχρὰ καὶ λεπτή, τίς ἐστιν;" 12

Πρεσβύτης "ὁ μὲν Ὀδυρμὸς καλεῖται," ἔφη, "ἡ δὲ Ἀθῡμίᾱ, ἀδελφὴ δ' ἐστὶν 13
αὕτη αὐτοῦ. τούτοις οὖν παραδίδοται καὶ μετὰ τούτων συμβιοῖ τῑμωρούμενος· εἶτα 14
ἐνταῦθα πάλιν εἰς τὸν ἕτερον οἶκον ῥίπτεται, εἰς τὴν Κακοδαιμονίᾱν, καὶ ὧδε τὸν 15
λοιπὸν βίον καταστρέφει ἐν πάσῃ κακοδαιμονίᾳ, ἂν μὴ ἡ Μετάνοια αὐτῷ ἐπιτύχῃ 16
ἐκ προαιρέσεως συναντήσασα." 17

---

16 **λοιπός, λοιπή, λοιπόν,** *remaining.*
καταστρέφω, *I turn down; I bring to an end.*
ἂν = ἐὰν.
ἂν μή, *unless.*
μετάνοια, μετανοίᾱς, ἡ, [μετα-, *change* + ὁ νοῦς], *change of mind;*
repentance.
ἐπιτυγχάνω, ἐπιτεύξομαι, ἐπέτυχον + dat., *I happen upon, meet (up) with.*
ἂν ... ἐπιτύχῃ: if-clause of a present general condition.
17 **προαίρεσις, προαιρέσεως, ἡ,** *choosing one thing before another; choice;*
purpose.
ἐκ προαιρέσεως: *of [her own] choice, for [her own] purpose.*
συναντάω, συναντήσω, συνήντησα, *I meet face to face, encounter.*

(β)

Exercise 22 η

Translate the underlined clauses into Greek using the verbs supplied and introducing the indirect statements with ὅτι:

1. I know <u>that (my) friend will be here</u>. (πάρειμι)

   _____

2. The man said <u>that he would return</u>. (ἐπανέρχομαι)

   _____

3. The woman said <u>that the girl had gone away to the spring</u>. (ἀπέρχομαι)

   _____

4. The girl said <u>that she would bring water</u>. (κομίζω)

   _____

5. The messenger announced <u>that the enemy was advancing</u>. (προέρχομαι)

   _____

6. We have heard <u>that they are nearby (ἐγγύς)</u>. (εἰμί)

   _____

7. The old man said <u>that the slave had not worked</u>. (πονέω)

   _____

8. The slave had said <u>that he was tired</u>. (κάμνω)

   _____

9. The boys said <u>that the dog had run away</u>. (ἀποτρέχω)

   _____

10. The father said <u>that the dog was staying in the field</u>. (μένω)

   _____

Exercise 22 θ

Translate the underlined clauses into Greek using the verbs supplied:

1.   She does not know <u>who he is</u>. (εἰμί)

_____

2.   Do you know <u>where we are going</u>? (ἔρχομαι)

_____

3.   The girl did not know <u>why her father had gone</u>. (ἀπέρχομαι)

_____

4.   The father seeks to know <u>how long (= how much time) his daughter would be away</u>. (ἄπειμι)

_____

5.   The slave asked <u>when he would stop working</u>. (παύομαι)

_____

6.   Does she know <u>what the stranger brought</u>? (κομίζω)

_____

7.   The mother asks <u>where (her) children are</u>. (εἰμί)

_____

8.   The man did not know <u>who was knocking on</u> the door. (κόπτω)

_____

9.   The boys asked <u>from where the dog had returned</u>. (ἐπανέρχομαι)

_____

10. The mother asked <u>how much water the girl had brought</u>. (κομίζω)

_____

Exercise 22 ι

Give an English equivalent of:

1. ἡ ἅμαξα _____   5. οὐδέποτε _____
2. τοσόσδε _____   6. ἐνδίδωμι _____
3. ὀδύρομαι _____   7. ὅπως _____
4. τὸ ἔαρ _____

1   εἶτα, adv., *then, next.*
     μετάνοια, μετανοίας, ἡ, [μετα-, *change* + ὁ νοῦς, *mind*], *change of mind;*
        repentance.
     συναντάω, συναντήσω, συνήντησα, *I meet face to face, encounter.*
2   ἐξαιρέω, ἐξαιρήσω, ἐξεῖλον, *I take out, remove.*
     συνίστημι, *I set together; I bring together as friends; I introduce/recommend*
        X *to* Y.
     ἕτερος, ἑτέρᾱ, ἕτερον, *one* or *the other* (of two); *other, another.*
3   δόξα, δόξης, ἡ, *notion; opinion; good reputation; honor.*
     ἀληθινός, ἀληθινή, ἀληθινόν, *true.*
     παιδείᾱ, παιδείᾱς, ἡ, *education.*
     ψευδοπαιδείᾱ, ψευδοπαιδείᾱς, ἡ, *false education.*
6   προσδέχομαι, προσδέξομαι, προσεδεξάμην, *I receive; I accept.*
7   καθαίρω, καθαρῶ, ἐκάθηρα, κεκάθαρμαι, ἐκαθάρθην, *I purge, cleanse,*
        purify.
     μακάριος, μακαρίᾱ, μακάριον, *blessed, happy.*
8   εὐδαίμων, εὔδαιμον [= with a good δαίμων, *spirit, fate, lot*], *fortunate, happy.*
     πάλιν, adv., *back; again; in turn.*
     πλανάω, πλανήσω, *I make* X *wander; I lead* X *astray; I deceive* X.
        πλανᾶται: passive.
     ψευδοδοξίᾱ, ψευδοδοξίᾱς, ἡ, *false opinion.*

Exercise 22 κ

Give the Greek equivalent of:

1. outside   _____   5. I receive   _____
2. tower   _____   6. family   _____
3. I yoke   _____   7. advice   _____
4. camp   _____

Exercise 22 λ

Translate into English on a separate sheet of paper:

ΚΕΒΗΤΟΣ ΠΙΝΑΞ

XI.

    Ξένος "εἶτα τί γίνεται, ἐὰν ἡ Μετάνοια αὐτῷ συναντήσῃ;"   1

    Πρεσβύτης "ἐξαιρεῖ αὐτὸν ἐκ τῶν κακῶν καὶ συνίστησιν αὐτῷ ἑτέρᾱν   2

Δόξαν τὴν εἰς τὴν Ἀληθινὴν Παιδείᾱν ἄγουσαν, ἅμα δὲ καὶ τὴν εἰς τὴν Ψευδο-   3

παιδείᾱν καλουμένην."   4

    Ξένος "εἶτα τί γίνεται;"   5

    Πρεσβύτης "ἐὰν μέν," φησί, "τὴν Δόξαν ταύτην προσδέξηται τὴν ἄξουσαν   6

αὐτὸν εἰς τὴν Ἀληθινὴν Παιδείᾱν, καθαρθεὶς ὑπ' αὐτῆς σῴζεται καὶ μακάριος καὶ   7

εὐδαίμων γίνεται ἐν τῷ βίῳ· εἰ δὲ μή, πάλιν πλανᾶται ὑπὸ τῆς Ψευδοδοξίᾱς."   8

Exercise 22 μ

Give the remaining principal parts of:

1. ζεύγνῡμι   _____   4. κρῑ́νω   _____

    _____   _____

    _____   _____

    _____   _____

               or _____

2. ἀποκτείνω   _____   5. ἀποκρῑ́νομαι   _____

    _____   _____

    _____   _____

3. μένω   _____

    _____

    _____

23
Η ΕΣΒΟΛΗ (α)

Exercise 23 α

Translate the underlined clauses into Greek using the verbs supplied:

1. ἡ γυνή φησι <u>that her daughter is walking to the spring</u>. (βαίνω)

   _____

2. ἡ γυνὴ πιστεύει <u>that her daughter will go to the spring</u>. (βαίνω)

   _____

3. ἡ γυνὴ ἐλπίζει <u>that her daughter went to the spring</u>. (βαίνω)

   _____

4. ἡ γυνὴ ἔφη <u>that she would go to the spring</u>. (βαίνω)

   _____

5. ὁ ἀνὴρ ἐπίστευε <u>that the boys had returned from the field</u>. (ἐπανέρχομαι)

   _____

6. ὁ ἀνὴρ ἔφη <u>that he himself was walking to the field</u>. (βαίνω)

   _____

7. ὁ ἀνὴρ οὐκ ἔφη <u>that he had seen the boys</u>. (ὁράω)

   _____

8. οἱ παῖδες ἤλπιζον <u>that they would not go to the field</u>. (βαίνω)

   _____

9. ἡ παρθένος ἤλπιζε <u>that she would see her friends</u>. (ὁράω)

   _____

10. <u>The girl said that her friends were not waiting at home</u>. (φημί, μένω)

   _____

Exercise 23 β

Translate the underlined clauses into Greek using the verbs supplied:

1. ἡ γυνὴ οἶδε <u>that her daughter is walking to the spring</u>. (βαίνω)

   _____

2. ἡ γυνὴ ἐπίσταται <u>that her daughter will go to the spring</u>. (βαίνω)

   _____

3. ἡ γυνὴ εἶδε <u>that her daughter had gone to the spring</u>. (βαίνω)

   _____

4. ἡ γυνὴ ἔγνω <u>that she would go to the spring</u>. (βαίνω)

   _____

5. ὁ ἀνὴρ ἔγνω <u>that the boys had returned from the field</u>. (ἐπανέρχομαι)

   _____

6. ὁ ἀνὴρ οἶδεν <u>that he himself is walking to the field</u>. (βαίνω)

   _____

7. ὁ ἀνὴρ οὐκ ἠπίστατο <u>that he had seen the boys</u>. (ὁράω)

   _____

8. οἱ παῖδες ἠπίσταντο <u>that they would not go to the field</u>. (βαίνω)

   _____

9. ἡ παρθένος ἠπίστατο <u>that she would see her friends</u>. (ὁράω)

   _____

10. ἡ παρθένος οἶδε <u>that her friends are not waiting at home</u>. (μένω)

   _____

Exercise 23 γ

Give an English equivalent of:

1. τάττω   _____   5. ὁ χῶρος   _____

2. τὸ φρούριον   _____   6. ἡ εἰσβολή   _____

3. ὁπότε   _____   7. καθέζομαι   _____

4. ἐπεξέρχομαι   _____   8. ᾗπερ   _____

1   Ἡρακλῆς, Ἡρακλέους, ὁ, *Heracles*.
         Ἡράκλεις: vocative case.
     ψευδοπαιδείᾱ, ψευδοπαιδείᾱς, ἡ, *false education*.
2   ποῖος, ποίᾱ, ποῖον, *what sort/kind of; of what sort/kind?*
3   ἕτερος, ἑτέρᾱ, ἕτερον, *one* or *the other* (of two); *other, another*.
     περίβολος, περιβόλου, ὁ, *enclosure*.
4   καὶ μάλα: *certainly; yes*.
5   οὐκοῦν, adv., *then* (introducing a question that expects the answer "yes" and
         carries the thought forward from a previous assent; contrast οὔκουν).
     παρά, prep. + acc., *beside, near, by*.
     εἴσοδος, εἰσόδου, ἡ, *entrance*.
     ἕστηκεν, *is standing* (perfect of ἵστημι).
6   πάνυ, adv., *very, very much*.
     καθάριος, καθάριον, *cleanly, neat, tidy, respectable*.
     εὔτακτος, -ον [cf. τάττω], *well-ordered, well-behaved*.
8   τοίνυν [τοι + νυν], particle, *therefore, accordingly; well then*.
     εἰκαῖος, εἰκαίᾱ, εἰκαῖον [cf. εἰκῇ, adv., *without plan/purpose; at random,
         recklessly*], *purposeless, heedless*.
     παιδείᾱ, παιδείᾱς, ἡ, *education*.
9   τοι, particle, *in truth, indeed*.
     ὁπόταν [ὁπότε + ἄν] + subjunctive, *whenever*.
10   ἀληθινός, ἀληθινή, ἀληθινόν, *true*.
     ὧδε, adv., *thus; here*.
     παραγῑνονται: = παραγίγνονται.
11   ἐπί, prep. + acc., *to*.

Exercise 23 δ

Translate into English on a separate sheet of paper:

ΚΕΒΗΤΟΣ ΠΙΝΑΞ

XII.

Ξένος "ὦ Ἡράκλεις, ὡς μέγας ὁ κίνδῠνος ἄλλος οὗτος. ἡ δὲ Ψευδοπαιδείᾱ, 1
ποίᾱ ἐστίν;" ἔφην ἐγώ. 2

Πρεσβύτης "οὐχ ὁρᾷς τὸν ἕτερον περίβολον ἐκεῖνον;" 3

Ξένος "καὶ μάλα," ἔφην ἐγώ. 4

Πρεσβύτης "οὐκοῦν ἔξω τοῦ περιβόλου παρὰ τὴν εἴσοδον γυνή τις ἕστηκεν, ἣ 5
δοκεῖ πάνυ καθάριος καὶ εὔτακτος εἶναι;" 6

Ξένος "καὶ μάλα." 7

Πρεσβύτης "ταύτην τοίνυν οἱ πολλοὶ καὶ εἰκαῖοι τῶν ἀνδρῶν Παιδείᾱν 8
καλοῦσιν· οὐκ ἔστι δέ, ἀλλὰ Ψευδοπαιδείᾱ," ἔφη. "οἱ μέν τοι σῳζόμενοι ὁπόταν 9
βούλωνται εἰς τὴν Ἀληθινὴν Παιδείᾱν ἐλθεῖν, ὧδε πρῶτον παραγῑνονται." 10

Ξένος "πότερον οὖν ἄλλη ὁδὸς οὐκ ἔστιν ἐπὶ τὴν Ἀληθινὴν Παιδείᾱν 11
ἄγουσα;" 12

Πρεσβύτης "οὐκ ἔστιν," ἔφη. 13

Exercise 23 ε

Give the Greek equivalent of:

1. (the) attack   _____
2. friendly   _____
3. I overlook   _____
4. district   _____

5. cause   _____
6. I cut   _____
7. the people   _____
8. trial   _____

Exercise 23 ζ

Give the remaining principal parts of:

1. καθέζομαι   _____   5. διαφθείρω   _____

2. τάττω   _____   _____

                     _____   _____

                     _____   **or** _____

                     _____   _____

                     _____   _____

3. τέμνω   _____   6. ἐγείρω   _____

                     _____   _____

                     _____   _____

                     _____   _____

                     _____   _____

4. αἴρω   _____   _____

                     _____

                     _____

                     _____

                     _____

(β)

Exercise 23η

Fill in the blanks with either the infinitive or the participle, as appropriate, of the verbs supplied; keep the same tense and voice as given. If there is more than one possibility, you need give only one form:

N.B.: Remember that for the infinitive and participle of ἔρχομαι Attic Greek uses the infinitive and participle of εἶμι.

1. τὸν Σωκράτην φημὶ τὸν ἄριστον ἄνθρωπον _____ . (εἰμί)

2. οἱ ἄνδρες εἶδον τὰς γυναῖκας οἴκαδε _____ . (ἔρχομαι)

3. πάντες πιστεύουσι τὸν ἄγγελον εἰς τὴν ἀγορὰν δι᾽ ὀλίγου _____ .
    (εἰσβήσομαι)

4. ὁ δοῦλος ἔφη τὸν ἰατρὸν δι᾽ ὀλίγου _____ . (παρέσομαι)

5. ὁ δεσπότης ἐλπίζει τοὺς δούλους πολλὰ _____ . (ποιήσω)

6. οἶδα ἡμᾶς μεγάλην ἀρετὴν _____ . (ἔδειξα)

7. οὐκ ἔφη οἴκαδε αὔριον _____ . (ἐπάνειμι)

8. ὁ ἄγγελος ἔφη τοὺς πολεμίους ἤδη _____ . (ἀφῑκόμην)

9. ἠκούσαμεν τοὺς παῖδας εἰς τὴν οἰκίᾱν _____ . (εἰσέρχομαι)

10. ἐλπίζομεν ἐν τῇ ἀγορᾷ τοὺς φίλους _____ . (εὑρήσω)

11. ἠπιστάμην τὸν Σωκράτην ἀγαθὸν ἄνδρα _____ . (εἰμί)

12. νομίζω τοὺς παῖδας οἴκαδε _____ . (ἔρχομαι)

Exercise 23θ

Choose one of the following forms of the articular infinitive to match the underlined English phrase in each of the sentences below:

(A) τὸ ἀδικεῖν. (B) τῷ ἀδικεῖν. (C) τοῦ ἀδικεῖν.

____ 1. <u>By being unjust</u> we harm ourselves.

____ 2. <u>Being unjust</u> is a harmful thing.

____ 3. He did this not from (ἀπὸ) <u>being unjust</u> but since he was afraid.

____ 4. We knew nothing about (περὶ) <u>being unjust</u>.

____ 5. Justice is not <u>being unjust</u>.

Exercise 23 ι

Choose the correct form of the relative pronoun to replace the underlined unattracted form in each sentence below and write the correct form in the blank:

ἧς, ᾗ, ἥν, ὧν, αἷς, ἅς, οὗ, ᾧ, ὅν, οἷς, οὕς, ὅ, ἅ

1. We saw the brother <u>of the woman whom</u> (τῆς γυναικὸς <u>ἥν</u>) _____ you saw.

2. They spoke <u>about those things that</u> (περὶ ἐκείνων <u>ἅ</u>) _____ you related.

3. We heard <u>the speaker whom</u> (τοῦ ῥήτορος <u>ὅν</u>) _____ you praised.

4. I am grateful <u>for these things which</u> (ἐπὶ τούτοις <u>ἅ</u>) _____ you did.

5. I gave those things <u>to the women whom</u> (ταῖς γυναιξὶν <u>ἅς</u>) _____ you mentioned.

Exercise 23 κ

Rewrite the following verb forms combining prefix and stem:

1. ἐν-   κρύπτω   _____

2. συν- μένω   _____

3. συν- φέρω   _____

4. ἐν-   λείπω   _____

5. συν- γίγνομαι   _____

6. ἐν-   βαίνω   _____

Exercise 23 λ

Give an English equivalent of:

1. ἡ ἔξοδος   _____   4. διαλύω   _____

2. οἴομαι   _____   5. τὸ στάδιον   _____

3. ἕκαστος   _____   6. ἐξαμαρτάνω   _____

Exercise 23 μ

Give the Greek equivalent of:

1. I remain in   _____   3. I allow   _____

2. Boeotians   _____   4. hope   _____

Exercise 23 v

Give the remaining principal parts of:

1. ἐάω   _____

     _____

     _____

     _____

     _____

2. οἴομαι   _____

     _____

3. αὐξάνω   _____

     _____

     _____

     _____

     _____

4. λαμβάνω   _____

     _____

     _____

     _____

     _____

5. μανθάνω   _____

     _____

     _____

1   ἔσω, prep. + gen., *inside*.
     περίβολος, περιβόλου, ὁ, *enclosure*.
     ἀνακάμπτω [κάμπτω, *I bend, turn*], *I bend back; I walk back and forth; I wander*.
3   ψευδοπαιδείᾱ, ψευδοπαιδείᾱς, ἡ, *false education*.
     ἐραστής, ἐραστοῦ, ὁ, *lover, devotee*.
     ἀπατάω, *I cheat; I deceive*.
         ἠπατημένοι: *deceived* (perfect passive participle).
4   ἀληθινός, ἀληθινή, ἀληθινόν, *true*.
     παιδείᾱ, παιδείᾱς, ἡ, *education*.
     συνομιλέω, *I associate* (with).
6   διαλεκτικός, διαλεκτικοῦ, ὁ, *one skilled in logical argument, dialectitian*.
7   μουσικός, μουσικοῦ, ὁ, *one skilled in music, musician*.
     ἀριθμητικός, ἀριθμητικοῦ, ὁ, *one skilled in numbers, mathematician*.
     γεωμέτρης, γεωμέτρου, ὁ, *measurer of land; one skilled in geometry, geometer*.
     ἀστρολόγος, ἀστρολόγου, ὁ, *one skilled in astronomy, astronomer*.
     κριτικός, κριτικοῦ, ὁ, *one skilled in judging; scholar; grammarian*.
8   ἡδονικός, ἡδονικοῦ, ὁ, *one skilled in pleasures; hedonist; member of the
         Cyrenaic or the Epicurean school of philosophy*.
     περιπατητικός, περιπατητικοῦ, ὁ, *one walking about while teaching;
         peripatetic; member of the Aristotelian school of philosophy*.
     παραπλήσιος, παραπλήσιον + dat., *resembling, similar* (to).

Exercise 23 ξ

Translate into English on a separate sheet of paper:

ΚΕΒΗΤΟΣ ΠΙΝΑΞ

XIII.

Ξένος "οὗτοι δὲ οἱ ἄνθρωποι οἱ ἔσω τοῦ περιβόλου ἀνακάμπτοντες, τίνες   1
εἰσίν;"   2

Πρεσβύτης "οἱ τῆς Ψευδοπαιδείας," ἔφη, "ἐρασταί, ἠπατημένοι καὶ οἰόμενοι   3
μετὰ τῆς Ἀληθινῆς Παιδείας συνομιλεῖν."   4

Ξένος "τίνες οὖν καλοῦνται οὗτοι;"   5

Πρεσβύτης "οἱ μὲν ποιηταί," ἔφη, "οἱ δὲ ῥήτορες, οἱ δὲ διαλεκτικοί, οἱ δὲ   6
μουσικοί, οἱ δὲ ἀριθμητικοί, οἱ δὲ γεωμέτραι, οἱ δὲ ἀστρολόγοι, οἱ δὲ κριτικοί, οἱ δὲ   7
ἡδονικοί, οἱ δὲ περιπατητικοὶ καὶ ὅσοι ἄλλοι τούτοις εἰσὶ παραπλήσιοι."   8

24
ΕΝ ΔΙΔΑΣΚΑΛΩΝ (α)

Exercise 24 α

Translate the underlined adjectives using the Greek adjectives supplied:

1. ἀνδρεῖος: the <u>brave</u> man _____
2. σώφρων: the <u>more prudent</u> women _____
3. ἀνδρεῖος: the <u>bravest</u> farmer _____
4. χαλεπός: the <u>more difficult</u> work (ἔργον) _____
5. σώφρων: the <u>most prudent</u> maiden _____
6. ἀληθής: the <u>true</u> story (λόγος) _____
7. ἀνδρεῖος: the <u>somewhat brave</u> barbarians _____
8. χαλεπός: the <u>most difficult</u> flight (φυγή) _____
9. ἀνδρεῖος: the <u>brave</u> girls _____
10. σώφρων: the <u>most prudent</u> parents _____
11. ἀληθής: the <u>truest</u> story (λόγος) _____
12. ἀνδρεῖος: the <u>braver</u> woman _____
13. σώφρων: the <u>rather prudent</u> farmers _____
14. ἀνδρεῖος: the <u>very brave</u> boy _____
15. ἀληθής: the <u>truer</u> friend (φίλη) _____
16. χαλεπός: the <u>more difficult</u> labors (πόνοι) _____

Exercise 24 β

Locate the Greek word in column B that best translates the underlined adjective in column A and write its letter in the blank:

A

1. ἀγαθός: the <u>better</u> (i.e., morally superior) man ____
2. ἀγαθός: the <u>stronger</u> women ____
3. κακός: the <u>bad</u> deed (ἔργον) ____
4. κακός: the <u>worst</u> ship (ναῦς) ____
5. κακός: the <u>worse</u> slave ____
6. κακός: the <u>worse</u> (i.e., inferior) water jars ____
7. ἀγαθός: the <u>better</u> (i.e., morally superior) women ____
8. κακός: the <u>worse</u> (i.e., more cowardly) boys ____
9. ἀγαθός: the <u>bravest</u> farmers ____
10. κακός: the <u>worst</u> man ____

B

a. ἄριστοι
b. βελτίονες
c. βελτίων
d. κακίονες
e. κακίων
f. κακόν
g. κρείττονες
h. χειρίστη
i. χείριστος
j. χείρονες

Exercise 24 γ

Give an English equivalent of:

1. ἡ παίδευσις ____
2. μελετάω ____
3. σμῑκρός ____
4. ὁ γραμματιστής ____
5. φοιτάω ____
6. περὶ πολλοῦ ποιοῦμαι ____
7. ἡ γυμναστική ____
8. ἄσμενος ____
9. ὁ κιθαριστής ____
10. *ζάω ____
11. ἄδικος ____
12. ὅπως ____

Exercise 24 δ

Give the Greek equivalent of:

1. shameful ____
2. I educate ____
3. every day ____
4. music ____
5. son ____
6. I consider of greatest importance ____
7. teacher ____
8. letter ____
9. sophist ____
10. I teach ____
11. parent ____
12. just ____

1   περιτρέχω, *I run around.*

2   ἀκρασίᾱ, ἀκρασίᾱς, ἡ [ἀ- + τὸ κράτος], *lack of power / control over one's passions; intemperance.*

3   αὐταὶ ἐκεῖναί: ἐκεῖναί is the subject; αὐταὶ is a predicate adjective, here meaning *the same.*

4   ὧδε, adv., *thus; here.*

5   νή + acc., adv. of swearing, *yes, by . . . !*
     σπανίως, adv., *seldom.*

6   περίβολος, περιβόλου, ὁ, *enclosure.*

7   δόξα, δόξης, ἡ, *notion; opinion; good reputation; honor.*
     αἱ Δόξαι: *Opinions.*

8   πόμα, πόματος, τό, *drink.*
     παρά, prep. + gen., *from.*
     ἀπάτη, ἀπάτης, ἡ, *trick; deceit; deception.*

9   ἄγνοια, ἀγνοίᾱς, ἡ, *ignorance.*
     ἀφροσύνη, ἀφροσύνης, ἡ, *mindlessness; foolishness.*
     οὐ μὴ ἀπέλθῃ: *will not go away* (the subjunctive, usually aorist as here, is used with οὐ μή to express an emphatic negative statement referring to the future).

10   λοιπός, λοιπή, λοιπόν, *remaining.*
     κακίᾱ, κακίᾱς, ἡ, *evil.*
     μέχρι, conj., *until.*
     ἄν: with the subjunctives, εἰσέλθωσιν (10) and πίωσι (11).
     ἀπογι(γ)νώσκω, *I depart from a judgment;* + gen., *I despair of, reject, repudiate.*
        ἀπογνόντες: aorist participle.
     ψευδοπαιδείᾱ, ψευδοπαιδείᾱς, ἡ, *false education.*
     εἰσέλθωσιν . . . πίωσι (11): aorist subjunctives introduced by μέχρι ἄν; translate as present indicatives.

11   ἀληθινός, ἀληθινή, ἀληθινόν, *true.*
     καθαρτικός, καθαρτική, καθαρτικόν, + gen., *cathartic, purifying.*
        τούτων καθαρτικὰς: *purifying* (them) *of these things,* i.e., of the bad things mentioned in the previous lines.
     εἶτα, adv., *then, next.*

12   καθαίρω, καθαρῶ, ἐκάθηρα, κεκάθαρμαι, ἐκαθάρθην, *I purge, cleanse, purify.*
        ὅταν (11) καθαρθῶσι (12) καὶ ἐκβάλωσι: *when(ever) they are purified and throw out* (indefinite temporal clause; see Ch. 22, Gr. 2, pp. 94 and 95).

14   παρά, prep. + dat., *with.*
     ἀπολύω, ἀπολύσω, ἀπέλῦσα, ἀπολέλυκα, ἀπολέλυμαι, ἀπελύθην, *I set free, release.*
     οὐδὲ . . . οὐδέν (15): *nor will any.*
     ἐλλείπω [ἐν- + λείπω], *I leave.*

15   μάθημα, μαθήματος, τό, *learning; branch of learning, academic discipline.*
        τούτων τῶν μαθημάτων: i.e., the teachings offered by those listed in ΚΕΒΗΤΟΣ ΠΙΝΑΞ XIII:6–8, p. 73.

Exercise 24 ε

Translate into English on a separate sheet of paper:

ΚΕΒΗΤΟΣ ΠΙΝΑΞ

XIV.

Ξένος "αἱ δὲ γυναῖκες ἐκεῖναι αἱ δοκοῦσαι περιτρέχειν ὅμοιαι ταῖς πρώταις,   1
ἐν αἷς ἔφης εἶναι τὴν ᾿Ακρασίᾶν, τίνες εἰσίν;"   2

Πρεσβύτης "αὐταὶ ἐκεῖναί εἰσιν," ἔφη.   3

Ξένος "πότερον οὖν καὶ ὧδε εἰσπορεύονται;"   4

Πρεσβύτης "νὴ Δία καὶ ὧδε, σπανίως δὲ καὶ οὐχὶ ὥσπερ ἐν τῷ πρώτῳ   5
περιβόλῳ."   6

Ξένος "πότερον οὖν καὶ αἱ Δόξαι;" ἔφην.   7

Πρεσβύτης "μένει γὰρ καὶ ἐν τούτοις τὸ πόμα, ὃ ἔπιον παρὰ τῆς ᾿Απάτης, καὶ   8
ἡ ἄγνοια μένει καὶ μετ᾿ αὐτῆς γε ἡ ἀφροσύνη, καὶ οὐ μὴ ἀπέλθῃ ἀπ᾿ αὐτῶν οὔθ᾿ ἡ   9
δόξα οὔθ᾿ ἡ λοιπὴ κακίᾱ, μέχρι ἂν ἀπογνόντες τῆς Ψευδοπαιδείᾱς εἰσέλθωσιν εἰς   10
τὴν ἀληθινὴν ὁδὸν καὶ πίωσι τᾱς τούτων καθαρτικᾱς δυνάμεις. εἶτα ὅταν   11
καθαρθῶσι καὶ ἐκβάλωσι τὰ κακὰ πάνθ᾿ ὅσα ἔχουσι καὶ τὰς δόξας καὶ τὴν   12
ἄγνοιαν καὶ τὴν λοιπὴν κακίᾱν πᾶσαν, τότε δὴ οὕτω σωθήσονται. ὧδε δὲ   13
μένοντες παρὰ τῇ Ψευδοπαιδείᾳ οὐδέποτε ἀπολυθήσονται οὐδὲ ἐλλείψει αὐτοὺς   14
κακὸν οὐδὲν ἕνεκα τούτων τῶν μαθημάτων."   15

Exercise 24 ζ

Give the remaining principal parts of:

1. διδάσκω   _____   4. κάμνω   _____

   _____   _____

   _____   _____

   _____   5. ἀφικνέομαι   _____

   _____   _____

2. *ζάω   _____   _____

   or _____   6. δείκνῡμι   _____

3. παιδεύω   _____   _____

   _____   _____

   _____   _____

   _____

(β)

Exercise 24η

Locate the Greek word in column B that best translates the underlined adjective in column A and write its letter in the blank:

A   B

1. the <u>most beautiful</u> tree ____   a. τάχιστος

2. the <u>most shameful</u> deed ____   b. ῥᾷον

3. the <u>more hostile</u> opponent ____   c. ὀλίγιστον

4. the <u>sweeter</u> fruit (καρπός) ____   d. φιλαίταται

5. the <u>swiftest</u> runner ____   e. αἴσχιστον

6. the <u>bigger</u> boy ____   f. πλείονες

7. the <u>smallest</u> child (τέκνον) ____   g. ἐχθίων

8. the <u>dearest</u> women ____   h. μείζων

9. the <u>easier</u> lesson (μάθημα) ____   i. κάλλιστον

10. <u>more</u> boys ____   j. ἡδίων

Exercise 24θ

Supply the correct forms of the Greek adjectives to translate the English adjectives. Sometimes two spellings of the same word are requested:

1. γιγνώσκω τοῦτον τὸν παῖδα ὄντα (stronger) _____ or

   _____ ἢ ἐκεῖνον. (κρείττων)

2. ἐπίσταμαι τοῦτον τὸν καρπὸν ὄντα (sweeter) _____ or

   _____ ἢ ἐκεῖνον. (ἡδίων)

3. ἀκούω τὸν (swifter) _____ or _____ κύνα.

   (θάττων)

4. καθεύδουσιν ὑπὸ τῷ (smaller) _____ δένδρῳ. (ἐλάττων)

5. φίλοι ἐσμὲν τῶν (bigger) _____ παίδων. (μείζων)

6. (More) _____ or _____ γυναῖκες πρὸς τὴν

   ἑορτὴν ἔρχονται. (πλείων)

7. γιγνώσκω τοῦτο (easier) _____ ὂν ἢ ἐκεῖνο. (ῥᾴων)

8. οἱ ἄνδρες ἦλθον ἐκ τοῦ (larger) _____ οἴκου. (μείζων)

9. δώσομεν τὰ χρήματα ταῖς (more beautiful) _____ παρθένοις.

   (καλλίων)

10.   ὁ Δικαιόπολις ἔχει (fewer) _____ or _____ φίλους ἢ
      ὁ Φίλιππος. (ἐλάττων)

Exercise 24 ι

Give an English equivalent of:

1. ὁ ῥυθμός _____
2. κιθαρίζω _____
3. παλαιός _____
4. ἡ διάνοια _____
5. πρός + dat. _____
6. ἡ σωφροσύνη _____

7. ἡ πρᾶξις _____
8. αὖ _____
9. ἐπιμελέομαι _____
10. ὁ ἔπαινος _____
11. χρήσιμος _____

Exercise 24 κ

Give the Greek equivalent of:

1. book _____
2. prosperous _____
3. voice _____
4. I am glad _____
5. on _____

6. body _____
7. harmony _____
8. useful; good _____
9. wickedness _____
10. pupil _____

Exercise 24 λ

Give the remaining principal parts of:

1. ἐπιμελέομαι _____
    _____
    _____

2. ἥδομαι _____
    _____

3. κιθαρίζω _____

4. γιγνώσκω _____
    _____
    _____
    _____

5. ἀποθνῄσκω _____
    _____

6. εὑρίσκω _____
    _____
    or _____
    _____
    or _____
    _____
    or _____
    _____
    or _____

1   ποῖος, ποία, ποῖον, *what sort/kind of; of what sort/kind?*
     ἐπί, prep. + acc., *to.*
     ἀληθινός, ἀληθινή, ἀληθινόν, *true.*
     παιδείᾱ, παιδείᾱς, ἡ, *education.*

2   ἐπικατοικέω [ἐπι- + κατα- + οἰκέω], *I dwell.*

5   οὐκοῦν, adv., *then* (introducing a question that expects the answer "yes" and
        carries the thought forward from a previous assent).
     θύρᾱν. . . . : supply ὁρᾷς.
     ἥτις: = ἥ, *which.*

6   πολύ, adv., *much.*
     ὀχλέω, *I disturb; I frequent, crowd.*
     πάνυ, adv., *very, very much.*
     ἀνοδίᾱ, ἀνοδίᾱς, ἡ, *pathless area, trackless waste.*

7   πετρώδης, πετρῶδες, *rocky.*

8   καὶ μάλα: *certainly; yes.*

9   οὐκοῦν, adv., *surely then* (here introducing a statement rather than a question).
     βουνός, βουνοῦ, ὁ, *hill, mound.*
     ὑψηλός, ὑψηλή, ὑψηλόν, *high.*
     ἀνάβασις, ἀναβάσεως, ἡ, *way up, ascent.*

10   κρημνός, κρημνοῦ, ὁ, *cliff, precipice.*
     ἔνθεν καὶ ἔνθεν: *on this side and on that side.*
     βαθεῖς: this word can mean *high* as well as *deep.*

12   τοίνυν [τοι + νυν], particle, *therefore, accordingly; well then.*

14   προσοράω, προσόψομαι, προσεῖδον, *I look at.*
        προσιδεῖν: an epexegetic (i.e., explanatory) infinitive limiting the adjective
          χαλεπή. The path is difficult *to look at* = *it looks difficult.*

15   πέτρᾱ, πέτρᾱς, ἡ, *rock; mass of rock; boulder* (compare ὁ πέτρος, *stone*).

16   κύκλος, κύκλου, ὁ, *circle.*
     ἀπόκρημνος, ἀπόκρημνον [ἀπο- + ὁ κρημνός, *cliff, precipice*], *precipitous,*
     steep.

Exercise 24 μ

Translate into English on a separate sheet of paper:

ΚΕΒΗΤΟΣ ΠΙΝΑΞ

XV.

Ξένος "ποία οὖν αὕτη ἡ ὁδός ἐστιν ἡ φέρουσα ἐπὶ τὴν Ἀληθινὴν Παιδείᾱν;"   1

Πρεσβύτης "ὁρᾷς ἄνω," ἔφη, "τόπον τινὰ ἐκεῖνον, ὅπου οὐδεὶς ἐπικατοικεῖ,   2
ἀλλ᾽ ἔρημος δοκεῖ εἶναι;"   3

Ξένος "ὁρῶ."   4

Πρεσβύτης "οὐκοῦν καὶ θύρᾱν τινὰ μῑκρὰν καὶ ὁδόν τινα πρὸ τῆς θύρᾱς, ἥτις   5
οὐ πολὺ ὀχλεῖται, ἀλλ᾽ ὀλίγοι πάνυ πορεύονται ὥσπερ δι᾽ ἀνοδίᾱς τινὸς καὶ   6
τραχείᾱς καὶ πετρώδους εἶναι δοκούσης;"   7

Ξένος "καὶ μάλα," ἔφην.   8

Πρεσβύτης "οὐκοῦν καὶ βουνός τις ὑψηλὸς δοκεῖ εἶναι καὶ ἀνάβασις στενὴ   9
πάνυ καὶ κρημνοὺς ἔχουσα ἔνθεν καὶ ἔνθεν βαθεῖς."   10

Ξένος "ὁρῶ."   11

Πρεσβύτης "αὕτη τοίνυν ἐστὶν ἡ ὁδός," ἔφη, "ἡ ἄγουσα πρὸς τὴν Ἀληθινὴν   12
Παιδείᾱν."   13

Ξένος "καὶ μάλα γε χαλεπὴ προσιδεῖν."   14

Πρεσβύτης "οὐκοῦν καὶ ἄνω ἐπὶ τοῦ βουνοῦ ὁρᾷς πέτρᾱν τινὰ μεγάλην καὶ   15
ὑψηλὴν καὶ κύκλῳ ἀπόκρημνον;"   16

Ξένος "ὁρῶ," ἔφην.   17

VOCABULARY
CHAPTERS 21–24

VERBS

-ω Verbs

ἀγορεύω	*I speak in the Assembly;* more generally, *I speak; I say*
ἀναγιγνώσκω, ἀναγνώσομαι, ἀνέγνων	*I read*
ἄρχω, ἄρξω, ἦρξα, ἦργμαι, ἤρχθην	+ gen., active or middle, *I begin;* + gen., active, *I rule*
βουλεύω, βουλεύσω, ἐβούλευσα, βεβούλευκα, βεβούλευμαι, ἐβουλεύθην	*I deliberate; I plan*
διαλύω	*I disband* (an army); *I disperse* (a fleet)
διδάσκω, διδάξω, ἐδίδαξα, δεδίδαχα, δεδίδαγμαι, ἐδιδάχθην	*I teach* someone (acc.) something (acc.); passive, *I am taught* something (acc.)
εἰσβάλλω	+ εἰς + acc., *I invade*
ἐμμένω	*I remain in*
ἐξαμαρτάνω	*I miss; I fail; I make a mistake*
ἐπιβουλεύω	+ dat., *I plot against*
θύω, θύσω, ἔθῦσα, τέθυκα, τέθυμαι, ἐτύθην	*I sacrifice*
κιθαρίζω, κιθαριῶ, ἐκιθάρισα	*I play the lyre*
λούω, λούσομαι, ἔλουσα, λέλουμαι	*I wash;* middle, *I wash myself, bathe*
νομίζω, νομιῶ, ἐνόμισα, νενόμικα, νενόμισμαι, ἐνομίσθην	*I think*
παιδεύω, παιδεύσω, ἐπαίδευσα, πεπαίδευκα, πεπαίδευμαι, ἐπαιδεύθην	*I educate*
προάγω	*I lead forward*
τάττω, τάξω, ἔταξα, τέταχα, τέταγμαι, ἐτάχθην	*I marshal, draw up in battle array; I station, post*
τέμνω, τεμῶ, ἔτεμον, τέτμηκα, τέτμημαι, ἐτμήθην	*I cut; I ravage*
ὑπάρχω	*I am; I exist; I am ready*

Deponent or Middle -ω Verbs

ἐπεξέρχομαι	+ dat., *I march out against, attack*
ἥδομαι, ἡσθήσομαι, ἥσθην	*I am glad, delighted;* + participle or dat., *I enjoy*
καθέζομαι, καθεδοῦμαι	*I sit down; I encamp*
ὀδύρομαι	*I grieve*
οἴομαι or οἶμαι, οἰήσομαι, ᾠήθην	*I think*

προσδέχομαι   *I receive, admit;*
                     I await, expect

ψηφίζομαι,
   ψηφιοῦμαι,
   ἐψηφισάμην,
   ἐψήφισμαι   *I vote*

-άω Contract Verbs

ἐάω, ἐάσω,
   εἴᾱσα , εἴᾱκα,
   εἴᾱμαι, εἰάθην   *I allow, let be*
*ζάω, ζήσω or
   ζήσομαι   *I live*
μελετάω   *I study; I practice*
περιοράω   *I overlook, disregard*
φοιτάω   *I go; I visit*

-έω Contract Verbs

πολεμέω   *I make war; I go to*
                 war

Deponent -έω Contract Verbs

ἐπιμελέομαι,
   ἐπιμελήσομαι,
   ἐπιμεμέλημαι,
   ἐπεμελήθην   + gen., *I take care for;*
              + ὅπως + future
              indicative, *I take*
              care (to see to it
              that)

-όω Contract Verbs

πληρόω   *I fill*

-μι Verbs

ἐνδίδωμι   *I give in, yield*
ζεύγνῡμι,
   ζεύξω,
   ἔζευξα,
   ἔζευγμαι,
   ἐζεύχθην or
   ἐζύγην   *I yoke*

Middle -μι Verbs

ἀνθίσταμαι,
   ἀντιστήσομαι,
   ἀντέστην,
   ἀνθέστηκα   + dat., *I stand up*
              against, withstand

ἀνίσταμαι,
   ἀναστήσομαι,
   ἀνέστην,
   ἀνέστηκα   *I stand up; I am*
              forced to move; I
              move; I evacuate

Athematic Verbs

πρόκειμαι,
   προκείσομαι   + dat., *I lie before*

NOUNS

1st Declension

αἰτίᾱ, -ᾱς, ἡ   *blame; responsibility;*
                cause

ἅμαξα, -ης, ἡ   *wagon*
ἀνάγκη, -ης, ἡ   *necessity*
ἁρμονίᾱ, -ᾱς, ἡ   *harmony*
ἀρχή, -ῆς, ἡ   *beginning; rule;*
               empire

βουλή, -ῆς, ἡ   *plan; advice; Council*
γραμματιστής,
   γραμμα-
   τιστοῦ, ὁ   *schoolmaster*
γυμναστική,
   -ῆς, ἡ   *gymnastics*
διάνοια,
   διανοίᾱς, ἡ   *intention; intellect*
δίκη,
   δίκης, ἡ   *custom; justice; right;*
              lawsuit; penalty
εἰσβολή,
   -ῆς, ἡ   *invasion*
ἐκκλησίᾱ,
   -ᾱς, ἡ   *assembly*
ἰδιώτης,
   -ου, ὁ   *private person*
κιθαριστής,
   -οῦ, ὁ   *lyre player*
μαθητής,
   -οῦ, ὁ   *pupil*
μουσική,
   -ῆς, ἡ   *music*
πεῖρα,
   -ᾱς, ἡ   *trial; attempt; test*
πονηρίᾱ,
   -ᾱς, ἡ   *fault; wickedness*
προσβολή,
   -ῆς, ἡ   *attack*
σοφιστής,
   -οῦ, ὁ   *wise man; sophist*
στρατιά,
   -ᾶς, ἡ   *army*
σωφροσύνη,
   -ης, ἡ   *soundness of mind,*
              prudence; modera-
              tion, self-control
τῑμή, -ῆς, ἡ   *honor*

φυλακή, -ῆς, ἡ   *guard; garrison*
φωνή, -ῆς, ἡ   *voice; speech*
χώρᾱ, -ᾱς, ἡ   *land*

2nd Declension

βιβλίον,
   -ου, τό   *book*
δῆμος, -ου, ὁ   *the people; township;*
                deme
διδάσκαλος,
   -ου, ὁ   *teacher*
ἔξοδος, -ου, ἡ   *going out; marching*
                forth; military
                expedition
ἔπαινος,
   -ου, ὁ   *praise*
οἰκεῖοι, -ων, οἱ   *the members of the*
                household; family;
                relations
πύργος, -ου, ὁ   *tower*
ῥυθμός, -οῦ, ὁ   *rhythm*
στάδιον,
   -ου, τό, pl.,
   τὰ στάδια or
   οἱ στάδιοι   *stade*
στρατόπεδον,
   -ου, τό   *camp; army*
τρόπος, -ου, ὁ   *manner; way*
υἱός, -οῦ, ὁ   *son*
φρούριον,
   -ου, τό   *garrison*
χωρίον,
   -ου, τό   *place; district*
χῶρος, -ου, ὁ   *place*

3rd Declension

ἀνάστασις,
   ἀναστάσεως, ἡ   *forced move; move;*
                evacuation
γράμμα,
   γράμματος, τό   *letter* (of the
                alphabet); pl.,
                writing
δύναμις,
   δυνάμεως, ἡ   *power; strength;*
                forces (military)
ἔαρ, ἦρος, τό   *spring*
ἐλπίς,
   ἐλπίδος, ἡ   *hope; expectation*
οἴκησις,
   οἰκήσεως, ἡ   *dwelling*

παίδευσις,
   παιδεύσεως, ἡ   *education*
πρᾶξις,
   πρᾱξεως, ἡ   *deed*
πρέσβεις,
   πρέσβεων, οἱ   *ambassadors*
πρέσβυς,
   πρέσβεως, ὁ   *old man;*
                ambassador
ῥήτωρ,
   ῥήτορος, ὁ   *speaker; politician*
σῶμα,
   σώματος, τό   *body*
τεκών,
   τεκόντος, ὁ   *parent*

PRONOUNS

ὅστις, ἥτις,
   ὅ τι   *often in indefinite or*
                general clauses
                with ἄν *and sub-*
                junctive, anyone
                who, whoever;
                anything that,
                whatever; pl., all
                that; whoever;
                whatever

ADJECTIVES

1st/2nd Declension

αἰσχρός,
   -ά, -όν   *shameful*
ἄσμενος,
   -η, -ον   *glad(ly)*
δίκαιος,
   -ᾱ, -ον   *just*
δυνατός,
   -ή, -όν   *possible; capable*
ἕκαστος,
   -η, -ον,   *each*
ἑκάτερος,
   -ᾱ, -ον   *each* (of two)
ἐπιτήδειος,
   -ᾱ, -ον   *friendly;* + infin.,
                suitable for
μύριοι, -αι, -α   *10,000*
μῡρίοι, -αι, -α   *numberless,*
                countless
νέος, -ᾱ, -ον   *young; new*
ὄλβιος, -ᾱ, -ον   *happy; blest;*
                prosperous

ὅμοιος, -ᾱ, -ον   + dat., *like*

ὅσος, -η, -ον   *as great as; as much as;* pl., *as many as*

παλαιός, -ά, -όν   *old; of old*

σμῑκρός, -ά, -όν   *small*

τελευταῖος, -ᾱ, -ον   *last*

τοιόσδε, τοιᾱ́δε, τοιόνδε   *such* (as the following)

τοιοῦτος, τοιαύτη, τοιοῦτο,   *such*

τοσόσδε, τοσήδε, τοσόνδε   *so great;* pl., *so many*

χρήσιμος, -η, -ον   *useful*

χρηστός, -ή, -όν   *useful; good*

χρόνιος, -ᾱ, -ον   *lengthy*

2nd Declension

ἄδικος, -ον   *unjust*

ἀδύνατος, -ον   *impossible; incapable*

PREPOSITIONS

ἐκτός   + gen., *outside*

ἕνεκα   + preceding gen., *for the sake of; because of*

ἐπί   + gen., *toward, in the direction of; on;* + dat., *at;* of price, *for;* + acc., *at; against; onto, upon*

κατά   + acc., *down;* distributive, *each; by; on; according to;* of time, *at*

πρός   + dat., *at; near; by; in addition to;* + acc., *to, toward; upon; against*

ADVERBS

αὖ   *again*

ᾗπερ   *where*

ἰδίᾳ   *privately*

πεζῇ   *on foot*

οὐδέποτε   *never*

CONJUNCTIONS

ἐάν   + subjunctive, *if*

ἐπειδάν   in indefinite or general clauses with subjunctive, *when(ever)*

ἐπειδή   *when; since*

ἵνα   + subjunctive, *so that, in order to* (expressing purpose)

ὁπόταν   + subjunctive, *when(ever)*

ὁπότε   *when*

ὅπως   + subjunctive, *so that, in order to;* + future indicative, *(to see to it) that*

πρίν   + indicative or + ἄν and subjunctive, *until;* + infin., *before*

EXPRESSIONS

ἀνάγκη ἐστί(ν)   *it is necessary*

καθ᾽ ἡμέρᾱν   *every day*

πάντα ὅσα   *all that, whatever*

πάντες ὅσοι   *all that, whoever*

περὶ πλείστου ποιοῦμαι   *I consider of greatest importance*

περὶ πολλοῦ ποιοῦμαι   *I consider of great importance*

PROPER NAMES & ADJECTIVES

Ἀχαρναί, -ῶν, αἱ   *Acharnae*

Ἀχαρνῆς, Ἀχαρνέων, οἱ   *inhabitants of Acharnae, the Acharnians*

Βοιωτοί, -ῶν, οἱ	*Boeotians*		Πνύξ, Πυκνός, ἡ	*the Pnyx* (the hill in Athens on which the Assemblies were held)
Πελοποννήσιοι, -ων, οἱ	*Peloponnesians*			

25
Ο ΚΡΟΙΣΟΣ
ΤΟΝ ΣΟΛΩΝΑ ΞΕΝΙΖΕΙ (α)

Exercise 25 α

Transform the following present and future indicative forms into the equivalent forms of the optative:

1.	λύουσι(ν)	_____	11.	δηλοῦμαι	_____
2.	λῡόμεθα	_____	12.	τῑμῶσι(ν)	_____
3.	λύσεται	_____	13.	λύεται	_____
4.	λύεσθε	_____	14.	δηλώσεις	_____
5.	τῑμᾶτε	_____	15.	γίγνομαι	_____
6.	δηλοῦσι(ν)	_____	16.	φιλήσεται	_____
7.	φιλῶ	_____	17.	ἀρῶ	_____
8.	τῑμᾶται	_____	18.	φιλεῖτε	_____
9.	βούλονται	_____	19.	τῑμήσονται	_____
10.	τῑμηθήσεσθε	_____	20.	φιλεῖ:	
				she loves	_____

Exercise 25 β

Transform the following aorist indicative forms into the equivalent forms of the optative. If there is more than one spelling of a form, you need give only one:

1.	ἔλῡσα	_____	9.	ἐλίπετο	_____
2.	ἐλύσατο	_____	10.	ἐτῑμήσαντο	_____
3.	ἐλύθης	_____	11.	ἐγενόμην	_____
4.	ἐτίμησε(ν)	_____	12.	ἔβημεν	_____
5.	ἐνῑκήθην	_____	13.	ἐφιλήσασθε	_____
6.	ἐφίλησας	_____	14.	ἔμεινα	_____
7.	ἐλάβετε	_____	15.	ἤρατε	_____
8.	ἐδηλώθη	_____	16.	ἐδήλωσαν	_____

Exercise 25 γ

Fill in the blank with the optative form of the verb given, keeping the same tense. Supply ἄν where needed. If there is more than one spelling of a form, you need give only one. Label each of the uses of the independent optative as either: Potential Optative (PO) or Optative of Wish (OW):

1. ὦ Φίλιππε, (may you find) _____ τοὺς φίλους. (ηὗρον) ___

2. ἡ γυνὴ τὸ δεῖπνον (would prepare) _____ . (παρεσκεύασα)

    ___

3. (I hope you will prepare) _____ τὸ δεῖπνον, ὦ γύναι.

    (παρεσκεύασα) ___

4. εἰ γὰρ ἡ μήτηρ σε (may help) _____ . (ὠφελέω) ___

5. ἴσως ὁ πατήρ σε (may help) _____ . (ὠφελέω) ___

6. ἡ μήτηρ σοι (would be angry) _____ . (ὀργίζομαι) ___

7. εἴθε μὴ ὁ πατήρ σοι (be angry) _____ . (ὀργίζομαι) ___

8. ὁ νεᾱνίᾱς τὸ δῶρον (may receive) _____ . (ἐδεξάμην) ___

9. (May he receive) _____ τὸ δῶρον . (ἐδεξάμην) ___

10. ὁ αὐτουργὸς τὸν βοῦν (may find) _____ . (ηὗρον) ___

Exercise 25 δ

Fill in the blank with the optative form of the verb given. Supply ἄν if needed. If there is more than one spelling of a form, you need give only one. Label each of the subordinate clauses as one of the following: Purpose (P), Fear (F), Indefinite Temporal (IT), or Indefinite Relative (IR):

1. οἱ ἄνδρες Ἀθήνᾱζε ἦλθον ἵνα τοὺς φίλους (they might find) _____ .

    (ηὗρον) ___

2. οἱ δοῦλοι ἐφοβοῦντο μὴ ὁ δεσπότης (might become angry) _____ .

    (ὀργίζομαι) ___

3. ἡ γυνὴ οἴκοι ἔμεινεν ὡς τὸ δεῖπνον (she might prepare) _____ .

    (παρεσκεύασα) ___

4. οἱ παῖδες ἡδέως ἐδέχοντο δῶρα ἅτινα ὁ πατὴρ (provided) _____ .

    (παρέσχον) ___

5. ὁ Ξανθίᾱς τοὺς βοῦς ἐζεύγνῡ ὁπότε ἐν τῷ ἀγρῷ (he worked) _____ .

    (ἐπόνησα) ___

6. ὁ πατὴρ πόνου ἐπαύσατο ἵνα τοῖς τέκνοις (he might speak with)

    _____ . (διελεξάμην) ___

7. ὁ δοῦλος ἐχρῆτο βουσὶν οὕστινας ἐν τῷ ἀγρῷ (he found) _____ .

    (ηὗρον) ___

8. μέγας κίνδῦνος ἦν μὴ οἱ πολέμιοι (might attack) _____ .

    (προσέβαλον) ___

Exercise 25 ε

Give an English equivalent of:

1. ἡ βασιλείᾱ   _____   5. ξενίζω   _____

2. οἷός τ' εἰμί   _____   6. ἡ θεωρίᾱ   _____

3. καταστρέφω   _____   7. μετά   _____

4. ἡ τελευτή   _____   8. ἀποδημέω   _____

Exercise 25 ζ

Give the Greek equivalent of:

1. through   _____   5. wisdom   _____

2. servant   _____   6. I bury   _____

3. I judge   _____   7. treasury   _____

4. palace   _____   8. I lead around   _____

Exercise 25 η

Give the remaining principal parts of:

1. θάπτω   _____   5. ξενίζω   _____

    _____   _____

    _____   6. δύναμαι   _____

2. καταστρέφω   _____

    _____   _____

    _____   7. κρῑνω   _____

    _____   _____

3. ἐπίσταμαι   _____

    _____   _____

4. κεῖμαι   _____

1   ἑστηκυίᾱς: *standing* (perfect participle, feminine accusative plural, of ἵστημι).
    πέτρᾱ, πέτρᾱς, ἡ, *rock; mass of rock; boulder.*
    λιπαρός, λιπαρά, λιπαρόν, *shining, radiant.*
2   εὐεκτέω, *I am in good condition / good health.*
    ἐκτετάκᾱσι: *they have stretched out* (perfect active, 3rd person plural, of
        ἐκτείνω, ἐκτενῶ, ἐξέτεινα, ἐκτέτακα, ἐκτέταμαι, ἐξετάθην,
        I stretch forth / out).
    προθύμως, adv., *eagerly.*
4   ἐγκράτεια, ἐγκρατείᾱς, ἡ [cf. κρατέω, ἡ ἀκρασίᾱ, *intemperance,* and τὸ
        κράτος], *self-control.*
    καρτερίᾱ, καρτερίᾱς, ἡ [cf. καρτερός, καρτερά, καρτερόν, *strong,* and
        καρτερέω, *I am strong; I endure*], *patience; endurance.*
5   ἀδελφή, ἀδελφῆς, ἡ, *sister.*
7   παρακαλέω, *I summon; I exhort, encourage.*
8   ἀποδειλιάω [cf. δειλός, δειλή, δειλόν, *cowardly,* and ἡ δειλίᾱ, *cowardice],I play
        the coward; I shrink back, flinch.*
    βραχύ, adv., *for a short time.*
    καρτερέω, *I am strong; I endure.*
    εἶτα, adv., *then, next.*
11 αὐτᾱς: i.e., Ἐγκράτειαν and Καρτερίᾱν (line 4).
12 κρημνός, κρημνοῦ, ὁ, *cliff, precipice.*
    προσκαταβαίνω, *I go down to meet.*
    ἕλκω, ἕλξω, εἵλκυσα, εἵλκυκα, εἵλκυσμαι, εἱλκύσθην, *I drag.*
13 αὐτᾱς: = ἑαυτᾱς.
    διαναπαύομαι [δια- + ἀνα- + παύομαι], *I rest a while.*
    μῑκρὸν: supply χρόνον.
14 ἰσχύς, ἰσχύος, ἡ, *strength, might.*
    θάρσος, θάρσους, τό, *daring, courage.*
    ἐπαγγέλλω, *I proclaim, announce;* middle, *I promise* (unasked); *I offer* (of my own
        free will).
    καταστήσειν: *will place / bring* (future active infinitive of καθίστημι; infinitive in
        indirect statement; αὐτοὺς is its object).
15 ἀληθινός, ἀληθινή, ἀληθινόν, *true.*
    παιδείᾱ, παιδείᾱς, ἡ, *education.*
    δεικνύουσιν: = δεικνύᾱσιν.
    ὁμαλός, ὁμαλή, ὁμαλόν, *even, smooth.*
16 εὐπόρευτος, εὐπόρευτον [πορεύομαι], *easy to travel.*
    καθαρός, καθαρά, καθαρόν + gen., *clean, pure.*
17 ἐμφαίνει, impersonal, *it is manifest / plain.*
    νή + acc., adv. of swearing, *yes, by …!*

Exercise 25 θ

Translate into English on a separate sheet of paper:

ΚΕΒΗΤΟΣ ΠΙΝΑΞ

XVI.

Πρεσβύτης "ὁρᾷς οὖν καὶ γυναῖκας δύο ἑστηκυίας ἐπὶ τῆς πέτρας, λιπαρὰς 1
καὶ εὐεκτούσᾱς τῷ σώματι, ὡς ἐκτετάκᾱσι τὰς χεῖρας προθύμως;" 2

Ξένος "ὁρῶ, ἀλλὰ τίνες καλοῦνται," ἔφην, "αὗται;" 3

Πρεσβύτης "ἡ μὲν Ἐγκράτεια καλεῖται," ἔφη, "ἡ δὲ Καρτερίᾱ· εἰσὶ δὲ 4
ἀδελφαί." 5

Ξένος "τί οὖν τὰς χεῖρας ἐκτετάκᾱσι προθύμως οὕτως;" 6

Πρεσβύτης "παρακαλοῦσιν," ἔφη, "τοὺς παραγῑνομένους ἐπὶ τὸν τόπον 7
θαρρεῖν καὶ μὴ ἀποδειλιᾶν λέγουσαι ὅτι βραχὺ ἔτι δεῖ καρτερῆσαι αὐτούς, εἶτα 8
ἥξουσιν εἰς ὁδὸν καλήν." 9

Ξένος "ὅταν οὖν παραγένωνται ἐπὶ τὴν πέτρᾱν, πῶς ἀναβαίνουσιν; ὁρῶ γὰρ 10
ὁδὸν φέρουσαν οὐδεμίαν ἐπ' αὐτᾱς." 11

Πρεσβύτης "αὗται ἀπὸ τοῦ κρημνοῦ προσκαταβαίνουσι καὶ ἕλκουσιν αὐτοὺς 12
ἄνω πρὸς αὑτᾱς, εἶτα κελεύουσιν αὐτοὺς διαναπαύσασθαι. καὶ μετὰ μῑκρὸν 13
διδόᾱσιν ἰσχὺν καὶ θάρσος καὶ ἐπαγγέλλονται αὐτοὺς καταστήσειν πρὸς τὴν 14
Ἀληθινὴν Παιδείᾱν καὶ δεικνύουσιν αὐτοῖς τὴν ὁδόν, ὡς ἔστι καλή τε καὶ ὁμαλὴ 15
καὶ εὐπόρευτος καὶ καθαρὰ παντὸς κακοῦ, ὥσπερ ὁρᾷς." 16

Ξένος "ἐμφαίνει νὴ Δία." 17

(β)

Exercise 25 ι

Transform the following present and future indicative forms into the equivalent forms of the optative:

1. τίθεται   _____
2. ἐστί(ν)   _____
3. ἱστᾶσι(ν)   _____
4. δώσω   _____
5. ἵεμεν   _____
6. ἵτε   _____

7. δείκνυσαι   _____
8. τίθεσθε   _____
9. ἐσόμεθα   _____
10. ἵεται   _____
11. στήσεις   _____
12. δίδονται   _____

Exercise 25 κ

Transform the following aorist indicative forms into the equivalent forms of the optative:

1. ἔθετο   _____
2. ἧκα   _____
3. ἐδόμην   _____
4. εἷσαν   _____

5. ἔστης   _____
6. ἔδωκε   _____
7. εἵμην   _____
8. ἔθεμεν   _____

Exercise 25 λ

Fill in the blanks with the optative forms of the verbs given. If there is more than one spelling of a form, you need give only one:

1. ἡ παρθένος οὐκ ἠπίστατο τί ἡ φίλη (had gone away) _____ .
   (ἀπῆλθον)

2. οἱ πολῖται εἶπον ὅτι ὁ Σόλων νόμους βελτίονας (would make)
   _____ . (ποιήσει)

3. ὁ στρατηγὸς ἠρώτησε πῶς οἱ ὁπλῖται (were faring) _____ .
   (πράττουσιν)

4. ὁ ἀνὴρ εἶπεν ὅτι ὁ δοῦλος τὸ ἔργον (had done) _____ . (ἐποίησεν).

Exercise 25 μ

Give an English equivalent of:

1. ὁ πλοῦτος _____
2. ἱκανός _____
3. καταφρονέω _____
4. ἡ εὐδαιμονίᾱ _____

5. ἡ εὐχή _____
6. ἕλκω _____
7. ἡ ῥώμη _____
8. ἀμφότερος _____

Exercise 25 ν

Give the remaining principal parts of:

1. ἕλκω _____
   _____
   _____
   _____
   _____

2. ἐάω _____
   _____
   _____
   _____
   _____

3. ἕπομαι _____
   _____

4. ἐργάζομαι _____
   or _____
   _____
   _____

5. ἔχω _____
   or _____
   _____
   _____

1   ἔμπροσθεν, prep. + gen., *in front of.*
        ἄλσος, ἄλσους, τό, *grove.*

2   λειμωνοειδής, λειμωνοειδές [ὁ λειμών, *meadow* + τὸ εἶδος, *form, shape*],
           meadow-like, grassy and flowery.
        φῶς, φωτός, τό, *light.*
        καταλαμπόμενος, καταλαμπομένη, καταλαμπόμενον, *illuminated.*

3   καὶ μάλα: *certainly; yes.*

4   κατανοέω, *I observe, see.*
        λειμών, λειμῶνος, ὁ, *meadow.*
        περίβολος, περιβόλου, ὁ, *enclosure.*
        ἕτερος, ἑτέρᾱ, ἕτερον, *one* or *the other* (of two); *other.*

7   εὐδαίμων, εὔδαιμον [= with a good δαίμων, *spirit, fate, lot*], *fortunate, happy.*
        οἰκητήριον, οἰκητηρίου, τό, *dwelling.*
        ὧδε, adv., *thus; here.*
        διατρίβω [δια- + τρίβω, *I rub, wear away, beat; I spend*], *I spend / pass time.*

9   εἶεν, particle, *well, quite so, very good.*

Exercise 25 ξ

Translate into English on a separate sheet of paper:

ΚΕΒΗΤΟΣ ΠΙΝΑΞ

XVII.

Πρεσβύτης "ὁρᾷς οὖν," ἔφη, "καὶ ἔμπροσθεν τοῦ ἄλσους ἐκείνου τόπον τινά, ὃς   1
δοκεῖ καλός τε εἶναι καὶ λειμωνοειδὴς καὶ φωτὶ πολλῷ καταλαμπόμενος;"   2

Ξένος "καὶ μάλα."   3

Πρεσβύτης "κατανοεῖς οὖν ἐν μέσῳ τῷ λειμῶνι περίβολον ἕτερον καὶ πύλην   4
ἑτέρᾱν;"   5

Ξένος "ἔστιν οὕτως. ἀλλὰ τίς καλεῖται ὁ τόπος οὗτος;"   6

Πρεσβύτης "εὐδαιμόνων οἰκητήριον," ἔφη· "ὧδε γὰρ διατρίβουσιν αἱ Ἀρεταὶ   7
πᾶσαι καὶ ἡ Εὐδαιμονίᾱ."   8

Ξένος "εἶεν," ἔφην ἐγώ, "ὡς καλὸν λέγεις τὸν τόπον εἶναι."   9

26
Ο ΚΡΟΙΣΟΣ
ΤΟΝ ΠΑΙΔΑ ΑΠΟΛΛΥΣΙΝ (α)

Exercise 26 α

Fill in the blanks with the correct forms of the verbs given, choosing the appropriate tense, mood, person, and number. If there is more than one possible form or spelling of a form, you need give only one. Supply either εἰ or ἐάν, as appropriate, along with your verbs in the if-clauses.

N.B.: Remember that for the future of ἔρχομαι Attic Greek uses εἶμι.

1. Present Particular:

   If the slave <u>returns home</u> (νοστέω) _____ now, <u>he is</u> (εἰμί) _____ _____ foolish.

2. Future More Vivid (Particular):

   If you return home (νοστέω) _____ , Philip, <u>you will see</u> (ὁράω) _____ your mother.

3. Past Particular:

   <u>If</u> Philip <u>returned home</u> (νοστέω) _____ yesterday, <u>he</u> surely <u>saw</u> (ὁράω) _____ his mother.

4. Future More Vivid (General):

   <u>If</u> Philip (ever) <u>returns home</u> (νοστέω) _____ , <u>he will see</u> (ὁράω) _____ his mother.

5. Present General:

   <u>If</u> (ever) Philip <u>returns home</u> (νοστέω) _____ , <u>he</u> (always) <u>sees</u> (ὁράω) _____ his mother.

6. Future Minatory:

   <u>If you go away from</u> home (ἀπέρχομαι) _____ , Philip, <u>you will see</u> (ὁράω) _____ a monster!

7. Past General:

   <u>If</u> (ever) Philip <u>returned home</u> (νοστέω) _____ , <u>he</u> (always) <u>saw</u> (ὁράω) _____ his mother.

Exercise 26 β

Fill in the blanks with the correct forms of the verbs given, choosing the appropriate tense, mood, person, and number. If there is more than one possible form or spelling of a form, you need give only one. Supply εἰ and ἄν as needed. Identify the type of condition used in each sentence as Past Contrary to Fact (Past CTF), Present Contrary to Fact (Present CTF), or Future Remote (FR).

N.B.: Remember that for the optative and the imperfect of ἔρχομαι Attic Greek uses forms of εἶμι.

1. If Philip <u>were working</u> (πονέω) _____ in the field, Xanthias <u>would be helping</u> (συλλαμβάνω) _____ him.

    _____

2. If Philip <u>should work/were to work</u> (πονέω) _____ in the field, Xanthias <u>would help</u> (συλλαμβάνω) _____ him.

    _____

3. If Philip <u>had worked</u> (πονέω) _____ in the field, Xanthias <u>would have helped</u> (συλλαμβάνω) _____ him.

    _____

4. If Melissa <u>should go/were to go</u> (ἔρχομαι) _____ to the spring, Myrrhine <u>would go</u> (συνέρχομαι) _____ with her.

    _____

5. If Melissa <u>had gone</u> (ἔρχομαι) _____ to the spring, Myrrhine <u>would have gone</u> (συνέρχομαι) _____ with her.

    _____

6. If Melissa <u>were going</u> (ἔρχομαι) _____ to the spring at this time, Myrrhine <u>would be going</u> (συνέρχομαι) _____ with her. _____

1   οὐκοῦν, adv., *then* (introducing a question that expects the answer "yes" and
         carries the thought forward from a previous assent).
     παρά, prep. + acc., *beside, near, by.*
2   καθεστηκώς, καθεστηκυῖα, καθεστηκός, *calm, composed* (perfect active
         participle of καθίστημι).
     πρόσωπον, προσώπου, τό, *face, countenance.*
         τὸ πρόσωπον: accusative of respect.
     κεκριμένος, κεκριμένη, κεκριμένον, *distinguished* (perfect passive participle
         of κρῑνω).
     ἡλικίᾱ, ἡλικίᾱς, ἡ, *age, time of life.*
         μέσῃ . . . τῇ ἡλικίᾳ: supply ἐν.
     στολή, στολῆς, ἡ, *robe.*
3   ἁπλοῦς, ἁπλῆ, ἁπλοῦν, *simple.*
     ἀκαλλώπιστος, ἀκαλλώπιστον [ἀ- + τὸ κάλλος, *beauty* + ἡ ὤψ, *face*],
         unadorned.
     ἕστηκε: *she stands* (perfect of ἵστημι).
     στρογγύλος, στρογγύλη, στρογγύλον, *round.*
4   τετράγωνος, τετράγωνον [ἡ τετράς, *the number four* + ἡ γωνίᾱ, *corner, angle*],
         four-angled, square.
     κειμένου: *placed* (= passive of τίθημι).
6   ἐμφαίνει, impersonal, *it is manifest/plain.*
     οὕτως ἔχειν: another example of ἔχω plus adverb equalling εἰμί plus adjective;
         literally, *to hold thus,* better English, *to be so.*
7   τοίνυν [τοι + νυν], particle, *therefore, accordingly; well then.*
     παιδείᾱ, παιδείᾱς, ἡ, *education.*
8   πειθώ, πειθοῦς, ἡ, *persuasion.*
10   σημεῖον, σημείου, τό, *sign, emblem.*
     βέβαιος, βεβαίᾱ, βέβαιον, *firm; secure.*
11   διδομένων: *of the things being given* [by her] = *of the things that she gives*
         (present passive participle of δίδωμι); the genitive is dependent on ἡ δόσις.
     δόσις, δόσεως, ἡ, *gift.*
12   ἃ: supply ἐκεῖνα as antecedent.
13   θάρσος, θάρσους, τό, *daring, courage.*
     ἀφοβίᾱ, ἀφοβίᾱς, ἡ, *fearlessness.*
15   ἐπιστήμη, ἐπιστήμης, ἡ [cf. ἐπίσταμαι], *knowledge, understanding.*
     τοῦ . . . παθεῖν: articular infinitive; the object of the infinitive is μηδὲν . . .
         δεινόν.
             ἄν . . . παθεῖν: *that one would suffer* (the infinitive with ἄν expresses
                 potentiality).

Exercise 26γ

Give an English equivalent of:

1. καθαίρω   _____   7. ἄκων   _____
2. τὸ οἰκίον   _____   8. ἀπόλλῡμι   _____
3. τὸ δόρυ   _____   9. ὁπόθεν   _____
4. ὀνομάζω   _____   10. δέομαι   _____
5. ὁ ὄνειρος   _____   11. ἐπί + acc.   _____
6. ὁ μὲν ἕτερος . . .   (of purpose)
   ὁ δὲ ἕτερος   _____

Exercise 26 δ

Translate into English on a separate sheet of paper:

ΚΕΒΗΤΟΣ ΠΙΝΑΞ

XVIII.

Πρεσβύτης "οὐκοῦν παρὰ τὴν πύλην ὁρᾷς," ἔφη, "ὅτι γυνή τίς ἐστι καλὴ καὶ   1
καθεστηκυῖα τὸ πρόσωπον, μέσῃ δὲ καὶ κεκριμένῃ ἤδη τῇ ἡλικίᾳ, στολὴν δ' ἔχουσα   2
ἁπλῆν τε καὶ ἀκαλλώπιστον; ἕστηκε δὲ οὐκ ἐπὶ στρογγύλου λίθου, ἀλλ' ἐπὶ   3
τετραγώνου ἀσφαλῶς κειμένου. καὶ μετὰ ταύτης ἄλλαι δύο εἰσί, θυγατέρες τινὲς   4
δοκοῦσαι εἶναι."   5

Ξένος "ἐμφαίνει οὕτως ἔχειν."   6

Πρεσβύτης "τούτων τοίνυν ἡ μὲν ἐν τῷ μέσῳ Παιδείᾱ ἐστίν, ἡ δὲ Ἀλήθεια, ἡ   7
δὲ Πειθώ."   8

Ξένος "τί δὲ ἕστηκεν ἐπὶ λίθου τετραγώνου αὕτη;"   9

Πρεσβύτης "σημεῖον," ἔφη, "ὅτι ἀσφαλής τε καὶ βεβαίᾱ ἡ πρὸς αὐτὴν ὁδός   10
ἐστι τοῖς ἀφικνουμένοις καὶ τῶν διδομένων ἀσφαλὴς ἡ δόσις τοῖς λαμβάνουσι."   11

Ξένος "καὶ τίνα ἐστίν, ἃ δίδωσιν αὕτη;"   12

Πρεσβύτης "θάρσος καὶ ἀφοβίᾱ," ἔφη ἐκεῖνος.   13

Ξένος "ταῦτα δὲ τίνα ἐστίν;"   14

Πρεσβύτης "ἐπιστήμη," ἔφη, "τοῦ μηδὲν ἄν ποτε δεινὸν παθεῖν ἐν τῷ βίῳ."   15

Exercise 26 ε

Give the Greek equivalent of:

1. I slay   _____
2. with regard to   _____
3. marriage   _____
4. the other (of two) _____
5. I show   _____

6. truth   _____
7. I stand near   _____
8. retribution   _____
9. I perish   _____
10. I learn by
    inquiry   _____

Exercise 26 ζ

Give the remaining principal parts of:

1. ἀπόλλῡμι   _____
                     _____

   Middle: _____
                     _____
                     _____

   Perfect: _____
                     _____

2. δέομαι   _____

3. ἐφίσταμαι   _____

4. καθαίρω   _____
                     _____
                     _____

5. ὀνομάζω   _____
                     _____
                     _____

6. φονεύω   _____
                     _____

7. πυνθάνομαι   _____
                     _____

8. φαίνω   _____
   or   _____
                     _____

9. γίγνομαι   _____
                     _____

10. γιγνώσκω   _____
                     _____
                     _____

11. διδάσκω   _____
                     _____
                     _____

12. πίπτω   _____
                     _____

(β)

Exercise 26η

Translate the underlined word or phrase, and then on the second line identify the use of the accusative case with one of the following descriptors:

Absolute, Adverbial, Direct Object,
Duration of Time, Extent of Space, Respect

1. The oxen are plowing <u>τὸν ἀγρόν</u>. _____

   _____

2. She ran <u>τάχιστα</u> to the spring. _____

   _____

3. Grandfather was not strong
   <u>τοὺς ὀφθαλμούς</u>. _____

   _____

4. They worked <u>εἴκοσιν ἡμέρᾱς</u>. _____

   _____

5. <u>ἐξὸν</u> that we do this, we will. _____

   _____

6. Their house is <u>τέτταρας σταδίους</u>
   away. _____

   _____

7. The man was Greek <u>τὸ γένος</u>. _____

   _____

8. <u>τί</u> are you running away? _____

   _____

9. <u>πολὺ</u> she wishes to marry. _____

   _____

10. <u>δέον</u> to find the child, they hurried
    into the house. _____

    _____

1   Ἡρακλῆς, Ἡρακλέους, ὁ, *Heracles*.
    Ἡράκλεις: vocative case.
  δῶρον, δώρου, τό, *gift*.
  ἕνεκεν [= ἕνεκα], prep. + gen., *for the sake of, on account of, because of.*

2   περίβολος, περιβόλου, ὁ, *enclosure*.
  ἕστηκεν: *she stands* (perfect of ἵστημι).

3   θεραπεύω, *I heal.*
  ποτίζω, *I make* X (acc.) *drink* Y (acc.).
    ποτίζει: supply αὐτούς.

4   καθαρτικός, καθαρτική, καθαρτικόν, *cathartic, purifying.*
  εἶτα, adv., *then, next.*

7   ὡς ἄν: *As if, As it were*, introducing the comparison with a patient and his doctor
    in the remainder of this sentence.
  εἴ . . . ἐτύγχανε (8), . . . ἄν . . . ἐξέβαλλε: *if someone should happen . . . , he
    would. . . .* (a future remote or future less vivid condition, here having the form
    of a present contrary to fact condition, with imperfect indicative in the if-clause
    and imperfect indicative with ἄν in the main clause; see Ch. 26, Gr. 1b, p. 164).
  φιλοτίμως, adv., *extremely.*

8   καθαρτικά, καθαρτικῶν, τά, *purgatives.*

9   νοσοποιέω, *I cause illness / sickness.*
    νοσοποιοῦντα: *things causing illness.*
  ἀνάληψις, ἀναλήψεως, ἡ, *taking up; recovery.*
  ὑγίεια, ὑγιείας, ἡ, *health.*
  κατέστησεν: sigmatic 1st aorist of καθίστημι.
    ἄν . . . κατέστησεν: *he would bring.*

10   εἰ . . . μὴ ἐπείθετο . . . , . . . ἄν . . . ἐξώλετο: *if he were not to comply with
    . . . , . . . he would perish.*
  οἷς: = ἐκείνοις ἅ, *those things that* (for attraction of the relative pronoun to the case
    of the antecedent, see Ch. 23, Gr. 6a, p. 119).
  ἐπιτάττω, *I order.*
    ἐπέταττεν: supply ὁ ἰᾱτρὸς as subject.
  εὐλόγως, adv., *reasonably, rightly.*
  ἀπωσθείς: aorist passive participle of ἀπωθέω, *I push off / reject.*
  ἐξώλετο: with ἄν, *would perish* (aorist middle of ἐξόλλῡμι).

11   νόσος, νόσου, ἡ, *sickness, disease.*

13   τὸν αὐτὸν . . . τρόπον: *in the same way* (adverbial accusative).
  τοίνυν [τοι + νυν], particle, *therefore, accordingly; well then.*
  παιδείᾱ, παιδείᾱς, ἡ, *education.*

14   ποτίζω, *I make* X (acc.) *drink of* Y (dat.).
    ποτίζει: repeat αὐτόν as direct object; note the different construction from
        that in line 3.
  ἐκκαθαίρω, aorist, ἐξεκάθᾱρα, *I clean out, purge.*

16   ποῖος, ποίᾱ, ποῖον, *what sort / kind of; of what sort / kind?*

17   ἄγνοια, ἀγνοίᾱς, ἡ, *ignorance.*
  πλάνος, πλάνου, ὁ, *wandering; error.*
  ἐπεπώκει: *he had drunk* (pluperfect of πίνω).
  παρά, prep. + gen., *from.*
  ἀπάτη, ἀπάτης, ἡ, *trick; deceit; deception.*

Exercise 26θ

Translate into English on a separate sheet of paper:

ΚΕΒΗΤΟΣ ΠΙΝΑΞ

XIX.

Ξένος "ὦ Ἡράκλεις ὡς καλά," ἔφην, "τὰ δῶρα. ἀλλὰ τίνος ἕνεκεν οὕτως 1
ἔξω τοῦ περιβόλου ἔστηκεν;" 2

Πρεσβύτης "ὅπως τοὺς παραγῑνομένους," ἔφη, "θεραπεύῃ καὶ ποτίζῃ τὴν 3
καθαρτικὴν δύναμιν. εἶθ' ὅταν καθαρθῶσιν, οὕτως εἰσάγει τούτους πρὸς τὰς 4
Ἀρετάς." 5

Ξένος "πῶς τοῦτο;" ἔφην ἐγώ, "οὐ γὰρ συνῑημι." 6

Πρεσβύτης "ἀλλὰ συνήσεις," ἔφη. "ὡς ἄν, εἴ τις φιλοτῑμως κάμνων 7
ἐτύγχανε, πρὸς ῑατρὸν ἂν δήπου γενόμενος πρότερον καθαρτικοῖς ἐξέβαλλε τὰ 8
νοσοποιοῦντα, εἶτα οὕτως ἂν ὁ ῑατρὸς αὐτὸν εἰς ἀνάληψιν καὶ ὑγίειαν κατέστησεν, 9
εἰ δὲ μὴ ἐπείθετο οἷς ἐπέταττεν, εὐλόγως ἂν δήπου ἀπωσθεὶς ἐξώλετο ὑπὸ τῆς 10
νόσου." 11

Ξένος "ταῦτα μὲν συνῑημι," ἔφην ἐγώ. 12

Πρεσβύτης "τὸν αὐτὸν τοίνυν τρόπον," ἔφη, "καὶ πρὸς τὴν Παιδείαν ὅταν τις 13
παραγένηται, θεραπεύει αὐτὸν καὶ ποτίζει τῇ ἑαυτῆς δυνάμει, ὅπως ἐκκαθάρῃ 14
πρῶτον καὶ ἐκβάλῃ τὰ κακὰ πάντα, ὅσα ἔχων ἦλθε." 15

Ξένος "ποῖα ταῦτα;" 16

Πρεσβύτης "τὴν ἄγνοιαν καὶ τὸν πλάνον, ὃν ἐπεπώκει παρὰ τῆς Ἀπάτης, 17
καὶ τὴν ἀλαζονείαν καὶ τὴν ἐπιθῡμίαν καὶ τὴν ἀκρασίαν καὶ τὸν θῡμὸν καὶ τὴν 18
φιλαργυρίᾱν καὶ τὰ λοιπὰ πάντα, ὧν ἀνεπλήσθη ἐν τῷ πρώτῳ περιβόλῳ." 19

---

18 **ἀλαζονείᾱ, ἀλαζονείᾱς, ἡ,** *boastfulness.*
ἐπιθῡμίᾱ, ἐπιθῡμίᾱς, ἡ, *desire, longing.*
ἀκρασίᾱ, ἀκρασίᾱς, ἡ [ἀ- + τὸ κράτος], *lack of power/control over one's
passions; intemperance.*
θῡμός, θῡμοῦ, ὁ, *spirit; passion; wrath.*

19 **φιλαργυρίᾱ, φιλαργυρίᾱς, ἡ,** *avarice, greed.*
λοιπός, λοιπή, λοιπόν, *remaining.*
ἀνεπλήσθη: *he was filled up* (with) + gen., (aorist passive indicative, 3rd person
singular, of ἀναπίμπλημι, *I fill up*).

Exercise 26ι

Translate the sentences below:

1. συζευκτέοι (*yoked together*) οἱ βόες.   _____

2. καλητέοι ὑμῖν οἱ φίλοι.   _____

3. δραμητέον ἡμῖν.   _____

4. σοὶ βαδιστέα ἐστὶν πρὸς τὴν κρήνην.   _____

5. ἐμοὶ τοῦτο οὐ ποιητέον.   _____

Exercise 26κ

Give an English equivalent of:

1. μεταπέμπομαι   _____   5. μέλει   _____
2. ἡ δειλίᾱ   _____   6. ἐπεί   _____
3. ποῖος;   _____   7. τὸ θηρίον   _____
4. ὁ φόνος   _____   8. μεθῑ́ημι   _____

Exercise 26λ

Give the Greek equivalent of:

1. guard   _____   5. despair   _____
2. hunt   _____   6. I oblige   _____
3. I reveal   _____   7. saying   _____
4. circle   _____   8. from (i.e., at the hand of)   _____

Exercise 26μ

Give the remaining principal parts of:

1. μέλει   _____   4. γίγνομαι   _____

  _____   _____

2. χαρίζομαι   _____   _____

  _____   5. ἐγείρω   _____

3. διαφθείρω   _____   _____

  _____   _____

  or _____   _____

  _____   6. λείπω   _____

  _____   _____

            _____

            _____

27
Ο ΚΡΟΙΣΟΣ ΕΠΙ ΤΟΝ ΚΥΡΟΝ ΣΤΡΑΤΕΥΕΤΑΙ (α)

Exercise 27 α

Using the verbs supplied, write perfect middle or passive participles that translate the English phrases correctly:

1. ἡ θυγάτηρ <u>having been freed</u> (λύω) _____

2. ἡ γυνὴ <u>having feared</u> (φοβέομαι) _____

3. τὰς γυναῖκας <u>having been loved</u> (φιλέω) _____

4. τὰ ἔργα <u>having been done</u> (ποιέω) _____

5. οἱ πολῖται <u>having been honored</u> (τῑμάω) _____

6. ὁ πατὴρ <u>having ransomed</u> (λύομαι) _____

Exercise 27 β

Translate the following English phrases with the correct form of the perfect middle or passive. For indicative forms, give the pluperfect as well:

1. λύομαι: he/she has/had been loosened Pf. _____
   Plpf. _____

2. λύομαι: you (pl.) have/had been loosened Pf. _____
   Plpf. _____

3. φιλέω: I have/had been loved Pf. _____
   Plpf. _____

4. φιλέω: they have/had been loved Pf. _____
   Plpf. _____

5. φιλέω: we have/had been loved Pf. _____
   Plpf. _____

6. τῑμάω: you (sing.) have/had been honored Pf. _____
   Plpf. _____

7. τῑμάω: he/she has/had been honored Pf. _____
   Plpf. _____

8. τῑμάω: I (fem.) have been honored
   (subjunctive) Pf. _____

9. δηλόω: they (masc.) have been shown
    (optative)   Pf.   _____

10. δηλόω: to have been shown   Pf.   _____

11. δηλόω: we have/had been shown   Pf.   _____

         Plpf.   _____

12. δηλόω: it has/had been shown   Pf.   _____

         Plpf.   _____

13. ἀφικνέομαι: we have/had arrived   Pf.   _____

         Plpf.   _____

14. ἀφικνέομαι: you (sing., fem.) have
    arrived (subjunctive)   Pf.   _____

15. ἀφικνέομαι: we (fem.) have arrived
    (optative)   Pf.   _____

16. βουλεύομαι: they have/had deliberated   Pf.   _____

         Plpf.   _____

17. βουλεύομαι: it has/had been planned   Pf.   _____

         Plpf.   _____

18. βουλεύομαι: to have planned   Pf.   _____

Exercise 27γ

Translate the English prepositional phrases into Greek to express agency with the given verb forms:

1. τῑμᾶται by the men: ἄνδρες   _____

2. τετίμηται by the men: ἄνδρες   _____

3. ἐλύθη by her (= the) father: πατήρ   _____

4. ἐλύ̈ετο by her (= the) father: πατήρ   _____

5. ἐλέλυτο by her (= the) father: πατήρ   _____

Exercise 27 δ

Give an English equivalent of:

1. τὸ μαντεῖον _____
2. αὐτίκα _____
3. ἀγωνίζομαι _____
4. τὸ στράτευμα _____
5. οὐδέτερος _____
6. ἀντιόομαι _____
7. τὸ χρηστήριον _____

8. πρός + acc. _____
9. παρακαλέω _____
10. τὸ μέτρον _____
11. πάνυ _____
12. τὸ ἀνάθημα _____
13. μέμφομαι _____
14. ἄλλοι ἄλλοσε _____

Exercise 27 ε

Give the Greek equivalent of:

1. gift _____
2. oath _____
3. I approach _____
4. to another place _____
5. I gather _____
6. Pythia _____
7. I dissolve _____

8. for (of time) _____
9. number _____
10. I cross _____
11. alliance _____
12. I speak _____
13. fierce _____
14. oracular
    response _____

Exercise 27 ζ

Give the remaining principal parts of:

1. ἀγείρω _____
   _____

2. ἀγωνίζομαι _____
   _____
   _____

3. ἀντιόομαι _____
   _____

4. μέμφομαι _____
   _____
   or _____

5. αἱρέω _____
   _____
   _____
   _____
   _____

6. ἔρχομαι infin. _____
   participle _____
   imperfect _____
   future _____
   aorist _____
   perfect _____
7. τρέχω _____
   _____
   _____
   _____

1   "ὅταν . . . καθαρθῇ, . . . αὐτὸν ἀποστέλλει;": for the subjects and object,
        see ΚΕΒΗΤΟΣ ΠΙΝΑΞ XIX:13–19, p. 103.
    ποῦ: = ποῖ.
    ἀποστέλλω, *I send off/away.*
2   ἔνδον, adv., *within, inside.*
    ἐπιστήμη, ἐπιστήμης, ἡ [cf. ἐπίσταμαι], *understanding, knowledge.*
4   ἔσω, prep. + gen., *inside.*
    εὐειδής, εὐειδές, *well-formed, graceful.*
5   εὔτακτος, -ον [cf. τάττω], *well-ordered, well-behaved, neat.*
    στολή, στολῆς, ἡ, *robe.*
    ἀτρύφερος, ἀτρύφερον, *not luxurious; plain, simple.*
    ἁπλοῦς, ἁπλῆ, ἁπλοῦν, *simple.*
6   ἄπλαστος, ἄπλαστον, *unfashioned, natural, genuine.*
    οὐδαμῶς, adv., *in no way.*
    καλλωπίζω, *I beautify my face* (ὤψ).
        κεκαλλωπισμένος: perfect passive participle.
    καθάπερ, adv., *just as, as.*
9   ἀδελφή, ἀδελφῆς, ἡ, *sister.*
    ἀνδρείᾱ, ἀνδρείᾱς, ἡ, *courage, bravery.*
    δικαιοσύνη, δικαιοσύνης, ἡ, *uprightness, righteousness, justice.*
    καλοκἀγαθίᾱ, καλοκἀγαθίᾱς, ἡ, *rectitude, honor, honorable behavior.*
    εὐταξίᾱ, εὐταξίᾱς, ἡ, *good order, propriety.*
10 ἐγκράτεια, ἐγκρατείᾱς, ἡ [cf. κρατέω, ἡ ἀκρασίᾱ, *intemperance,* and τὸ
        κράτος], *self-control.*
    πρᾳότης, πρᾳότητος, ἡ, *mildness, modesty.*
11 κάλλιστε (vocative), *most noble/honorable.*
12 συνῆτε: *you understand* (aorist subjunctive of συνίημι; see Ch. 21, Gr. 4, p. 86 for
        the form of the uncompounded verb).
    ἕξις, ἕξεως, ἡ, *habit.*
    περιποιέομαι, *I acquire.*
        περιποιήσησθε: aorist subjunctive.
    ὧν: supply ἐκείνων (genitive with ἕξιν) as antecedent (for omission of the
        antecedent and attraction [ἀκούετε would normally take the accusative of the
        thing heard], see Ch. 23, Gr. 6c, p. 119).
13 προσέχω, *I direct; I apply.*
        προσέχω (+ τὸν νοῦν, stated or implied), *I pay attention to.*
14 τοιγαροῦν [τοι + γάρ + οὖν], particle, *for that reason, therefore.*

Exercise 27 η

Translate into English on a separate sheet of paper:

ΚΕΒΗΤΟΣ ΠΙΝΑΞ

ΧΧ.

Ξένος "ὅταν οὖν καθαρθῇ, ποῦ αὐτὸν ἀποστέλλει;"   1

Πρεσβύτης "ἔνδον," ἔφη, "πρὸς τὴν Ἐπιστήμην καὶ πρὸς τὰς ἄλλᾱς Ἀρετᾱς."   2

Ξένος "ποίᾱς ταύτᾱς;"   3

Πρεσβύτης "οὐκ ὁρᾷς," ἔφη, "ἔσω τῆς πύλης χορὸν γυναικῶν, ὡς εὐειδεῖς   4
δοκοῦσιν εἶναι καὶ εὔτακτοι καὶ στολὴν ἀτρύφερον καὶ ἁπλῆν ἔχουσιν· ἔτι τε ὡς   5
ἄπλαστοί εἰσι καὶ οὐδαμῶς κεκαλλωπισμέναι καθάπερ αἱ ἄλλαι;"   6

Ξένος "ὁρῶ," ἔφην. "ἀλλὰ τίνες αὖται καλοῦνται;"   7

Πρεσβύτης "ἡ μὲν πρώτη Ἐπιστήμη," ἔφη, "καλεῖται. αἱ δὲ ἄλλαι ταύτης   8
ἀδελφαί, Ἀνδρείᾱ, Δικαιοσύνη, Καλοκἀγαθίᾱ, Σωφροσύνη, Εὐταξίᾱ, Ἐλευθερίᾱ,   9
Ἐγκράτεια, Πρᾳότης."   10

Ξένος "ὦ κάλλιστε," ἔφην ἔγωγε, "ὡς ἐν μεγάλῃ ἐλπίδι ἐσμέν."   11

Πρεσβύτης "ἐὰν συνῆτε," ἔφη, "καὶ ἕξιν περιποιήσησθε ὧν ἀκούετε."   12

Ξένος "ἀλλὰ προσέξομεν," ἔφην ἔγωγε, "ὡς μάλιστα."   13

Πρεσβύτης "τοιγαροῦν," ἔφη, "σωθήσεσθε."   14

(β)

Exercise 27θ

Transform the verb given to the perfect middle / passive:

1. θάπτω   _____
2. ξενίζω   _____
3. ἀγγέλλω   _____
4. ψεύδομαι   _____
5. σκοπέω   _____
6. γράφω   _____
7. σπεύδω   _____
8. ἀφικνέομαι   _____

Exercise 27ι

Translate the following English phrases with the correct form of the perfect middle / passive. For indicative forms, give the pluperfect as well:

1. λείπω: he/she has/had been left   Pf.   _____

    Plpf. _____

2. λείπω: to have been left   Pf.   _____
3. λείπω: we have/had been left   Pf.   _____

    Plpf. _____

4. κρίνω: you (sing.) have/had been judged   Pf.   _____

    Plpf. _____

5. κρίνω: (ὁ ἄνθρωπος) having been judged   Pf.   _____
6. κρίνω: they (masc.) have/had been judged   Pf.   _____

    Plpf. _____

7. ἀγγέλλω: it has/had been announced   Pf.   _____

    Plpf. _____

8. ἀγγέλλω: they (neut.) have/had been

    announced   Pf.   _____

    Plpf. _____

9. πείθω: you (pl.) have/had been persuaded   Pf.   _____

    Plpf. _____

10. πείθω: we (fem.) have been persuaded

    (optative)   Pf.   _____

11. πείθω: I have/had been persuaded   Pf. _____

                 Plpf. _____

12. φαίνω: they (masc.) have/had appeared   Pf. _____

                 Plpf. _____

13. φαίνω: it has/had appeared   Pf. _____

                 Plpf. _____

14. φαίνω: (ἡ γυνὴ) having appeared   Pf. _____

15. δέχομαι: we have/had received   Pf. _____

                 Plpf. _____

16. δέχομαι: you (sing., fem.) have received
(subjunctive)   Pf. _____

17. δέχομαι: to have received   Pf. _____

Exercise 27 κ

Give an English equivalent of:

1. ἄχρηστος _____   6. ἀνέχομαι _____
2. κτείνω _____   7. ἡ κάμηλος _____
3. ἡ ἵππος _____   8. φείδομαι _____
4. ὄπισθεν _____   9. τὸ ἱππικόν _____
5. κατὰ τάχος _____

Exercise 27 λ

Give the Greek equivalent of:

1. I command _____   5. infantry _____
2. I ride a horse _____   6. cowardly _____
3. tribe _____   7. backward _____
4. I turn around _____   8. horse _____

1   **παραλαμβάνω**, *I receive.*
     ποῦ: = ποῖ.
5   **ποῖος, ποία, ποῖον**, *what sort/kind of; of what sort/kind?*
6   **ὑψηλόν, ὑψηλοῦ, τό**, *height, high place.*
7   **περίβολος, περιβόλου, ὁ**, *enclosure.*
9   **οὐκοῦν**, adv., *then* (introducing a question that expects the answer "yes" and
         carries the thought forward from a previous assent).
     ἐπί, prep. + gen., *in; near.*
     προπύλαιον προπυλαίου, τό, *gateway.*
     καθεστηκώς, καθεστηκυῖα, καθεστηκός, *stationed* (perfect active participle
         of καθίστημι); this word is used in a different sense in ΚΕΒΗΤΟΣ ΠΙΝΑΞ
         XVIII:2, p. 99.
     εὐειδής, εὐειδές, *well-formed, comely, graceful.*
10   **θρόνος, θρόνου, ὁ**, *throne.*
     ὑψηλός, ὑψηλή, ὑψηλόν, *high.*
     κοσμέω, *I put in order; I adorn.*
     ἐλευθέρως, adv., *freely; in the manner of a free-born person.*
     ἀπεριέργως [ἀ- + περι- + τὸ ἔργον], *not excessively busily; artlessly; simply.*
11   **στεφανόω**, *I crown.*
         ἐστεφανωμένος, ἐστεφανωμένη, ἐστεφανωμένον, *crowned.*
     στέφανος, στεφάνου, ὁ, *crown.*
     εὐανθής, εὐανθές [εὐ- + τὸ ἄνθος, *flower*], *made of beautiful flowers.*
12   **ἐμφαίνει**, impersonal, *it is manifest/plain.*
13   **τοίνυν** [τοι + νυν], particle, *therefore, accordingly; well then.*

Exercise 27 μ

Give the remaining principal parts of:

1. λέγω   _____   3. εἴρω   _____
                   _____   _____
                   _____   _____
                   _____   _____
2. ἔπω   _____

Exercise 27v

Translate into English on a separate sheet of paper:

ΚΕΒΗΤΟΣ ΠΙΝΑΞ

XXI.

Ξένος "ὅταν οὖν παραλάβωσιν αὐτὸν αὗται, ποῦ ἄγουσι;"   1

Πρεσβύτης "πρὸς τὴν μητέρα," ἔφη.   2

Ξένος "αὕτη δὲ τίς ἐστιν;"   3

Πρεσβύτης "Εὐδαιμονίᾱ," ἔφη.   4

Ξένος "ποίᾱ δ' ἐστὶν αὕτη;"   5

Πρεσβύτης "ὁρᾷς τὴν ὁδὸν ἐκείνην τὴν φέρουσαν ἐπὶ τὸ ὑψηλὸν ἐκεῖνο, ὅ ἐστιν   6
ἀκρόπολις τῶν περιβόλων πάντων;"   7

Ξένος "ὁρῶ."   8

Πρεσβύτης "οὐκοῦν ἐπὶ τοῦ προπυλαίου γυνὴ καθεστηκυῖα εὐειδής τις   9
κάθηται ἐπὶ θρόνου ὑψηλοῦ, κεκοσμημένη ἐλευθέρως καὶ ἀπεριέργως καὶ   10
ἐστεφανωμένη στεφάνῳ εὐανθεῖ πάνυ καλῷ;"   11

Ξένος "ἐμφαίνει οὕτως."   12

Πρεσβύτης "αὕτη τοίνυν ἐστὶν ἡ Εὐδαιμονίᾱ," ἔφη.   13

28
Ο ΑΠΟΛΛΩΝ
ΤΟΝ ΚΡΟΙΣΟΝ ΣΩΙΖΕΙ (α)

Exercise 28 α

Translate the following English phrases with the correct form of the perfect active. For indicative forms, give the pluperfect as well. If there is more than one spelling of a form, you need give only the more common:

1. λύω: to have freed   Pf. _____
2. λύω: we have/had freed   Pf. _____

                      Plpf. _____

3. λύω: (ἡ γυνὴ) having freed   Pf. _____
4. λύω: I (masc.) have freed (subjunctive)   Pf. _____
5. λύω: he/she has/had freed   Pf. _____

                      Plpf. _____

6. λύω: you (pl., fem.) have freed (optative)   Pf. _____
7. πείθω: we have/had persuaded   Pf. _____

                      Plpf. _____

8. πείθω: you (sing.) have/had persuaded   Pf. _____

                      Plpf. _____

9. πείθω: they (masc.) have persuaded (optative)   Pf. _____
10. πείθω: to have persuaded   Pf. _____
11. πείθω: (οἱ ἄνθρωποι) having persuaded   Pf. _____
12. πείθω: she has persuaded (subjunctive)   Pf. _____

Exercise 28 β

Translate the following English phrases with the correct form of the perfect active. For indicative forms, give the pluperfect as well. If there is more than one spelling of a form, you need give only the more common:

1. τῑμάω: he/she has/had honored   Pf. _____

                      Plpf. _____

2. φιλέω: (ἡ γυνὴ) having loved   Pf. _____
3. τρέχω: they have/had run   Pf. _____

                      Plpf. _____

4.   βάλλω: we have/had thrown   Pf.   _____
                                         Plpf. _____

5.   κρίνω: to have judged   Pf.   _____

6.   μανθάνω: I (masc.) have learned
     (subjunctive)   Pf.   _____

7.   δηλόω: they have/had shown   Pf.   _____
                                         Plpf. _____

8.   νομίζω: to have thought   Pf.   _____

9.   μένω: we (fem.) have waited (optative) Pf. _____

10. καλέω: (ὁ ἄνθρωπος) having called   Pf.   _____

11. εὑρίσκω: we have/had found   Pf.   _____
                                         Plpf. _____

12. ἀποθνῄσκω: to have died = to be dead Pf.   _____

13. ἵστημι: they are/were standing   Pf.   _____
        (N.B. Pluperfect augments to εἰ-.) Plpf. _____

14. βαίνω: I am/was set   Pf.   _____
                                         Plpf. _____

Exercise 28 γ

Match the following verb forms with their translations:

1. ___ ἐλελύκει(ν)   A. we had freed
2. ___ ἐλελύκετε   B. you (pl.) had loved
3. ___ ἐλελύκεμεν   C. you (sing.) had loved
4. ___ ἐλελύκη   D. he/she had loved
5. ___ ἐλελύκεσαν   E. you (pl.) had freed
6. ___ ἐπεφιλήκεμεν   F. he/she had freed
7. ___ ἐπεφιλήκης   G. I had loved
8. ___ ἐπεφιλήκετε   H. they had freed
9. ___ ἐπεφιλήκει(ν)   I. I had freed
10. ___ ἐπεφιλήκη   K. we had loved

Exercise 28 δ

Using the verbs supplied, write the perfect and pluperfect forms that translate the English phrases correctly:

1. γράφω: we have/had written   Pf. _____
                                         Plpf. _____

2. γράφω: you (sing.) have/had written Pf. _____
                                         Plpf. _____

3. γίγνομαι: I have/had become   Pf. _____
                                         Plpf. _____

4. ἄγω: they have/had driven   Pf. _____
                                         Plpf. _____

5. ἀποκτείνω: we have/had killed   Pf. _____
                                         Plpf. _____

6. δείκνῡμι: you (pl.) have/had shown   Pf. _____
                                         Plpf. _____

7. ἔρχομαι: he/she has/had come   Pf. _____
    (N.B. Pluperfect augments to εἰ-.)   Plpf. _____

8. κρύπτω: I have/had hidden   Pf. _____
                                         Plpf. _____

9. τάττω: you (pl.) have/had stationed   Pf. _____
                                         Plpf. _____

10. τρέπω: we have/had turned   Pf. _____
                                         Plpf. _____

11. λείπω: I have/had left   Pf. _____
                                         Plpf. _____

12. φέρω: they have/had carried   Pf. _____
                                         Plpf. _____

13. πέμπω: we have/had sent   Pf. _____
                                         Plpf. _____

14. πέμπω: you (sing.) have/had sent   Pf. _____
                                         Plpf. _____

15. γίγνομαι: they have/had become   Pf. _____
                                         Plpf. _____

16. λείπω: I have/had left   Pf. _____
                                         Plpf. _____

Exercise 28 ε

Give an English equivalent of:

1. τὸ δέος   _____
2. ἀναιρέομαι   _____
3. πορθέω   _____
4. εἴτε . . . εἴτε _____

5. ἡ ζωή   _____
6. ἁλίσκομαι   _____
7. ὁ δαίμων   _____
8. κατακαίω or
   κατακάω   _____

Exercise 28 ζ

Give the Greek equivalent of:

1. I mount   _____
2. funeral pyre   _____
3. after   _____
4. I put an end to _____

5. citadel   _____
6. I proclaim   _____
7. horseman   _____
8. (it) makes a
   difference to   _____

Exercise 28 η

Give the remaining principal parts of:

1. ἁλίσκομαι   _____
                    _____
            or _____
                    _____
            or _____

2. κατακαίω or
   κατακάω   _____
                    _____
                    _____
                    _____
                    _____

3. φέρω   _____
                    _____
            or _____
                    _____
                    _____
                    _____

1   ὧδε, adv., *thus; here.*

     ποιεῖ: the subject is ἡ Εὐδαιμονίᾱ: see ΚΕΒΗΤΟΣ ΠΙΝΑΞ XXI:13, p. 113.

2   στεφανόω, *I crown.*

4   ποῖος, ποία, ποῖον, *what sort / kind of; of what sort / kind?*

5   ἅ: governing singular verbs, as is usual for neuter plurals.

6   κατεσθίω [κατα- + ἐσθίω], *I eat up, devour.*

     κολάζω, *I punish.*

     ἀπορρίπτω, ἀπορρίψω, ἀπέρρῑψα, *I throw away.*

7   ἐκεῖνα: neuter plural subject of δουλεύουσι. The plural verb (rather than the usual
         singular with a neuter plural subject) may be used here to emphasize the
         number of monsters now enslaved to the victor.

     δουλεύω + dat., *I serve* X *as a slave, I am a slave* to X.

     καθάπερ, adv., *just as, as.*

Exercise 28 θ

Translate into English on a separate sheet of paper:

ΚΕΒΗΤΟΣ ΠΙΝΑΞ

XXII.

    Ξένος "ὅταν οὖν ὧδέ τις παραγένηται, τί ποιεῖ;"   1

    Πρεσβύτης "στεφανοῖ αὐτόν," ἔφη, "τῇ ἑαυτῆς δυνάμει ἥ τε Εὐδαιμονίᾱ καὶ   2
αἱ ἄλλαι Ἀρεταὶ πᾶσαι ὥσπερ τοὺς νενῑκηκότας τοὺς μεγίστους ἀγῶνας."   3

    Ξένος "καὶ ποίους ἀγῶνας νενίκηκεν αὐτός;" ἔφην ἐγώ.   4

    Πρεσβύτης "τοὺς μεγίστους," ἔφη, "καὶ τὰ μέγιστα θηρία, ἃ πρότερον αὐτὸν   5
κατήσθιε καὶ ἐκόλαζε καὶ ἐποίει δοῦλον. ταῦτα πάντα νενίκηκε καὶ ἀπέρρῑψεν   6
ἀφ' ἑαυτοῦ καὶ κεκράτηκεν ἑαυτοῦ, ὥστε ἐκεῖνα νῦν τούτῳ δουλεύουσι, καθάπερ   7
οὗτος ἐκείνοις πρότερον."   8

(β)

Exercise 28 ι

Match the following verb forms with their translations:

1. ____ μέμνημαι   A . I am likely to

2. ____ ἕστηκα   B . I am by nature

3. ____ ἔοικα   C . I know

4. ____ εἴωθα   D . I remember

5. ____ ὡς ἔοικε(ν)   E . I am afraid

6. ____ οἶδα   F . I stand

7. ____ πέφυκα   G . as it seems

8. ____ δέδοικα   H . I am accustomed to

Exercise 28 κ

Translate the following English phrases with the correct form of the verb οἶδα. If there is more than one spelling of a form, you need give only one:

1. he/she knows   _____   6. you (pl.) know   _____

2. we know   _____   7. they know   _____

3. you (sing.) knew _____   8. he/she knew   _____

4. they knew   _____   9. we knew   _____

5. I will know   _____   10. they will know   _____

Exercise 28 λ

Translate the following English phrases with the correct form of the verb οἶδα:

1. to know   _____

2. (αἱ γυναῖκες) knowing   _____

3. I know (subjunctive)   _____

4. we know (optative)   _____

5. (ὁ ἄνθρωπος) knowing   _____

6. know! (sing.)   _____

7. (τῶν ἀνθρώπων) knowing   _____

8. know! (pl.)   _____

9. they know (subjunctive)   _____

10. they know (optative)   _____

Exercise 28 μ

Give an English equivalent of:

1. ἀναστενάζω   _____
2. ἀντί + gen.   _____
3. ἔσχατος   _____
4. ἐνθῡμέομαι   _____

5. ἡ νεφέλη   _____
6. μέμνημαι   _____
7. ὁ ὄλβος   _____
8. περὶ οὐδενὸς
   ποιοῦμαι   _____

Exercise 28 ν

Give the Greek equivalent of:

1. I remind X   _____
2. I repent   _____
3. silence   _____
4. I stand near   _____

5. I call upon   _____
6. quietness   _____
7. I choose   _____
8. foolish   _____

Exercise 28 ξ

Give the remaining principal parts of:

1. ἀναμιμνήσκω   _____
                     _____
                     _____
                     _____
                     _____

2. ἐνθῡμέομαι   _____
                     _____
                     _____

3. παρίσταμαι   _____
                     _____

4. βούλομαι   _____
                   _____

5. ἐθέλω   _____
                _____

6. μάχομαι   _____
                  _____

7. χαίρω   _____
                _____
                _____

1 ποῖος, ποία, ποῖον, *what sort/kind of; of what sort/kind?*
   ἐπιποθέω, *I desire.*
2 ἄγνοια, ἀγνοίας, ἡ, *ignorance.*
   πλάνος, πλάνου, ὁ, *wandering; error.*
4 πονηρός, πονηρά, πονηρόν, *toilsome, painful, grievous.*
5 εἶτα, adv., *then, next.*
   λύπη, λύπης, ἡ [λῡπέω, *I grieve, pain*], *pain* (of body); *pain* (of mind); *grief.*
   ὀδυρμός, ὀδυρμοῦ, ὁ [cf. ὀδύρομαι, *I grieve*], *lamentation.*
   φιλαργυρίᾱ, φιλαργυρίας, ἡ, *avarice, greed.*
6 ἀκρασίᾱ, ἀκρασίας, ἡ [ἀ- + τὸ κράτος], *lack of power/control over one's passions; intemperance.*
   λοιπός, λοιπή, λοιπόν, *remaining.*
   κακίᾱ, κακίᾱς, ἡ, *evil.*
8 ὦ, exclamation + gen., *oh; what.*
9 στέφανος, στεφάνου, ὁ, *crown.*
   στεφανόω, *I crown.*
10 εὐδαιμονικός, εὐδαιμονική, εὐδαιμονικόν, *making one happy, conferring happiness.*
   νεᾱνίσκος, νεᾱνίσκου, ὁ, *young man.*
11 εὐδαίμων, εὔδαιμον [= with a good δαίμων, *spirit, fate, lot*], *fortunate, happy.*
   μακάριος, μακαρίᾱ, μακάριον, *blessed, happy.*
   ἕτερος, ἑτέρᾱ, ἕτερον, *one* or *the other* (of two); *other, another.*
14 αὐτῷ: = ἑαυτῷ.

Exercise 28 o

Translate into English on a separate sheet of paper:

ΚΕΒΗΤΟΣ ΠΙΝΑΞ

XXIII.

Ξένος "ποῖα ταῦτα λέγεις τὰ θηρία; πάνυ γὰρ ἐπιποθῶ ἀκοῦσαι."   1

Πρεσβύτης "πρῶτον μέν," ἔφη, "τὴν Ἄγνοιαν καὶ τὸν Πλάνον. ἢ οὐ δοκεῖ σοι   2
ταῦτα θηρία;"   3

Ξένος "καὶ πονηρά γε," ἔφην ἐγώ.   4

Πρεσβύτης "εἶτα τὴν Λύπην καὶ τὸν Ὀδυρμὸν καὶ τὴν Φιλαργυρίᾱν καὶ τὴν   5
Ἀκρασίᾱν καὶ τὴν λοιπὴν ἅπασαν Κακίᾱν. πάντων τούτων κρατεῖ καὶ οὐ   6
κρατεῖται ὥσπερ πρότερον."   7

Ξένος "ὦ καλῶν ἔργων," ἔφην ἐγώ, "καὶ καλλίστης νίκης. ἀλλ᾽ ἐκεῖνο ἔτι   8
μοι εἰπέ· τίς ἡ δύναμις τοῦ στεφάνου, ᾧ ἔφης στεφανοῦσθαι αὐτόν;"   9

Πρεσβύτης "εὐδαιμονική, ὦ νεᾱνίσκε. ὁ γὰρ στεφανωθεὶς ταύτῃ τῇ δυνάμει   10
εὐδαίμων γίνεται καὶ μακάριος καὶ οὐκ ἔχει ἐν ἑτέροις τὰς ἐλπίδας τῆς   11
εὐδαιμονίᾱς, ἀλλ᾽ ἐν αὑτῷ."   12

VOCABULARY
CHAPTERS 25–28

VERBS

-ωVerbs

ἀγείρω, ἀγερῶ, ἤγειρα	*I gather*
ἀναμιμνήσκω, ἀναμνήσω, ἀνέμνησα	*I remind* someone (acc.) *of* something (acc. or gen.)
μέμνημαι	*I have reminded myself = I remember*
μνησθήσομαι	*I will remember*
ἐμνήσθην	*I remembered*
ἀναστενάζω	*I groan aloud*
ἀναστρέφω	*I turn around*
ἀποφαίνω	*I show; I reveal; I prove*
διαβαίνω	*I cross*
διαφέρει	impersonal + dat., *(it) makes a difference to*
ἕλκω, ἕλξω, εἵλκυσα, εἵλκυκα, εἵλκυσμαι, εἱλκύσθην	*I drag*
ἐπιβαίνω	+ gen., *I get up on, mount;* + dat., *I board*
θάπτω, θάψω, ἔθαψα, τέθαμμαι, ἐτάφην	*I bury*
ἱππεύω, ἱππεύσω, ἵππευσα	*I am a horseman; I ride a horse*
καθαίρω, καθαρῶ, ἐκάθηρα, κεκάθαρμαι, ἐκαθάρθην	*I purify*
κατακαίω or κατακᾶω, κατακαύσω, κατέκαυσα, κατακέκαυκα, κατακέκαυμαι, κατεκαύθην	*I burn completely*
καταλύω	*I dissolve; I break up; I destroy*
καταπαύω	*I put an end to*
καταστρέφω, καταστρέψω, κατέστρεψα, κατέστραμμαι, κατεστράφην	*I overturn;* middle, *I subdue*
κρίνω, κρινῶ, ἔκρῑνα, κέκρικα, κέκριμαι, ἐκρίθην	*I judge*
κτείνω, κτενῶ, ἔκτεινα, ἔκτονα	*I kill*
μέλει, μελήσει, ἐμέλησε, μεμέληκε	impersonal + dat., X *is a care to; there is a care to* X (dat.) *for* Y (gen.)
μεταγιγνώσκω	*I change my mind; I repent*
ξενίζω, ξενιῶ, ἐξένισα, ἐξενίσθην	*I entertain*
ὀνομάζω, ὀνομάσω, ὠνόμασα, ὠνόμακα, ὠνόμασμαι, ὠνομάσθην	*I name; I call*
περιάγω	*I lead around*
προλέγω	*I proclaim*
προστάττω	*I command*
φαίνω, φανῶ or φανοῦμαι, ἔφηνα, πέφασμαι	*I show*

φονεύω,
φονεύσω,
ἐφόνευσα,
πεφόνευκα,
πεφόνευμαι,
ἐφονεύθην   *I slay*

Deponent or Middle -ω Verbs

ἀγωνίζομαι,
ἀγωνιοῦμαι,
ἠγωνισάμην,
ἠγώνισμαι   *I contend*

ἀλίσκομαι,
ἀλώσομαι,
ἐάλων or ἥλων,
ἐάλωκα or
ἥλωκα   *I am caught; I am taken*

ἀνέχομαι,
ἀνέξομαι,
ἠνεσχόμην   *I endure; I am patient*

ἐπέρχομαι   *I approach; + dat., I attack*

μέμφομαι,
μέμψομαι,
ἐμεμψάμην or
ἐμέμφθην   *+ dat. or acc., I blame, find fault with*

μεταπέμπομαι   *I send for*

πυνθάνομαι,
πεύσομαι,
ἐπυθόμην,
πέπυσμαι   *I inquire; I learn by inquiry; I hear; I find out about X (acc.) from Y (gen.)*

φείδομαι,
φείσομαι,
ἐφεισάμην   *+ gen., I spare*

χαρίζομαι,
χαριοῦμαι,
ἐχαρισάμην,
κεχάρισμαι   *+ dat., I show favor to; I oblige*

-έω Contract Verbs

ἀποδημέω   *I am abroad; I go abroad*

ἐπικαλέω   *I call upon; middle, I call upon X to help*

καταφρονέω   *+ gen., I despise*
παρακαλέω   *I summon*
πορθέω   *I sack*
φωνέω   *I speak*

Deponent or Middle -έω Contract Verbs

αἱρέομαι   *I choose*
ἀναιρέομαι   *I take up; I pick up*
δέομαι,
δεήσομαι,
ἐδεήθην   *I ask for X (acc.) from Y (gen.); + infin., I beg; + gen., I want*

ἐνθῡμέομαι,
ἐνθῡμήσομαι,
ἐντεθύμημαι,
ἐνεθῡμήθην   *I take to heart; I ponder*

Deponent -όω Contract Verbs

ἀντιόομαι,
ἀντιώσομαι,
ἠντιώθην   *+ dat., I oppose*

-μι Verbs

ἀπόλλῡμι,
ἀπολῶ,
ἀπώλεσα   *I destroy; I ruin; I lose*

μεθίημι   *I set loose; I let go*

Middle-μι Verbs

ἀπόλλυμαι,
ἀπολοῦμαι,
ἀπωλόμην   *I perish*
Perfect:
ἀπολώλεκα   *I have ruined,*
ἀπόλωλα   *I am ruined*

ἐφίσταμαι,
ἐπέστην   *+ dat., I stand near; of dreams, I appear to*

παρίσταμαι,
παρέστην,
παρέστηκα   *+ dat., I stand near, stand by; I help*

NOUNS

1st Declension

ἄγρᾱ, -ᾱς, ἡ	*hunt; hunting*
ἀθῡμίᾱ, -ᾱς, ἡ	*lack of spirit; despair*
ἀλήθεια, -ᾱς, ἡ	*truth*
βασιλείᾱ, -ᾱς, ἡ	*kingdom*
δειλίᾱ, -ᾱς, ἡ	*cowardice*
εὐδαιμονίᾱ, -ᾱς, ἡ	*happiness; prosperity; good luck*
εὐχή, -ῆς, ἡ	*prayer*
ζωή, -ῆς, ἡ	*life*
ἡσυχίᾱ, -ᾱς, ἡ	*quietness*
θεωρίᾱ, -ᾱς, ἡ	*viewing; sight-seeing*
νεφέλη, -ης, ἡ	*cloud*
πυρᾱ́, -ᾱς, ἡ	*funeral pyre*
ῥώμη, -ης, ἡ	*strength*
σῑγή, -ῆς, ἡ	*silence*
σοφίᾱ, -ᾱς, ἡ	*wisdom*
συμμαχίᾱ, -ᾱς, ἡ	*alliance*
τελευτή, -ῆς, ἡ	*end*
φήμη, -ης, ἡ	*saying; report; voice; message*

2nd Declension

ἀριθμός, -οῦ, ὁ	*number*
βασίλεια, -ων, τά	*palace*
γάμος, -ου, ὁ	*marriage*
δῶρον, -ου, τό	*gift*
θηρίον, -ου, τό	*beast, wild beast*
θησαυρός, -οῦ, ὁ	*treasure; treasury*
ἱππικόν, -οῦ, τό	*cavalry*
ἵππος, -ου, ἡ	*cavalry*
ἵππος, -ου, ὁ	*horse*
κάμηλος, -ου, ἡ	*camel*
κύκλος, -ου, ὁ	*circle*
μαντεῖον, -ου, τό	*oracle*
μέτρον, -ου, τό	*measure*
οἰκίον, -ου, τό	*house; palace (often in plural for a single house or palace)*

ὄλβος, -ου, ὁ	*happiness, bliss; prosperity*
ὄνειρος, -ου, ὁ	*dream*
ὅρκιον, -ου, τό	*oath; pl., treaty*
πεζός, -οῦ, ὁ	*infantry*
πλοῦτος, -ου, ὁ	*wealth*
φόνος, -ου, ὁ	*murder*
χρησμός, -οῦ, ὁ	*oracular response*
χρηστήριον, χρηστη-ρίου, τό	*oracle (either the seat of the oracle or the oracular response)*

3rd Declension

ἀκρόπολις, ἀκροπόλεως, ἡ	*citadel*
ἀνάθημα, ἀναθή-ματος, τό	*temple offering*
δαίμων, δαίμονος, ὁ	*spirit; god; the power controlling one's destiny, fate, lot*
δέος, δέους, τό	*fear*
δόρυ, δόρατος, τό	*spear*
ἔθνος, ἔθνους, τό	*tribe; people*
θεράπων, θερά-ποντος, ὁ	*attendant; servant*
ἱππεύς, ἱππέως, ὁ	*horseman; cavalryman*
νέμεσις, νεμέσεως, ἡ	*retribution*
στράτευμα, στρατεύ-ματος, τό	*army*
φύλαξ, φύλακος, ὁ	*guard*

ADJECTIVES

1st/2nd Declension

ἀμφότερος, -ᾱ, -ον	*both*
δειλός, -ή, -όν	*cowardly*
ἔσχατος, -η, -ον	*furthest; extreme*

ἕτερος,
-ᾱ, -ον   *one* or *the other* (of
two)
ἱκανός,
-ή, -όν   *sufficient; capable*
καρτερός,
-ᾱ, -όν   *strong; fierce*
οὐδέτερος,
-ᾱ, -ον   *neither*
ποῖος; ποίᾱ;
ποῖον;   *what kind of?*

2nd Declension
ἀνόητος, -ον   *foolish*
ἄχρηστος, -ον   *useless*

3rd/1st Declension
ἄκων, ἄκουσα,
ἄκον   *unwilling(ly);
involuntary(-ily)*

PREPOSITIONS

ἀντί   + gen., *instead of;
against*
ἐπί   + gen., *toward, in the
direction of; on;* +
dat., *upon, on; at;*
of price, *for;* + acc.,
*at; against; onto,
upon;* of direction
or purpose, *to; for;*
of time, *for*
κατά   + acc., *down;*
distributive, *each,
every; by; on; ac-
cording to;* of time,
*at; through; with
regard to; after*
ὄπισθε(ν)   + gen., *behind*
πρός   + gen., *from* (i.e., *at
the hand of*); +
dat., *at, near, by; in
addition to;* + acc.,
*to, toward; upon;
onto; against; with*
(i.e., *in relation to*)

ADVERBS

ἄλλοσε   *to another place; to
other places*

αὐτίκα   *straightway, at once*
μετά   *afterward; later*
ὄπισθε(ν)   *behind*
ὀπίσω   *backward*
ὁπόθεν   *whence, from where*
πάνυ   *altogether; very;
exceedingly*

CONJUNCTIONS

εἴτε . . . εἴτε   *either . . . or*
ἐπεί   *when; since*

EXPRESSIONS

ἄλλοι ἄλλοσε   *some to some places
. . . others to other
places*
κατὰ τάχος   *quickly*
οἷός τ' εἰμί   *I am able*
ὁ μὲν ἕτερος . . .
ὁ δὲ ἕτερος   *the one . . . the other*
περὶ οὐδενὸς
ποιοῦμαι   *I consider of no
importance*

PROPER NAMES &
ADJECTIVES

Ἀλυάττης,
Ἀλυάττεω, ὁ   *Alyattes*
Δελφοί,
-ῶν, οἱ   *Delphi*
Μῡσοί, -ῶν, οἱ   *Mysians*
Ὄλυμπος,
-ου, ὁ   *Mount Olympus
(here, a mountain
in Mysia)*
Πῡθίᾱ, -ᾱς, ἡ   *Pythia (the Delphic
priestess of Apollo)*
Σάρδεις,
Σάρδεων, αἱ;
Ionic, Σάρδιες,
Σαρδίων, αἱ   *Sardis*

29
ΜΕΓΑ ΤΟ ΤΗΣ
ΘΑΛΑΣΣΗΣ ΚΡΑΤΟΣ (α)

1   **νίκημα, νικήματος, τό,** *victory.*
    στεφανόω, *I crown.*

3   **ὑπολαμβάνω,** *I take under protection.*

4   **διατρίβω** [δια- + τρίβω, *I rub, wear away, beat; I spend*], *I spend / pass time.*

5   **ἀθλίως,** adv., *wretchedly.*
    ναυαγέω, *I suffer shipwreck.*
    πλανάω, πλανήσω, *I make* X *wander; I lead* X *astray; I deceive* X; passive,
        I wander, stray.*

6   **κατακρατέω,** *I overpower.*
    ἀκρασίᾱ, ἀκρασίᾱς, ἡ [ἀ- + τὸ κράτος], *lack of power / control over one's
        passions; intemperance.*

7   **ἀλαζονείᾱ, ἀλαζονείᾱς, ἡ,** *boastfulness.*
    φιλαργυρίᾱ, φιλαργυρίᾱς, ἡ, *avarice, greed.*
    ἕτερος, ἑτέρᾱ, ἕτερον, *one* or *the other* (of two); *other, another;* pl., *others.*
    κενοδοξίᾱ, κενοδοξίᾱς, ἡ, *empty / false doctrine.*

8   **ἐξ ὧν:** picked up by τῶν δεινῶν.
    ἐκλύω, *I set free.*

9   **ὧδε,** adv., *thus; here.*
    ταράττω, *I trouble, disturb.*

10   **ἐπιλανθάνομαι** or **ἐπιλήθομαι, ἐπιλήσομαι, ἐπελαθόμην,** *I forget.*
    παρά, prep. + gen., *from.*

11   **Δαιμόνιον, Δαιμονίου, τό:** = Δαίμων, Δαίμονος, ὁ.
    πρόσταγμα, προστάγματος, τό, *command.*

Exercise 29 α

Translate into English on a separate sheet of paper:

ΚΕΒΗΤΟΣ ΠΙΝΑΞ

XXIV.

Ξένος "ὡς καλὸν τὸ νίκημα λέγεις.   ὅταν δὲ στεφανωθῇ, τί ποιεῖ ἢ ποῖ   1
βαδίζει;"   2

Πρεσβύτης "ἄγουσιν αὐτὸν ὑπολαβοῦσαι αἱ Ἀρεταὶ πρὸς τὸν τόπον ἐκεῖνον,   3
ὅθεν ἦλθε πρῶτον, καὶ δεικνύουσιν αὐτῷ τοὺς ἐκεῖ διατρίβοντας ὡς κακῶς   4
διατρίβουσι καὶ ἀθλίως ζῶσι καὶ ὡς ναυαγοῦσιν ἐν τῷ βίῳ καὶ πλανῶνται καὶ   5
ἄγονται κατακεκρατημένοι ὥσπερ ὑπὸ πολεμίων, οἱ μὲν ὑπ' Ἀκρασίας, οἱ δὲ ὑπ'   6
Ἀλαζονείας, οἱ δὲ ὑπὸ Φιλαργυρίας, ἕτεροι δὲ ὑπὸ Κενοδοξίας, οἱ δὲ ὑφ' ἑτέρων   7
Κακῶν.   ἐξ ὧν οὐ δύνανται ἐκλῦσαι ἑαυτοὺς τῶν δεινῶν, οἷς δέδενται, ὥστε   8
σωθῆναι καὶ ἀφικέσθαι ὧδε, ἀλλὰ ταράττονται διὰ παντὸς τοῦ βίου.   τοῦτο δὲ   9
πάσχουσι διὰ τὸ μὴ δύνασθαι τὴν ἐνθάδε ὁδὸν εὑρεῖν· ἐπελάθοντο γὰρ τὸ παρὰ τοῦ   10
Δαιμονίου πρόσταγμα."   11

Exercise 29 β

Give an English equivalent of:

1. ὁ κόλπος   _____
2. στέλλω   _____
3. ἡ ταραχή   _____
4. μήτε . . . μήτε   _____
5. ἡ ἕως   _____
6. ἐπιγίγνομαι   _____

7. τὸ πνεῦμα   _____
8. ἐπιτίθεμαι   _____
9. ἐπὶ τὴν ἕω   _____
10. τὸ πλοῖον   _____
11. ἐκπνέω   _____
12. ἡ ναυμαχίᾱ   _____

Exercise 29 γ

Give the Greek equivalent of:

1. stern (of a ship)   _____
2. in the middle of   _____
3. I bring together   _____
4. bow (of a ship)   _____
5. I guard   _____

6. mainland   _____
7. I sail by   _____
8. inward   _____
9. I attempt   _____
10. position   _____

Exercise 29 δ

Give the remaining principal parts of:

1. ἐκπνέω   _____
   and _____
   _____
   _____

2. ἐπιτίθεμαι   _____
   _____

3. στέλλω   _____
   _____
   _____
   _____
   _____

4. ὁράω   _____
   _____
   or _____
   _____
   or _____
   _____

(β)

Exercise 29 ε

Give an English equivalent of:

1. χωρέω _____
2. καταδύω _____
3. ἀποστέλλω _____
4. ἡ παρασκευή _____

5. προσπίπτω _____
6. ἐξαρτύω _____
7. τὸ τρόπαιον _____
8. ταράττω _____

Exercise 29 ζ

Give the remaining principal parts of:

1. ἐξαρτύω _____
   _____
   _____
   _____
   _____

2. καταδύω _____
   _____
   _____
   _____
   _____

   athematic aorist _____

3. ταράττω _____
   _____
   _____
   _____
   _____

4. ἀκούω _____
   _____
   _____

5. ἐλαύνω _____
   _____
   _____
   _____

6. ἐσθίω _____
   _____

1   τοῦτο: *about this* (accusative of respect with ἀπορῶ).
     πάλιν, adv., *back; again; in turn.*
3   ἀκριβῶς, adv., *clearly.*
     ᾔδει: *he was aware, knew* (3rd person singular pluperfect = imperfect of οἶδα; see
         Ch. 28, Gr. 9, pp. 219–220).
4   ἐνδοιάζω, *I am in doubt, am at a loss.*
     ἄγνοια, ἀγνοίᾱς, ἡ, *ignorance.*
     πλάνος, πλάνου, ὁ, *wandering; error.*
     ἐπεπώκει: pluperfect of πίνω.
5   διό, conj. = δι' ὅ, *wherefore, for which reason, therefore.*
6   διατρίβω [δια- + τρίβω, *I rub, wear away, beat; I spend*], *I spend/pass time.*
     ἀπολαμβάνω, *I take from; I receive.*
         ἀπειληφὼς: *having received*, i.e., from the Virtues (perfect active participle,
             nominative singular masculine, of ἀπολαμβάνω; see Ch. 23β PP, p. 115).
     ἐπιστήμη, ἐπιστήμης, ἡ [cf. ἐπίσταμαι], *knowledge, understanding.*
7   συμφέρω, *I bring together;* impersonal, *it is profitable, useful, beneficial,
         advantageous.*
         συμφέροντα, συμφερόντων, τά, *things that are beneficial/
             advantageous.*

Exercise 29η

Translate into English on a separate sheet of paper:

ΚΕΒΗΤΟΣ ΠΙΝΑΞ

XXV.

Ξένος "ὀρθῶς μοι δοκεῖς λέγειν. ἀλλὰ καὶ τοῦτο πάλιν ἀπορῶ, διὰ τί   1
δεικνύουσιν αὐτῷ τὸν τόπον ἐκεῖνον αἱ Ἀρεταί, ὅθεν ἥκει τὸ πρότερον."   2

Πρεσβύτης "οὐκ ἀκριβῶς ᾔδει οὐδὲ ἠπίστατο," ἔφη, "οὐδὲν τῶν ἐκεῖ, ἀλλ'   3
ἐνεδοίαζε καὶ διὰ τὴν ἄγνοιαν καὶ τὸν πλάνον, ὃν δὴ ἐπεπώκει, τὰ μὴ ὄντα   4
ἀγαθὰ ἐνόμιζεν ἀγαθὰ εἶναι καὶ τὰ μὴ ὄντα κακὰ κακά. διὸ καὶ ἔζη κακῶς,   5
ὥσπερ οἱ ἄλλοι οἱ ἐκεῖ διατρίβοντες. νῦν δὲ ἀπειληφὼς τὴν ἐπιστήμην τῶν   6
συμφερόντων αὐτός τε καλῶς ζῇ καὶ τούτους θεωρεῖ ὡς κακῶς πράττουσιν."   7

(γ)

1   **ποῦ**: = ποῖ.
     ἔτι, adv., *still; yet; hereafter.*

2   **ὅπου**: = ὅποι, adv., *where, whither.*
     ἀσφάλεια, ἀσφαλείᾱς, ἡ, *safety.*

3   **Κωρύκιος, Κωρυκίᾱ, Κωρύκιον**, *Corycian.*
     ἄντρον, ἄντρου, τό, *cave.*
         τὸ Κωρύκιον ἄντρον: a cave on Mt. Parnassus. When Xerxes of Persia
            invaded Greece in 481 B.C., the people of Delphi used this cave as a place
            of refuge (Herodotus 8.36).
     οὗ ἂν: = οἷ ἂν, *wherever.*
     πάντα: *with respect to all things.*

4   **βιόω, βιώσομαι**, *I live.*
     ὑποδέχομαι, *I receive.*
     ἀσμένως, adv., *gladly.*

5   **καθάπερ**, adv., *just as, as.*

6   **κἀκείνᾱς**: = καὶ ἐκείνᾱς.

7   **μὴ τι πάθῃ**: for clauses of fearing, see Ch. 22, Gr. 1, p. 92.

8   **διοχλέω**, *I disturb.*
         οὐ μὴ διοχληθήσεται: again οὐ μή introducing a strong negative
            statement with regard to future time; cf. ΚΕΒΗΤΟΣ ΠΙΝΑΞ XIV:9, p. 77,
            where οὐ μή is used with the subjunctive with this same sense.
     οὐδὲν: *in any way* (adverbial accusative).
     ὀδύνη, ὀδύνης, ἡ [ὀδυνάω, *I cause pain*], *pain* (of body); *pain* (of mind); *grief;*
         distress.
     λύπη, λύπης, ἡ [λῡπέω, *I grieve, pain*], *pain* (of body); *pain* (of mind); *grief.*

9   **ἀκρασίᾱ, ἀκρασίᾱς, ἡ** [ἀ- + τὸ κράτος], *lack of power/control over one's*
     passions; intemperance.
     φιλαργυρίᾱ, φιλαργυρίᾱς, ἡ, *avarice, greed.*
     πενίᾱ, πενίᾱς, ἡ, *poverty.*

10   **κυριεύω** + gen., *I am master* (of).
     ἐπάνω, prep. + gen., *above.*

11   **ἐχιόδηκτος, ἐχιοδήκτου, ὁ** [ὁ ἔχις, *snake* + δάκνω, *I bite*], *one bitten by a*
     snake.
         οἱ ἐχιόδηκτοι: it was thought that those who were bitten by snakes and
            survived were henceforth immune from the venom of snakes.
     τὰ . . . θηρία: i.e., snakes.

12   **κακοποιέω**, *I do harm to.*
     μέχρι, prep. + gen., *even to, as far as.*
         μέχρι θανάτου: *up to (the point of) death.*
     ἀντιφάρμακον, ἀντιφαρμάκου, τό, *antidote.*

Exercise 29 θ

Translate into English on a separate sheet of paper:

ΚΕΒΗΤΟΣ ΠΙΝΑΞ

XXVI.

Ξένος "ἐπειδὰν οὖν θεωρήσῃ πάντα, τί ποιεῖ ἢ ποῦ ἔτι βαδίζει;"   1

Πρεσβύτης "ὅπου ἂν βούληται," ἔφη. "πανταχοῦ γὰρ ἔστιν αὐτῷ ἀσφάλεια   2
ὥσπερ τῷ τὸ Κωρύκιον ἄντρον ἔχοντι, καὶ πανταχοῦ, οὗ ἂν ἀφίκηται, πάντα   3
καλῶς βιώσεται μετὰ πάσης ἀσφαλείᾱς. ὑποδέξονται γὰρ αὐτὸν ἀσμένως πάντες   4
καθάπερ τὸν ἰᾱτρὸν οἱ πάσχοντες."   5

Ξένος "πότερον οὖν κἀκείνᾱς τὰς γυναῖκας, ἃς ἔφης θηρία εἶναι, οὐκέτι   6
φοβεῖται, μή τι πάθῃ ὑπ' αὐτῶν;"   7

Πρεσβύτης "οὐ μὴ διοχληθήσεται οὐδὲν οὔτε ὑπὸ Ὀδύνης οὔτε ὑπὸ Λύπης οὔτε   8
ὑπ' Ἀκρασίᾱς οὔτε ὑπὸ Φιλαργυρίᾱς οὔτε ὑπὸ Πενίᾱς οὔτε ὑπὸ ἄλλου Κακοῦ   9
οὐδενός. ἁπάντων γὰρ κυριεύει καὶ ἐπάνω πάντων ἐστὶ τῶν πρότερον αὐτὸν   10
λῡπούντων καθάπερ οἱ ἐχιόδηκτοι. τὰ γὰρ θηρία δήπου τὰ πάντας τοὺς ἄλλους   11
κακοποιοῦντα μέχρι θανάτου ἐκείνους οὐ λῡπεῖ διὰ τὸ ἔχειν ἀντιφάρμαχον αὐτούς.   12
οὕτω καὶ τοῦτον οὐκέτι οὐδὲν λῡπεῖ διὰ τὸ ἔχειν ἀντιφάρμαχον."   13

Exercise 29 ι

Give an English equivalent of:

1. τὸ πάθος	_____	5. οὗπερ	_____
2. πρόθῡμος	_____	6. κατέχω	_____
3. παρακελεύομαι	_____	7. ἡ ἧττα	_____
4. ἡ εὐρυχωρίᾱ	_____	8. ὁρμίζω	_____

(δ)

2   **ἐκεῖθεν**, adv., *from that place.*
    βουνός, βουνοῦ, ὁ, *hill, mound.*
    στεφανόω, *I crown.*
3   **ἔμφασις, ἐμφάσεως, ἡ,** *appearance, impression.*
    εὐφροσύνη, εὐφροσύνης, ἡ, *mirth, happiness.*
    ἀστεφάνωτος, ἀστεφάνωτον, *uncrowned.*
    λύπη, λύπης, ἡ [λῡπέω, *I grieve, pain*], *pain* (of body); *pain* (of mind); *grief.*
4   **κνήμη, κνήμης, ἡ,** *the lower leg.*
    τρίβω, τρίψω, ἔτρῑψα, τέτρῐφα, τέτρῑμμαι, ἐτρίβην or **ἐτρίφθην,** *I wear out*
        (by rubbing).
5   **παιδείᾱ, παιδείᾱς, ἡ,** *education.*
6   **εὐφραίνω,** *I delight;* passive, *I am happy.*
    ἀπογιγνώσκω, *I depart from a judgment;* passive, *I am rejected.*
7   **ἀνακάμπτω** [κάμπτω, *I bend, turn*], *I bend back; I walk back and forth; I wander;*
        I turn back.
    ἀθλίως, adv., *wretchedly.*
    διάκειμαι + adv., *I am in a certain state.*
        κακῶς διάκειμαι, *I am in a bad state.*
    ἀποδειλιάω, *I play the coward.*
8   **καρτερίᾱ, καρτερίᾱς, ἡ** [cf. καρτερός, καρτερά, καρτερόν, *strong,* and
        καρτερέω, *I am strong; I endure*], *patience; endurance.*
    πάλιν, adv., *back; again; in turn.*
    πλανάω, πλανήσω, *I make X wander; I lead X astray; I deceive X;* passive,
        I wander, stray.
9   **ἀνοδίᾱ, ἀνοδίᾱς, ἡ,** *pathless area, trackless waste.*
10 **ἀκολουθέω,** *I follow.*
11 **ὀδύνη, ὀδύνης, ἡ** [ὀδυνάω, *I cause pain*], *pain* (of body); *pain* (of mind); *grief;*
        distress.
    ἀδοξίᾱ, ἀδοξίᾱς, ἡ, *ill-repute, disgrace.*
12 **ἄγνοια, ἀγνοίᾱς, ἡ,** *ignorance.*

Exercise 29κ

Give an English equivalent of:

1. ὑπεκφεύγω   _____   6. τὸ σημεῖον   _____
2. περί + dat.   _____   7. ἅμα ἔῳ   _____
3. τὸ κέρας   _____   8. ἐπιβοηθέω   _____
4. διαφεύγω   _____   9. κενός   _____
5. παραβοηθέω   _____

Exercise 29λ

Translate into English on a separate sheet of paper:

ΚΕΒΗΤΟΣ ΠΙΝΑΞ

XXVII.

Ξένος "καλῶς ἐμοὶ δοκεῖς λέγειν. ἀλλ' ἔτι τοῦτό μοι εἰπέ. τίνες εἰσὶν οὗτοι οἱ   1
δοκοῦντες ἐκεῖθεν ἀπὸ τοῦ βουνοῦ παραγίνεσθαι; καὶ οἱ μὲν αὐτῶν ἐστεφανωμένοι   2
ἔμφασιν ποιοῦσιν εὐφροσύνης τινός, οἱ δὲ ἀστεφάνωτοι λύπης καὶ ταραχῆς καὶ τὰς   3
κνήμᾱς καὶ τὰς κεφαλὰς δοκοῦσι τετρῖφθαι, κατέχονται δὲ ὑπὸ γυναικῶν τινων."   4

Πρεσβύτης "οἱ μὲν ἐστεφανωμένοι οἱ σεσωσμένοι εἰσὶ πρὸς τὴν Παιδείᾱν καὶ   5
εὐφραίνονται τετυχηκότες αὐτῆς. οἱ δὲ ἀστεφάνωτοι οἱ μὲν ἀπεγνωσμένοι ὑπὸ τῆς   6
Παιδείᾱς ἀνακάμπτουσι κακῶς καὶ ἀθλίως διακείμενοι· οἱ δὲ ἀποδεδειλιακότες   7
καὶ οὐκ ἀναβεβηκότες πρὸς τὴν Καρτερίᾱν πάλιν ἀνακάμπτουσι καὶ πλανῶνται   8
ἀνοδίᾳ."   9

Ξένος "αἱ δὲ γυναῖκες αἱ μετ' αὐτῶν ἀκολουθοῦσαι, τίνες εἰσὶν αὗται;"   10

Πρεσβύτης "Λῦπαι," ἔφη, "καὶ Ὀδύναι καὶ Ἀθῡμίαι καὶ Ἀδοξίαι καὶ   11
Ἄγνοιαι."   12

Exercise 29μ

Give the Greek equivalent of:

1. I turn around   _____
2. weapons   _____
3. I put out to sea   _____
4. I lie at anchor   _____

5. I go into   _____
6. I save   _____
7. I intercept   _____
8. past (prep.)   _____

Exercise 29ν

Give the remaining principal parts of:

1. ἐπιστρέφω   _____
2. ἀναμιμνῄσκω   _____

_____

_____

_____

_____

_____

(ε)

1   ἀκολουθέω + dat., *I follow.*
2   νή + acc., adv. of swearing, *yes, by ... !*
    πάντα: neuter plural subject of ἐπακολουθοῦσιν. The plural verb, rather than the
        usual singular with a neuter plural subject, may be used here because the
        πάντα κακὰ of line 1 are to be identified with the personifications (αἱ γυναῖκες)
        in the previous section.
    ἐπακολουθέω, *I follow after.*
3   περίβολος, περιβόλου, ὁ, *enclosure.*
    ἡδυπάθεια, ἡδυπαθείᾱς, ἡ, *sweet experience; luxury.*
    ἀκρασίᾱ, ἀκρασίᾱς, ἡ [ἀ- + τὸ κράτος], *lack of power/control over one's
        passions; intemperance.*
4   αἰτιάομαι, *I accuse, blame.*
    κακῶς λέγω, *I slander.*
    παιδείᾱ, παιδείᾱς, ἡ, *education.*
5   ταλαίπωρος, ταλαίπωρον, *suffering, miserable.*
    ἄθλιος, ἀθλίᾱ, ἄθλιον, *wretched.*
    κακοδαίμων, κακόδαιμον, *unhappy.*
6   ἀπολείπω, *I leave behind, abandon.*
    ἀπολαύω + gen., *I enjoy.*
8   ποῖος, ποίᾱ, ποῖον, *what sort/kind of; of what sort/kind?*
9   ἀσωτίᾱ, ἀσωτίᾱς, ἡ [ἀ- + σῴζω], *wastefulness, prodigality, profligacy.*
    κεφάλαιον, κεφαλαίου, τό, *head; the main point, the sum of the matter.*
        ἐπὶ κεφαλαίου: *in sum, to be brief.*
10 εὐωχέω, *I treat well;* middle, *I feast.*
    βόσκημα, βοσκήματος, τό, pl., *cattle.*
    τρόπον: *in the manner.*
    ἀπόλαυσις, ἀπολαύσεως, ἡ, *enjoyment.*
    ἡγέομαι, *I lead; I think; I consider.*

Exercise 29 ξ

Give an English equivalent of:

1. ἐναντίος   _____   6. ἡ κώπη   _____

2. φθάνω   _____   7. ἀτάκτως   _____

3. ἡ τροπή   _____   8. σφάζω   _____

4. πλήν   _____   9. ἡ ὁλκάς   _____

5. καταφεύγω   _____   10. περιμένω   _____

Exercise 29 ο

Translate into English on a separate sheet of paper:

ΚΕΒΗΤΟΣ ΠΙΝΑΞ

XXVIII.

 Ξένος "πάντα κακὰ λέγεις αὐτοῖς ἀκολουθεῖν."   1

 Πρεσβύτης "νὴ Δία πάντα," ἔφη, "ἐπακολουθοῦσιν. ὅταν δὲ οὗτοι   2
παραγένωνται εἰς τὸν πρῶτον περίβολον πρὸς τὴν Ἡδυπάθειαν καὶ τὴν Ἀκρασίᾶν,   3
οὐχ ἑαυτοὺς αἰτιῶνται, ἀλλ' εὐθὺς κακῶς λέγουσι καὶ τὴν Παιδείᾶν καὶ τοὺς   4
ἐκεῖσε βαδίζοντας, ὡς ταλαίπωροι καὶ ἄθλιοί εἰσι καὶ κακοδαίμονες, οἳ τὸν βίον   5
τὸν παρ' αὐταῖς ἀπολιπόντες κακῶς ζῶσι καὶ οὐκ ἀπολαύουσι τῶν παρ' αὐταῖς   6
ἀγαθῶν."   7

 Ξένος "ποῖα δὲ λέγουσιν ἀγαθὰ εἶναι;"   8

 Πρεσβύτης "τὴν ἀσωτίᾶν καὶ τὴν ἀκρασίᾶν, ὡς εἴποι ἄν τις ἐπὶ κεφαλαίου.   9
τὸ γὰρ εὐωχεῖσθαι βοσκημάτων τρόπον ἀπόλαυσιν μεγίστων ἀγαθῶν ἡγοῦνται   10
εἶναι."   11

Exercise 29 π

Give a Greek equivalent of:

1.	disordered	_____	5. I pursue	_____
2.	I stand firm	_____	6. at (of time)	_____
3.	wrecked ship	_____	7. help	_____
4.	from where	_____	8. disorder	_____

Exercise 29 ρ

Give the remaining principal parts of:

1. σφάζω   _____   3. λανθάνω   _____

       _____   _____

       _____

       _____   4. τυγχάνω   _____

2. φθάνω   _____

       _____   _____

     or _____

Exercise 29 ς

Rewrite the following sentences as indirect statements using the introductory words provided:

A. ἡ Μέλιττα τὰς φίλᾱς εἶδεν, ἐπεὶ πρὸς τὴν κρήνην ἔβαινεν.

    1. λέγω ὅτι _____ .

    2. φημί   _____ .

    3. οἶδα   _____ .

B. ὁ Φίλιππος τοὺς φίλους ἂν εἶδεν, εἰ πρὸς τὴν ἀγορὰν ἔβη.

    1. λέγω ὅτι _____ .

    2. φημί   _____ .

    3. οἶδα   _____ .

30
ΑΧΑΡΝΗΣ (α)

Exercise 30 α

Give an English equivalent of:

1. ποθέω _____

2. ἡ καρδίᾱ _____

3. κύριος _____

4. λαλέω _____

5. οὐδεπώποτε _____

6. λοιδορέω _____

7. οἱ πρυτάνεις _____

Exercise 30 β

Give the Greek equivalent of:

1. I cause pain _____

2. simply _____

3. I hate _____

4. I love _____

5. next _____

6. I bite _____

Exercise 30 γ

Give the remaining principal parts of:

1. δάκνω _____

_____

_____

_____

2. ὀδυνάω _____

_____

1   ἕτερος, ἑτέρᾱ, ἕτερον, *one* or *the other* (of two); *other, another;* pl., *others.*
     ἐκεῖθεν, adv., *from that place.*
     ἱλαρός, ἱλαρά, ἱλαρόν, *cheerful.*
3   δόξα, δόξης, ἡ, *notion; opinion; good reputation; honor.*
     παιδείᾱ, παιδείᾱς, ἡ, *education.*
4   ἀνακάμπτω [κάμπτω, *I bend, turn*], *I bend back; I walk back and forth; I wander;*
         I turn back.
5   ἀναγγέλλω, *I carry back tidings; I report.*
     εὐδαίμων, εὔδαιμον [= with a good δαίμων, *spirit, fate, lot*], *fortunate , happy.*
6   εἴσω, adv., *inward, within.*
8   θέμις, ἡ, *that which is established by custom, right.*
     ἐπιστήμη, ἐπιστήμης, ἡ [cf. ἐπίσταμαι], *knowledge, understanding.*
9   παραλαμβάνω, *I receive.*
10   πάλιν, adv., *back; again; in turn.*
     φορτίον, φορτίου, τό, *load, burden;* pl., *wares, cargo.*
     ἐξαιρέω, ἐξαιρήσω, ἐξεῖλον, *I take out;* middle, of ships, *discharge* their
         cargo.
11   γεμίζω + gen., *I fill full* (of), *load* (with).

Exercise 30 δ

Translate into English on a separate sheet of paper:

ΚΕΒΗΤΟΣ ΠΙΝΑΞ

XXIX.

Ξένος "αἱ δὲ ἕτεραι γυναῖκες αἱ ἐκεῖθεν παραγῑνόμεναι ἱλαραί τε καὶ   1
γελῶσαι, τίνες καλοῦνται;"   2

Πρεσβύτης "Δόξαι," ἔφη, "καὶ ἀγαγοῦσαι πρὸς τὴν Παιδείᾱν τοὺς εἰσ-   3
ελθόντας πρὸς τὰς Ἀρετὰς ἀνακάμπτουσιν ὅπως ἑτέρους ἀγάγωσι, καὶ   4
ἀναγγέλλουσιν ὅτι εὐδαίμονες ἤδη γεγόνᾱσιν οὓς τότε ἀπήγαγον."   5

Ξένος "πότερον οὖν," ἔφην ἐγώ, "αὗται εἴσω πρὸς τὰς Ἀρετὰς οὐκ εἰσ- 6
πορεύονται;"   7

Πρεσβύτης "οὐ γὰρ θέμις Δόξαν εἰσπορεύεσθαι πρὸς τὴν Ἐπιστήμην, ἀλλὰ τῇ 8
Παιδείᾳ παραδιδόᾱσιν αὐτούς. εἶτα ὅταν ἡ Παιδείᾱ παραλάβῃ, ἀνακάμπτουσιν 9
αὗται πάλιν ἄλλους ἄξουσαι, ὥσπερ αἱ νῆες τὰ φορτία ἐξελόμεναι πάλιν   10
ἀνακάμπτουσι καὶ ἄλλων τινῶν γεμίζονται."   11

(β)

2   **οὐδέπω**, adv., *not yet, not as yet.*
    Δαιμόνιον, Δαιμονίου, τό: = Δαίμων, Δαίμονος, ὁ.
4   **διό**, conj. = δι' ὅ, *wherefore, for which reason, therefore.*
5   **παραλείπω**, *I leave out.*
7   **ἐκτείνω, ἐκτενῶ, ἐξέτεινα, ἐκτέτακα, ἐκτέταμαι, ἐξετάθην**, *I stretch forth/out.*
    πάλιν, adv., *back; again; in turn.*
8   **στρογγύλος, στρογγύλη, στρογγύλον**, *round.*
    ἑστάναι: *to stand* (2nd perfect active infinitive of ἵστημι).
    ἄρτι, adv., *just; just now.*

Exercise 30 ε

Give an English equivalent of:

1. ἡ ἀσπίς   _____   7. κακοδαίμων   _____

2. χρῡσοῦς   _____   8. οἴχομαι   _____

3. αἰσθάνομαι   _____   9. ναὶ μὰ Δία   _____

4. πώποτε   _____   10. ὅλος   _____

5. ὁ ἀλαζών   _____   11. ἡ ὄρνις   _____

6. παρά + gen.   _____   12. ἄχθομαι   _____

Exercise 30 ζ

Translate into English on a separate sheet of paper:

ΚΕΒΗΤΟΣ ΠΙΝΑΞ

XXX.

 Ξένος "ταῦτα μὲν δὴ καλῶς μοι δοκεῖς," ἔφην, "ἐξηγεῖσθαι. ἀλλ᾽ ἐκεῖνο 1
οὐδέπω ἡμῖν δεδήλωκας, τί προστάττει τὸ Δαιμόνιον τοῖς εἰσπορευομένοις εἰς τὸν 2
Βίον ποιεῖν." 3

 Πρεσβύτης "θαρρεῖν," ἔφη. "διὸ καὶ ὑμεῖς θαρρεῖτε· πάντα γὰρ ἐξηγήσομαι 4
καὶ οὐδὲν παραλείψω." 5

 Ξένος "καλῶς λέγεις," ἔφην ἐγώ. 6

 Πρεσβύτης ἐκτείνας οὖν τὴν χεῖρα πάλιν, "ὁρᾶτε," ἔφη, "τὴν γυναῖκα 7
ἐκείνην, ἣ δοκεῖ τυφλή τις εἶναι καὶ ἐπὶ λίθου στρογγύλου ἑστάναι, ἣν καὶ ἄρτι ὑμῖν 8
εἶπον ὅτι Τύχη καλεῖται;" 9

 Ξένος "ὁρῶμεν." 10

Exercise 30 η

Give the Greek equivalent of:

1. oh misery! _____
2. clearly _____
3. I expect _____
4. month _____
5. immortal _____
6. before (of time
  or place) _____

7. I think _____
8. force _____
9. I do wrong _____
10. gold coin _____
11. forward _____

Exercise 30 θ

Give the remaining principal parts of:

1. αἰσθάνομαι _____

 _____

 _____

2. ἄχθομαι _____

 _____

(γ)

1   ταύτῃ: *this (woman)*, i.e., Fortune.
    κελεύει: the subject is ὁ Δαίμων; supply αὐτούς, *them*, i.e., the ones entering life, as
      object.
    βέβαιος, βεβαίᾱ, βέβαιον, *firm; secure.*
2   ἴδιος, ἰδίᾱ, ἴδιον, *peculiar; one's own.*
3   κωλύω, *I prevent.*
    κωλύει: supply αὐτήν as object.
    πάλιν, adv., *back; again; in turn.*
    ἕτερος, ἑτέρᾱ, ἕτερον, *one* or *the other* (of two); *other, another.*
    εἴωθε: *she is accustomed* (see Ch. 28, Gr. 8, p. 219).
4   κελεύει: supply αὐτούς as object.
    παρά, prep. + gen., *from.*
    δόσις, δόσεως, ἡ, *gift.*
5   ἴσος, ἴση, ἴσον, *equal; level-headed.*
    ἀθῡμέω, *I am disheartened/discouraged; I despair.*
6   ψέγω, *I blame.*
    ἐπαινέω, *I praise.*
    λογισμός, λογισμοῦ, ὁ, *calculation, reasoning.*
    εἰκῇ, adv., *without plan/purpose; at random; recklessly.*
7   ἔτυχε: gnomic aorist; translate as present, *as luck has it.*
    πάντα: repeat ποιεῖ with this as its direct object.
    ἔλεξα: = εἶπον.
    τὸ Δαιμόνιον: = ὁ Δαίμων.
    κελεύει: supply αὐτούς as object.
8   τραπεζίτης, τραπεζίτου, ὁ, *banker.*
9   καὶ γὰρ: *For in fact.*
10 ἀπαιτέω, *I ask* (for something) *back; passive, I am asked* (to return something).
    ἀγανακτέω, *I am displeased, vexed.*
11 μνημονεύω, *I remember, recall.*
    ἐπὶ τούτῳ . . . ἐφ' ᾧ: *on this condition . . . that.*
    θέμα, θέματος, τό, *deposit.*
12 τὸν θέμενον: *the one who had made the deposit, the depositor.*
    ὡσαύτως . . . ἔχειν: *to be in a similar state of mind.*
    τοίνυν [τοι + νυν], particle, *therefore, accordingly; well then.*
    κελεύει: supply αὐτούς, i.e., the ones entering life, as object.
13 φύσις, φύσεως, ἡ, *nature; natural disposition.*
14 πολλαπλάσιος, πολλαπλάσιον, *many times over.*
    πολλαπλάσια: translate as an adverb.
15 προϋπάρχω [προ- + ὑπάρχω, *I exist*], *I exist before, am preexistent.*
    τὰ προϋπάρχοντα: *things in their possession beforehand.*
    γοῦν (= γε οὖν), particle, *at least then; at all events.*
16 κελεύει: supply αὐτούς as object.
    συντόμως, adv., *speedily.*

Exercise 30 ι

Translate into English on a separate sheet of paper:

ΚΕΒΗΤΟΣ ΠΙΝΑΞ

XXXI.

Πρεσβύτης "ταύτῃ κελεύει," ἔφη, "μὴ πιστεύειν καὶ βέβαιον μηδὲν νομίζειν   1
μηδὲ ἀσφαλὲς εἶναι, ὅ τι ἂν παρ' αὐτῆς τις λάβῃ μηδὲ ὡς ἴδια ἡγεῖσθαι. οὐδὲν   2
γὰρ κωλύει πάλιν ταῦτα ἀφελέσθαι καὶ ἑτέρῳ δοῦναι. πολλάκις γὰρ εἴωθε   3
τοῦτο ποιεῖν. καὶ διὰ ταύτην οὖν τὴν αἰτίαν κελεύει πρὸς τὰς παρ' αὐτῆς δόσεις   4
ἴσους γίνεσθαι καὶ μήτε χαίρειν ὅταν διδῷ μήτε ἀθυμεῖν ὅταν ἀφέληται καὶ μήτε   5
ψέγειν αὐτὴν μήτε ἐπαινεῖν. οὐδὲν γὰρ ποιεῖ μετὰ λογισμοῦ, ἀλλ' εἰκῇ καὶ ὡς   6
ἔτυχε πάντα, ὥσπερ πρότερον ὑμῖν ἔλεξα. διὰ τοῦτο οὖν τὸ Δαιμόνιον κελεύει μὴ   7
θαυμάζειν, ὅ τι ἂν πράττῃ αὕτη, μηδὲ γίνεσθαι ὁμοίους τοῖς κακοῖς τραπεζίταις.   8
καὶ γὰρ ἐκεῖνοι ὅταν μὲν λάβωσι τὸ ἀργύριον παρὰ τῶν ἀνθρώπων, χαίρουσι καὶ   9
ἴδιον νομίζουσιν εἶναι, ὅταν δὲ ἀπαιτῶνται, ἀγανακτοῦσι καὶ δεινὰ οἴονται   10
πεπονθέναι, οὐ μνημονεύοντες ὅτι ἐπὶ τούτῳ ἔλαβον τὰ θέματα, ἐφ' ᾧ οὐδὲν   11
κωλύει τὸν θέμενον πάλιν κομίσασθαι. ὡσαύτως τοίνυν κελεύει ἔχειν τὸ   12
Δαιμόνιον καὶ πρὸς τὴν παρ' αὐτῆς δόσιν καὶ μνημονεύειν ὅτι τοιαύτην φύσιν ἔχει ἡ   13
Τύχη, ὥστε ἃ δέδωκεν ἀφελέσθαι καὶ ταχέως πάλιν δοῦναι πολλαπλάσια, αὖθις   14
δὲ ἀφελέσθαι ἃ δέδωκεν, οὐ μόνον δέ, ἀλλὰ καὶ τὰ προϋπάρχοντα. ἃ γοῦν δίδωσι,   15
λαβεῖν κελεύει παρ' αὐτῆς καὶ συντόμως ἀπελθεῖν βλέποντας πρὸς τὴν βεβαίαν   16
καὶ ἀσφαλῆ δόσιν."   17

Exercise 30 κ

Give an English equivalent of:

1. τὸ στόμα   _____   4. ἡ ἄμπελος   _____
2. σπένδω   _____   5. ἀνακράζω   _____
3. μιαρός   _____

Exercise 30 λ

Give the remaining principal parts of:

1. ἀνακράζω   _____

2. σπένδω   _____

_____

_____

(δ)

1 **ποῖος, ποία, ποῖον,** *what sort/kind of; of what sort/kind?*
   "ποίᾱν ταύτην;": = "ποίᾱν ταύτην τὴν δόσιν;"
2 **ἥν:** supply ἡ δόσις as antecedent.
   παιδείᾱ, παιδείᾱς, ἡ, *education.*
   ἥν: = ἐᾱν.
   διασῴζω, *I bring safely through.*
3 **αὕτη:** i.e., αὕτη ἡ δόσις.
4 **ἐπιστήμη, ἐπιστήμης, ἡ** [cf. ἐπίσταμαι], *knowledge, understanding.*
   συμφέρω, *I bring together;* impersonal, *it is profitable, useful, beneficial, advantageous.*
      συμφέροντα, συμφερόντων, τά, *things that are beneficial/ advantageous.*
   δόσις, δόσεως, ἡ, *gift.*
      δόσις: supply ἐστὶ.
5 **βέβαιος, βεβαίᾱ, βέβαιον,** *firm; secure.*
   ἀμεταμέλητος, ἀμεταμέλητον, *unrepented of, never causing regret.*
   κελεύει . . . κελεύει (7) . . . κελεύει (9): supply αὐτούς, i.e., the ones entering life, as objects.
   συντόμως, adv., *speedily.*
6 **ἀκρασίᾱ, ἀκρασίᾱς, ἡ** [ἀ- + τὸ κράτος, *power*], *lack of power/control over one's passions; intemperance.*
7 **ἡδυπάθεια, ἡδυπαθείᾱς, ἡ,** *sweet experience; luxury.*
   ἐντεύθεν, adv., *from there.*
   ἀπαλλάττομαι, *I get myself free from, escape.*
   μὴ . . . μηδὲ (8) . . . μηδέν: emphatic repetition of the negative.
8 **ψευδοπαιδείᾱ, ψευδοπαιδείᾱς, ἡ,** *false education.*
9 **αὐτοῦ,** adv., *here.*
   ἐνδιατρίβω (with χρόνον), *I spend time in* (a place).
10 **ἐφόδιον, ἐφοδίου, τό,** *supplies for traveling* (e.g., money and provisions).
   ἀληθινός, ἀληθινή, ἀληθινόν, *true; trustworthy, right.*
11 **τὸ Δαιμόνιον:** = ὁ Δαίμων.
   τοίνυν [τοι + νυν], particle, *therefore, accordingly; well then.*
   παρ' αὐτά: *contrary to them.*
12 **παρακούω** [παρα-, *amiss, wrong* + ἀκούω], *I hear wrongly/carelessly; I take no heed of.*

Exercise 30 μ

Give an English equivalent of:

1. μηνύω   _____   4. καταχέω   _____

2. ἡ εὐφημίᾱ   _____   5. καὶ μήν   _____

3. μακάριος   _____   6. ἀκολουθέω   _____

Exercise 30 v

Translate into English on a separate sheet of paper:

ΚΕΒΗΤΟΣ ΠΙΝΑΞ

XXXII.

Ξένος "ποίᾱν ταύτην;" ἔφην ἐγώ.   1

Πρεσβύτης "ἣν λήψονται παρὰ τῆς Παιδείᾱς, ἣν διασωθῶσιν ἐκεῖ."   2

Ξένος "αὕτη οὖν τίς ἐστιν;"   3

Πρεσβύτης "ἡ ἀληθὴς ἐπιστήμη τῶν συμφερόντων," ἔφη, "καὶ ἀσφαλὴς δόσις   4
καὶ βεβαίᾱ καὶ ἀμεταμέλητος. φεύγειν οὖν κελεύει συντόμως πρὸς ταύτην, καὶ   5
ὅταν ἔλθωσι πρὸς τὰς γυναῖκας ἐκείνᾱς, ἃς καὶ πρότερον εἶπον ὅτι Ἀκρασίᾱ καὶ   6
Ἡδυπάθεια καλοῦνται, καὶ ἐντεῦθεν κελεύει συντόμως ἀπαλλάττεσθαι καὶ μὴ   7
πιστεύειν μηδὲ ταύταις μηδέν, ἕως ἂν πρὸς τὴν Ψευδοπαιδείᾱν ἀφίκωνται.   8
κελεύει οὖν αὐτοῦ χρόνον τινὰ ἐνδιατρῖψαι καὶ λαβεῖν ὅ τι ἂν βούλωνται παρ'   9
αὐτῆς ὥσπερ ἐφόδιον, εἶτα ἐντεῦθεν ἀπιέναι πρὸς τὴν Ἀληθινὴν Παιδείᾱν   10
συντόμως. ταῦτά ἐστιν ἃ προστάττει τὸ Δαιμόνιον. ὅστις τοίνυν παρ' αὐτά τι ποιεῖ   11
ἢ παρακούει, ἀπόλλυται κακὸς κακῶς."   12

Exercise 30 ξ

Give the Greek equivalent of:

1. I sing _____
2. behind _____
3. household _____

4. I begin _____
5. very much _____
6. I keep holy
   silence _____

Exercise 30 o

Give the remaining principal parts of:

1. ἄδω _____
   _____
   _____

3. μηνΰω _____
   _____
   _____

2. καταχέω _____
   _____
   _____

Exercise 30 π

Give the principal parts of the following verbs in -μι:

1. δείκνῡμι _____   6. δίδωμι _____

_____   _____

_____   _____

_____   _____

_____   _____

2. ζεύγνῡμι _____   7. εἰμί

_____   8. ἵημι

_____   _____

or _____   _____

3. ἀνοίγνῡμι _____

_____   9. ἵστημι _____

_____   _____

_____   _____

4. ῥήγνῡμι _____

_____   10. τίθημι _____

_____   _____

_____   _____

5. σβέννῡμι _____   _____

_____

_____

_____

Exercise 30 ρ

Rewrite the following sentences as indirect statements using the introductory words provided. Use an optative substitution wherever you can:

A. Present Particular Condition:
ἡ Μέλιττα μώρᾱ ἐστίν, εἰ πρὸς τὴν κρήνην τήμερον βαίνει.

   1. εἶπεν ὅτι _____ .

   2. ἔφη   _____ .

   3. ᾔδει   _____ .

B. Past Contrary to Fact Condition:
ὁ Φίλιππος τοὺς φίλους ἂν εἶδεν, εἰ πρὸς τὴν ἀγορὰν ἔβη.

   1. εἶπεν ὅτι _____ .

   2. ἔφη   _____ .

   3. ᾔδει   _____ .

C. Future More Vivid Condition:
ἡ Μέλιττα τὰς φίλᾱς ὄψεται, ἐὰν πρὸς τὴν κρήνην βαίνῃ.

   1. εἶπεν ὅτι _____ .

   2. ἔφη   _____ .

   3. ᾔδει   _____ .

D. Future Less Vivid Condition:
ὁ Φίλιππος τοὺς φίλους ἂν ἴδοι, εἰ πρὸς τὴν ἀγορὰν βαίη.

   1. εἶπεν ὅτι _____ .

   2. ἔφη   _____ .

   3. ᾔδει   _____ .

VOCABULARY
CHAPTERS 29–30

VERBS

-ω Verbs

ἄδω, ἄσομαι, ἦσα, ἦσμαι, ἤσθην	*I sing*
ἀνακράζω, ἀνέκραγον	*I shout*
ἀπολαμβάνω	*I cut off, intercept*
ἀποστέλλω	*I send off*
δάκνω, δήξομαι, ἔδακον, δέδηγμαι, ἐδήχθην	*I bite; I sting*
διαφεύγω	*I escape*
ἐξαρτύω, ἐξαρτύσω, ἐξήρτῦσα, ἐξήρτῦκα, ἐξήρτῦμαι, ἐξηρτύθην	*I equip*
ἐπεισβαίνω	*I go into*
ἐπιδιώκω	*I pursue*
ἐπιστρέφω, ἐπεστράφην	*I turn around*
καταδύω, καταδύσω, κατέδῦσα, καταδέδυκα, καταδέδυμαι, κατεδύθην	*I sink*
κατέδῦν	*I sank;* of the sun, *set*
καταφεύγω	*I flee for refuge*
κατέχω	*I hold back*
μηνύω, μηνύσω, ἐμήνῦσα, μεμήνῦκα, μεμήνῦμαι, ἐμηνύθην	*I inform*
ὁρμίζω	*I bring* (a ship) *into harbor;* middle, *I come to anchor*
περιμένω	*I wait for*
προσπίπτω	+ dat., *I fall against; I fall on*

σπένδω, σπείσω, ἔσπεισα, ἔσπεισμαι	*I pour a libation;* middle, *I make a treaty; I make peace* (by pouring a libation with the other party)
στέλλω, στελῶ, ἔστειλα, ἔσταλκα, ἔσταλμαι, ἐστάλην	*I send; I equip; I take down* (sails)
συνάγω	*I bring together; I compress*
σφάζω and σφάττω, σφάξω, ἔσφαξα, ἔσφαγμαι, ἐσφάγην	*I slay*
ταράττω, ταράξω, ἐτάραξα, τετάραγμαι, ἐταράχθην	*I confuse*
ὑπεκφεύγω	*I escape*
ὑπομένω	*I await* (an attack); *I stand firm*
φθάνω, φθήσομαι, ἔφθασα or ἔφθην	+ acc. and/or participle, *I anticipate; I do* something *before* someone else

Deponent or Middle -ω Verbs

αἰσθάνομαι, αἰσθήσομαι, ᾐσθόμην, ᾔσθημαι	+ gen. or acc., *I perceive; I learn; I apprehend*

ἀνάγομαι	*I put out to sea*
ἀπάρχομαι	*I begin*
ἄχθομαι, ἀχθέσομαι, ἠχθέσθην	+ dat., *I am vexed (at); I am grieved (by)*
ἐπιγίγνομαι	*I come after*
οἴχομαι	present in perfect sense, *I have gone, have departed;* imperfect in pluperfect sense, *I had gone, had departed*
παρακελεύομαι	*I encourage, exhort*

-άω Contract Verbs

ἐράω	+ gen., *I love*
ὀδυνάω, ὀδυνηθήσομαι, ὠδυνήθην	*I cause pain;* passive, *I suffer pain*
προσδοκάω	*I expect*

-έω Contract Verbs

ἀδικέω	intransitive, *I do wrong;* transitive, *I wrong; I injure*
ἀκολουθέω	+ dat., *I follow*
ἐκπνέω, ἐκπνευσοῦμαι and ἐκπνεύσομαι, ἐξέπνευσα, ἐκπέπνευκα	*I blow out; I blow from*
ἐπιβοηθέω	+ dat., *I come to aid*
ἐπιχειρέω	+ dat., *I attempt; I attack*
εὐφημέω	*I keep holy silence*
καταχέω, καταχέω, κατέχεα, κατακέχυκα, κατακέχυμαι, κατεχύθην	*I pour* X (acc.) *over* Y (gen.)
λαλέω	*I talk; I chatter*
λοιδορέω	*I abuse*
ὁρμέω	*I lie at anchor*

παραβοηθέω	+ dat., *I come to* (X's) *aid*
παραπλέω	*I sail by; I sail past; I sail along*
ποθέω	*I long for*
στυγέω	*I hate*
φρουρέω	transitive, *I guard;* intransitive, *I am on guard*
χωρέω	*I go; I come*

Deponent or Middle -έω Contract Verbs

ἀφαιρέομαι	*I take away for myself; I save*
ἡγέομαι	+ dat., *I lead; I think, consider*

Middle -μι Verbs

ἐπιτίθεμαι, ἐπιθήσομαι, ἐπεθέμην	+ dat., *I attack*

NOUNS

1st Declension

ἀταξίᾱ, -ᾱς, ἡ	*disorder*
βίᾱ, -ᾱς, ἡ	*force; violence*
βοήθεια, -ᾱς, ἡ	*help; aid*
εὐρυχωρίᾱ, -ᾱς, ἡ	*broad waters*
εὐφημίᾱ, εὐφημίᾱς, ἡ	*call for holy silence*
ἧττα, -ης, ἡ	*defeat*
καρδίᾱ, καρδίᾱς, ἡ	*heart*
κώπη, -ης, ἡ	*oar*
ναυμαχίᾱ, -ᾱς, ἡ	*naval battle*
οἰκέται, οἰκετῶν, οἱ	*household*
παρασκευή, -ῆς, ἡ	*preparation*
πρύμνη, -ης, ἡ	*stern* (of a ship)
πρῷρα, -ᾱς, ἡ	*bow* (of a ship)
ταραχή, -ῆς, ἡ	*confusion*
τροπή, -ῆς, ἡ	*turn; turning; rout* (of the enemy)

2nd Declension

ἄμπελος, ἀμπέλου, ἡ	*grapevine*
ἤπειρος, -ου, ἡ	*land; mainland*

κόλπος, -ου, ὁ   *lap; gulf*
ναυάγιον, -ου, τό   *wrecked ship*
ὅπλα, -ων, τά   *weapons*
πλοῖον, -ου, τό   *boat*
σημεῖον,
   -ου, τό   *sign*
τρόπαιον,
   -ου, τό   *trophy*
χρῡσίον, -ου, τό   *gold coin; money;*
                        jewelry

Attic Declension

ἕως, ἕω, ἡ   *dawn*

3rd Declension

ἀλαζών,
   ἀλαζόνος,
   ὁ or ἡ   *imposter, charlatan,*
                        quack
ἀσπίς, ἀσπίδος, ἡ   *shield*
κέρας,
   κέρως, τό   *wing* (of a fleet or
                        army)
μήν, μηνός, ὁ   *month*
ὁλκάς,
   ὁλκάδος, ἡ   *merchant ship*
ὄρνῑς, ὄρνῑθος,
   ὁ or ἡ   *bird*
πάθος,
   πάθους, τό   *experience;*
                        misfortune
πνεῦμα,
   πνεύματος, τό   *breeze*
πρυτάνεις,
   πρυτάνεων, οἱ   *prytaneis =*
                        presidents
στόμα,
   στόματος, τό   *mouth*
τάξις,
   τάξεως, ἡ   *rank; position*

ADJECTIVES

1st/2nd Declension

ἐναντίος, -ᾱ, -ον   *opposed; opposite;*
                        hostile; as noun,
                        the enemy
κενός, -ή, -όν   *empty*
κύριος, -ᾱ, -ον   *having authority;*
                        legitimate; regular
μακάριος, -ᾱ, -ον   *blessed; happy*
μιαρός, -ᾱ́, -όν   *defiled; foul;*
                        villainous

ὅλος, -η, -ον   *whole, entire*
χρῡσοῦς, -ῆ, -οῦν   *golden*

2nd Declension

ἀθάνατος, -ον   *immortal*
ἄτακτος, -ον   *disordered*
πρόθῡμος, -ον   *eager*

3rd Declension

κακοδαίμων,
   κακοδαίμονος   *having an evil spirit,*
                        having bad luck

PREPOSITIONS

ἐξόπισθε(ν)   + gen., *behind*
παρά   + gen., *from;* + dat., *at*
                        the house of; + acc.,
                        of persons only, to;
                        along, past; in
                        respect of
περί   + gen., *about,*
                        concerning;
                        around; + dat.,
                        concerning; + acc.,
                        around
πλήν   + gen., *except, except*
                        for
ὑπό   + gen., *under;* of
                        agent, *by; because*
                        of; + dat., *under;* +
                        acc., *of motion,*
                        under; of time, *at*

ADVERBS

ἀτάκτως   *in disorder*
ἀτεχνῶς   *simply; really*
εἴσω (ἔσω)   *inward*
εἶτα   *then, next*
ἐξόπισθε(ν)   *behind*
μήν or καὶ μήν   *truly, indeed*
ὅθεν   *from where, whence*
ὅθενπερ   -περ added for
                        emphasis, *from*
                        where, whence
οὐδεπώποτε   *never yet*
οὗπερ   *where*
πρόσθε(ν)   *before* (of time or
                        place)
πώποτε   *ever*

σαφῶς   *clearly*
σφόδρα   *very much*

CONJUNCTIONS

μήτε   *and not*
μήτε . . . μήτε *neither . . . nor*

EXPRESSIONS

ἅμα ἕῳ   *at dawn*
εἰς τὸ πρόσθεν   *forward*
ἐπὶ τὴν ἕω   *at dawn*
κατὰ
  μέσον . . .   *in the middle of . . .*
ναὶ μὰ Δία   *yes, by Zeus!*
οἴμοι κακοδαίμων   *poor devil! oh misery!*

SUPPLEMENTARY GRAMMAR

Aspect, Time, and Tense

Aspect or the way an action is looked upon is very important in Greek. There are three aspects: (1) *progressive*, of action in process or ongoing, e.g., "John runs/is running/was running"; (2) *aorist*, of simple action, sometimes in past time, e.g., "John ran," and sometimes not, e.g., "Run, John!"; and (3) *perfective*, with emphasis on the enduring result of a completed action, e.g., "John has won the race" = "John won the race and is *now* the winner."

The various tenses usually designate time in the indicative mood:

Present Time:

Present Tense: λύω, *I loose(n), I am loos(en)ing*
   (for an exception, see the historic present below)
Perfect Tense: λέλυκα, *I have loos(en)ed*

Past Time:

Imperfect Tense: ἔλῦον, *I was loos(en)ing*
Aorist Tense: ἔλῦσα, *I loos(en)ed*
   (for an exception, see the gnomic aorist below)
Pluperfect Tense: ἐλελύκη, *I had loos(en)ed*

Future Time:

Future Tense: λύσω, *I will loos(en), I will be loos(en)ing*

In the following examples, note the relationships between aspect, tense, and time:

Progressive Aspect = Present Stem

Present (Progressive) Indicative:

   οἱ φύλακες τὰς πύλᾱς **κλείουσιν**.
   *The guards **are shutting** / **shut** the gates.*
   = an ongoing process in present time

Present (Progressive) Subjunctive:

   ἀνδρείως **μαχώμεθα**.
   ***Let us fight** (= **be fighting**) bravely.*
   = an ongoing action not limited to present time

   ὅστις ἂν ἔξω τῶν τειχῶν **μένῃ**, ἀποθανεῖται ὑπὸ τῶν πολεμίων.
   *Whoever **remains** outside the walls will be killed by the enemy.*
   = an ongoing action not limited to present time

Present (Progressive) Optative:

   ὠφελοίη σε ὁ θεός, ὦ παῖ.
   ***May** the god **help** you, son.*
   = an ongoing action over a period of time

   βουλοίμην ἄν τὸν ἰᾱτρὸν ἰδεῖν.
   ***I would like** to see the doctor.*
   = in process

εἰ ὁ Φίλιππος τοῦτο **λέγοι**, ἐψεύδετο.
*If Philip (ever) **said** this, he was (always) lying.*
= an ongoing action over a period of time

Present (Progressive) Imperative:

ἄκουε τὸν μῦθον.
***Listen to** the story!*
= an ongoing process that will take place over a period of time

Present (Progressive) Infinitive:

νῦν δέ—ὀψὲ γάρ ἐστιν—δεῖ ἡμᾶς **καθεύδειν**.
*But now—for it is late—it is necessary for us **to be sleeping**.*
= an ongoing process that will take place over a period of time

Present (Progressive) Participle:

ἡ Μέλιττα **φέρουσα** τὴν ὑδρίαν πταίει καὶ αὐτὴν καταβάλλει.
*Melissa, **carrying** her water jar, stumbles and drops it.*

ἡ Μέλιττα **φέρουσα** τὴν ὑδρίαν ἔπταισε καὶ αὐτὴν κατέβαλεν.
*Melissa, **carrying** her water jar, stumbled and dropped it.*
= an ongoing process taking place over a period of time (note that the
same progressive, i.e., present, participle is used whether the action of
the main verb is present or past)

θάλποντος τοῦ ἡλίου, ὑπὸ ἐλάᾳ κάθηνται.
*Since the sun **is hot**, they are sitting under an olive tree.*

θάλποντος τοῦ ἡλίου, ὑπὸ ἐλάᾳ ἐκάθηντο.
*Since the sun **was hot**, they were sitting under an olive tree.*
= an ongoing condition (note again that the same progressive, i.e.,
present, participle is used whether the action of the main verb is
present or past)

Present Tense: Special Usage

Historic Present:

βραδέως οὖν τῷ παιδὶ ἡγούμενοι **βαδίζουσι** πρὸς τὴν τοῦ
ἀδελφοῦ οἰκίαν. ἐπεὶ δ' ἀφίκοντο....
*Then, leading the boy, **they walked** (lit., **walk**) slowly to the
brother's house. And when they arrived....*
= present tense used in place of an expected past tense for the sake of
vividness; the present tense may be preserved in English
translation

Imperfect (Past Progressive) Indicative:

οἱ φύλακες τὰς πύλας **ἔκλειον**.
*The guards **were shutting** the gates.*
= an ongoing process in past time

οἱ βόες **ἔμενον** ἐν τῷ ἀγρῷ.
*The oxen **used to stay/were accustomed to staying** in the field.*
= repeated or habitual action in past time

Imperfect (Past Progressive) Indicative: Special Usages

Inchoative Imperfect:

εἰς τὸν ἀγρὸν εἰσελθόντες **ἐπόνουν**.
*Entering the field, **they began to work**.*
= the beginning of an action in past time

Conative Imperfect:

τὸν πατέρα **ἐπείθομεν** οἴκαδε ἐπανελθεῖν.
We tried to persuade *father to return home.*
= an attempt to do something in past time

Aorist Aspect = Aorist Stem

Aorist (Past) Indicative:

ὡς **ἀφῑκόμεθα**, οἱ φύλακες τὰς πύλᾱς **ἔκλεισαν**.
*When we **arrived**, the guards **shut** the gates.*
= simple actions in past time

Gnomic Aorist:

παθὼν νήπιος **ἔμαθεν**.
*A fool **learns** by experience.*
= a general, timeless truth; translated with a present tense

Ingressive Aorist:

ἡ Μυρρίνη **ἐδάκρῡσε**.
*Myrrhine **burst** into tears.*

ἡ Μυρρίνη **δακρῡσᾱσα** ἀπετρέψατο.
*Myrrhine, **bursting into tears**, turned away.*
= the entrance into a state or the beginning of an action in past time

Aorist Subjunctive:

ἐπειδὰν **ἐπανέλθῃ** ὁ πατήρ, πάντα μαθησόμεθα.
*When father **returns**, we will learn everything.*

φοβοῦμαι μὴ ἐν καιρῷ οὐκ **ἀφίκωμαι**.
*I am afraid that I **may** not **arrive** in time.*
= simple actions (not continuous or ongoing)

Aorist Optative:

μὴ εἰς κακὰ **πέσοιτε**, ὦ φίλοι.
*May you not **fall** into trouble, friends.*

ἐφοβούμην μὴ ἐν καιρῷ οὐκ **ἀφικοίμην**.
*I was afraid that I **might** not **arrive** in time.*

εἰ ὁ ῑᾱτρὸς τοῦτο **ποιήσειεν**, οὐκ ἂν **δέξαιτο** τὸν μισθόν.
*If the doctor **should do** this, he **would** not **receive** his pay.*
= simple actions (not continuous or ongoing)

Aorist Imperative:

λαβοῦ τῆς ἐμῆς χειρός.
***Take** my hand!*
= simple action (not continuous or ongoing)

Aorist Infinitive:

ὁ Δικαιόπολις τὸν πάππον ἔπεισεν οἴκαδε **ἐπανελθεῖν**.
*Dicaeopolis persuaded grandfather **to return** home.*
= simple action (not continuous or ongoing)

Aorist Infinitive in Indirect Statement:

ὁ νεᾱνίᾱς οὐκ ἔφη τὸν πατέρα αὐτοῦ ἐν τῷ ἀγρῷ **ἰδεῖν**.
*The young man said that he **had** not **seen** his father in the field.*
= simple action prior to that of the main verb

Aorist Participle:

ὁ δὲ ἀδελφὸς πρὸς τὴν θύρᾱν **ἐλθὼν** καὶ τὸν Δικαιόπολιν **ἰδών**, "χαῖρε, ὦ ἄδελφε," ἔφη.

*And his brother, **having come/after coming/coming** to the door and **having seen/after seeing/seeing** Dicaeopolis, said, "Greetings, brother."*

= simple actions prior to that of the main verb

ἀποκρῑνάμενος εἶπεν.

***Answering**, he said. He said **in reply**.*

= simple action without reference to time

ἡμέρᾱς **γενομένης**, ὁ πατὴρ τὸν παῖδα καλέσᾱς ἔπεμψεν ὡς ζητήσοντα τὰ πρόβατα.

*When day **came** /**At daybreak**/ When day **had come**, the father, calling his son, sent him to seek the sheep.*

= simple action prior to that of the main verb

Aorist Participle in Indirect Statement:

οἱ αὐτουργοὶ ἠπίσταντο εἰς μέγιστον κίνδῡνον **καταστάντες**.

*The farmers were aware that they **had fallen** into the greatest danger.*

= simple action prior to that of the main verb

Perfective Aspect = Perfect Stem

Present Perfective (= Perfect) Indicative:

οἱ δοῦλοι τοὺς βοῦς ἤδη **λελύκᾱσιν**.

*The slaves **have** already **loos(en)ed** the oxen.*

= enduring result of a completed action

Present Perfective (= Perfect) Subjunctive:

φοβούμεθα μὴ οἱ δοῦλοι τοὺς βοῦς ἤδη **λελυκότες ὦσιν**.

*We are afraid that the slaves **have** already **loos(en)ed** the oxen.*

= enduring result of a completed action

Present Perfective (= Perfect) Optative:

ἤρετο εἰ οἱ δοῦλοι τοὺς βοῦς ἤδη **λελυκότες εἶεν**.

*He asked whether the slaves **had** already **loos(en)ed** the oxen.*

= enduring result of a completed action

Present Perfective (= Perfect) Imperative:

τέθναθι.

Be dead!

= enduring result of a completed action

Present Perfective (= Perfect) Infinitive:

λέγει τοὺς δούλους τοὺς βοῦς ἤδη **λελυκέναι**.

*He says that the slaves **have** already **loos(en)ed** the oxen.*

= enduring result of a completed action

Present Perfective (= Perfect) Participle:

εἶδε τοὺς δούλους τοὺς βοῦς ἤδη **λελυκότας**.

*He saw that the slaves **had** already **loos(en)ed** the oxen.*

= enduring result of a completed action

Past Perfective (= Pluperfect) Indicative:

οἱ δοῦλοι τοὺς βοῦς **ἐλελύκεσαν** πρὶν καταδῦναι τὸν ἥλιον.

*The slaves **had loos(en)ed** the oxen before the sun set.*

= action completed in the past prior to some other action in the past

οἱ βόες **ἐλέλυντο** πρὶν καταδῦναι τὸν ἥλιον.
*The oxen **had been loos(en)ed** before the sun set.*
= a state that existed in the past prior to some other action in the past

Supplementary Grammar Exercise 1 (after Chapter 28)

The following extract from the story of Croesus and Atys (Herodotus 1.43–45) illustrates many of the the uses of aspect, tense, and time illustrated above. Note that all features of Herodotus's Ionic dialect are preserved in our quotation of this passage, including the open spellings of -ε- contract verbs.

Read the Greek passage carefully, and then fill in the blanks in the translation of the passage with the abbreviations of the descriptors below that describe each verb form:

ὁ μὲν δὴ [Ἄτῡς] (1) <u>βληθεὶς</u> τῇ αἰχμῇ (2) <u>ἐξέπλησε</u> τοῦ ὀνείρου τὴν φήμην, (3) <u>ἔθεε</u> δέ τις (4) <u>ἀγγελέων</u> τῷ Κροίσῳ τὸ (5) <u>γεγονός</u>, (6) <u>ἀφικόμενος</u> δὲ ἐς τὰς Σάρδῑς τήν τε μάχην καὶ τὸν τοῦ παιδὸς μόρον (7) <u>ἐσήμηνέ</u> οἱ. ὁ δὲ Κροῖσος τῷ θανάτῳ τοῦ παιδὸς (8) <u>συντεταραγμένος</u> μᾶλλόν τι (9) <u>ἐδεινολογέετο</u> ὅτι μιν (10) <u>ἀπέκτεινε</u> τὸν (= ὃν) αὐτὸς φόνου (11) <u>ἐκάθηρε</u>. (12) <u>περιημεκτέων</u> (*being aggrieved*) δὲ τῇ συμφορῇ δεινῶς (13) <u>ἐκάλεε</u> μὲν Δία καθάρσιον, (14) <u>μαρτυρόμενος</u> (*protesting*) τὰ (= ἃ) ὑπὸ τοῦ ξείνου (15) <u>πεπονθὼς εἴη</u>.... (16) <u>παρῆσαν</u> δὲ μετὰ τοῦτο οἱ Λῡδοὶ (17) <u>φέροντες</u> τὸν νεκρόν, ὄπισθε δὲ (18) <u>εἵπετο</u> οἱ ὁ φονεύς. (19) <u>στὰς</u> δὲ οὗτος πρὸ τοῦ νεκροῦ (20) <u>παρεδίδου</u> ἑωυτὸν Κροίσῳ (21) <u>προτείνων</u> τὰς χεῖρας, (22) <u>ἐπικατασφάξαι</u> μιν (23) <u>κελεύων</u> τῷ νεκρῷ, (24) <u>λέγων</u> τήν τε προτέρην ἑωυτοῦ συμφορήν, καὶ ὡς ἐπ' ἐκείνῃ τὸν (25) <u>καθήραντα</u> (26) <u>ἀπολωλεκὼς εἴη</u> . . . Κροῖσος δὲ τούτων (27) <u>ἀκούσας</u> τόν τε Ἄδρηστον (28) <u>κατοικτίρει</u>. . . καὶ (29) <u>λέγει</u> πρὸς αὐτόν. . . .

AOR. IND.: aorist indicative–simple action in past time
AOR. INF.: aorist infinitive–simple action
AOR. PART.: aorist participle–simple action prior to that of the main verb
FUT. PART.: future participle–purpose, here without ὡς
HIST. PRES.: historic present
IMP. IND.—CON.: imperfect indicative–conative
IMP. IND.—ONGOING: imperfect indicative–ongoing action in past time
PERF. OPT.: perfect optative in indirect statement–enduring result of a completed action
PERF. PART.: perfect participle–enduring result of a completed action
PRES. PART.: present participle–action in process

So Atys, <u>having been struck/after being struck/struck</u> (1: βληθεὶς: _____) by the spear point, <u>fulfilled</u> (2: ἐξέπλησε: _____) the warning of the dream, and someone <u>was running</u> (3: ἔθεε: _____) <u>to tell</u> (4: ἀγγελέων: _____) what <u>had happened</u> (5: γεγονός: _____), and <u>having arrived/after arriving/arriving</u> (6: ἀφικόμενος: _____) at Sardis he <u>reported</u> (7: ἐσήμηνέ: _____) to him the battle and the fate of his son. And Croesus, <u>confounded</u> (8: συντεταραγμένος: _____) by the death of his son, <u>was lamenting</u> (9: ἐδεινολογέετο: _____) all the more because the man had <u>killed</u> (10: ἀπέκτεινε:

_____; translated into English with *had* because of the secondary sequence)

him whom he himself <u>had purified</u> (11: ἐκάθηρε: _____; translated into

English with *had* because of the secondary sequence) of murder, and <u>being aggrieved</u>

(12: περιημεκτέων: _____) terribly at the disaster, <u>he was calling</u> (13: ἐκάλεε:

_____) on Zeus of purification, <u>protesting</u> (14: μαρτυρόμενος:

_____) what he <u>had suffered</u> (15: πεπονθὼς εἴη: _____) at the hands

of the stranger. . . . After this, the Lydians <u>were present</u> (16: παρῆσαν: : _____),

<u>carrying</u> (17: φέροντες: _____) the corpse, and the murderer <u>was following</u>

(18: εἵπετο: _____) it behind. And <u>having stopped; after stopping/stopping</u>

(19: στὰς: _____—it does not mean *standing*, which would require a perfect

participle), he <u>tried to hand</u> himself <u>over</u> (20: παρεδίδου: _____—Croesus

would not accept his surrender) to Croesus, <u>stretching out</u> (21: προτείνων:

_____) his hands, <u>telling him</u> (23: κελεύων: _____) <u>to slaughter</u> (22:

ἐπικατασφάξαι: _____) himself on top of the corpse, <u>telling</u> (24: λέγων:

_____) of his former disaster and (saying) that on top of that he <u>had destroyed</u>

(26: ἀπολωλεκὼς εἴη: _____; the destruction was complete and irrevocable;

translated into English with *had* because of the secondary sequence) the man who <u>had</u>

<u>purified</u> (25: τὸν καθήραντα: _____; translated into English with *had* because

of the secondary sequence) him. . . . But Croesus <u>having heard/after hearing/hearing</u>

(27: ἀκούσας: _____) <u>pities/pitied</u> (28: κατοικτίρει: _____) Adrastus

and <u>says/said</u> (29: λέγει: _____) to him. . . .

Articles

Articles at the Beginning of Clauses

The article + δέ is often used at the beginning of a clause to indicate a change of subject; the article is translated as a pronoun, e.g.:

ὁ οὖν Ἄργος ὑλακτεῖ καὶ διώκει τὸν λαγών, **ὁ δὲ** φεύγει ἀνὰ τὸ ὄρος.
*Then Argus barks and pursues the hare, **but it** (i.e., the hare) flees up the hill.*

ὁ δεσπότης τὸν δοῦλον καλεῖ, **ὁ δὲ** οὐ πάρεστιν.
*The master calls the slave, **but he** is not present.*

ὁ πατὴρ τὰς κόρᾱς καλεῖ, **αἱ δὲ** ταχέως προσχωροῦσιν.
*The father calls the girls, **and they** approach quickly.*

Articles with μέν . . . δέ also indicate a change of subject, e.g.:

ὁ μὲν διώκει, **ὁ δὲ** φεύγει.
***The one** pursues, and **the other** flees.*

αἱ μὲν διαλέγονται, **αἱ δὲ** σῑγῶσιν.
***Some** (women) talk, and **others** are silent.*

Articles Plus Modifiers

1. The article + an adjective can form a noun phrase, e.g.:

Adjectives:	Noun Phrases:
ἀνδρεῖος, -ᾱ, -ον = *brave*	οἱ ἀνδρεῖοι = *the brave men*
σώφρων, σῶφρον = *prudent*	αἱ σώφρονες = *the prudent women*
φίλος, -η, -ον = *dear*	οἱ φίλοι or αἱ φίλαι = *the friends*
πολέμιος, -ᾱ, -ον = *hostile*	οἱ πολέμιοι = *the enemy*
κακός, -ή, -όν = *bad, evil*	τὰ κακά = *evils, troubles*

2. The article + the neuter of an adjective is often used as an abstract noun, e.g.:

    τὸ καλόν = *beauty; virtue; honor*
    τὸ αἰσχρόν = *dishonor; disgrace; vice*
    τὸ ἀληθές or τὰ ἀληθῆ = *the truth*
    τὸ δίκαιον = *justice*
    τὸ ἕν = *the one = unity*

3. The article + an adverb, prepositional phrase, or genitive can form a noun phrase, e.g.:

    οἱ νῦν = *the now men = the men of today = the present generation*
    οἱ πάλαι = *the men of old*
    τὰ εἴσω = *the things inside = the inside*
    αἱ ἐν τῇ ἀγορᾷ = *the women in the agora*
    αἱ πρὸς τῇ κρήνῃ = *the women at the spring*
    ὁ τοῦ βασιλέως = *the (son) of the king = the king's son*
    τὰ τῆς πόλεως = *the things (i.e., the affairs) of the city = politics*
    τὰ τοῦ πολέμου = *the things (e.g., the resources) of/for war*
    τὰ τῆς τύχης = *the things (e.g., the ways) of fortune*

4. The article + a participle forms a noun phrase that may be translated by a relative clause in English, e.g.:

    οἱ παρόντες = *the ones being present = those who are present*
    οἱ ἐν τῷ ἀγρῷ ἐργαζόμενοι = *the in the field working (men) = the men who are working in the field*

ὁ ἱερεὺς ὁ τὴν θυσίαν ποιούμενος = *the priest who is making the sacrifice*

These participles are said to be *attributive*, serving as simple adjectives.

Attributive and Predicate Positions of Adjectives and Other Modifiers

Adjectives may stand in either an attributive or a predicate position with respect to the article-noun group that they modify, e.g.:

Attributive Position (between the article and the noun):	Predicate Position (outside the article-noun group):
ἡ **καλὴ** παρθένος ἡ παρθένος ἡ **καλή** *the **beautiful** girl*	**καλὴ** ἡ παρθένος. ἡ παρθένος **καλή**. *The girl is **beautiful**.*

In the example at the right above the adjective in the predicate position serves as the complement in a complete sentence.

Note the difference in meaning of the sentences below with the adjective first in the attributive and then in the predicate position:

οἱ Πέρσαι αἱροῦσι τὸ **ἔρημον** ἄστυ.
*The Persians take the **deserted** city.* (attributive position)

οἱ Πέρσαι αἱροῦσιν **ἔρημον** τὸ ἄστυ.
*The Persians take the city **deserted**.* (predicate position)

The adjective in the attributive position tells which city the Persians took: they took the *deserted* city. In the second example the adjective in the predicate position adds a comment about the city that the Persians took: it was *deserted*. Here the adjective ἔρημον is predicate to the direct object τὸ ἄστυ.

Demonstrative adjectives (οὗτος, αὕτη, τοῦτο, *this;* ἐκεῖνος, ἐκείνη, ἐκεῖνο, *that;* and ὅδε, ἥδε, τόδε, *this here*) always occupy the predicate position, e.g.:

ἐκείνη ἡ παρθένος
***that** girl*

The adjective πᾶς, πᾶσα, πᾶν may occupy either the predicate or the attributive position, with different meanings:

Predicate position:	**πάντες** οἱ θεοί or οἱ θεοὶ **πάντες** = ***all** the gods* **πᾶσα** ἡ ναῦς or ἡ ναῦς **πᾶσα** = *the **whole** ship*, i.e., all of its parts
Attributive position (rare):	ἡ **πᾶσα** πόλις = *the **whole** city* (regarded collectively as the sum total of its parts)

The adjective αὐτός, αὐτή, αὐτό may also occupy either the predicate or the attributive position, again with different meanings. When used to intensify or emphasize a noun, it occupies the predicate position, e.g.:

ὁ πάππος τὸν λύκον **αὐτὸν** ὁρᾷ.
ὁ πάππος **αὐτὸν** τὸν λύκον ὁρᾷ.
*The grandfather sees the wolf **itself**.*

αἱ μὲν κόραι τὰς ὑδρίας πληροῦσιν, αἱ δὲ γυναῖκες **αὐταὶ** οὔ.
αἱ μὲν κόραι τὰς ὑδρίας πληροῦσιν, **αὐταὶ** δὲ αἱ γυναῖκες οὔ.
*The girls fill their water jars, but the women **themselves** do not.*

When used to mean *same*, it occupies the attributive position, e.g.:

τὸν **αὐτὸν** λύκον   *the **same** wolf*

αἱ **αὐταὶ** γυναῖκες   *the **same** women*

Genitives of nouns, reflexive pronouns, prepositional phrases, and adverbs may occupy the same position as attributive adjectives, e.g.:

αἱ **τῶν βαρβάρων** νῆες   or   αἱ νῆες αἱ **τῶν βαρβάρων**
*the **barbarians'** ships*

Κροῖσος οὖν ἔθαψε τὸν **ἑαυτοῦ** παῖδα.
*Then Croesus buried **his own** son.*

οἱ **ἐν τῷ ἀγρῷ** δοῦλοι   or   οἱ δοῦλοι οἱ **ἐν τῷ ἀγρῷ**
*the slaves **in the field***

οἱ **νῦν** παῖδες   or   οἱ παῖδες οἱ **νῦν**
*the children **of today***

The possessive genitive of αὐτός, however, and the genitive of personal pronouns take the predicate position, e.g.:

ὁ πάππος πρὸς τὸν παῖδα τρέχει, ὁ δὲ τὴν μάχαιραν **αὐτοῦ** λαμβάνει.
*Grandfather runs to the boy, and he (the boy) takes **his** (the grandfather's) knife.*

"σὺ εἶ ὁ υἱός **μου** ὁ ἀγαπητός." (Luke 3.22)
*"You are **my** beloved son."*

Note Also: Substantive Use of Adjectives without Articles

Adjectives, especially in the plural, are often used as substantives, thus functioning as nouns, and can be translated by supplying words such as "men," "women," or "things," depending on the gender of the adjective, e.g.:

ἐν δὲ τῇ ὁδῷ **πολλοὺς** ὁρῶμεν.
*We see **many (men)** on the road.*

πρὸς τὴν κρήνην **πολλαὶ** ὑδρίας φέρουσιν.
***Many (women)** are carrying water jars to the spring.*

ἐν δὲ τῇ ὁδῷ **πολλὰ** καὶ **δεινὰ** πάσχουσιν.
*On the journey they suffer **many terrible (things)**.*

Note also that Greek uses the conjunction καί here, while English does not use a connective.

The adjective πᾶς, πᾶσα, πᾶν may be used as a substantive without a definite article, e.g.:

πάντες = *all people, everyone*
πάντα (n. pl.) = *all things, everything*

Supplementary Grammar Exercise 2 (after Chapter 24)

Translate into English. Show how the rules stated above are illustrated in these sentences:

1.   οἱ ἐν τῇ νήσῳ πολλὰ καὶ κακὰ ἔπασχον.

2.   οὐ σώφρων ὁ γέρων· οὐ γὰρ ἐπίσταται τὰ τῆς τύχης.

3.   οἱ νῦν οὐδὲν κακίους εἰσὶ τῶν προγόνων.

4.   πάντες οἱ σώφρονες ἐτίμων τοὺς ἐν ἐκείνῃ τῇ μάχῃ ἀποθανόντας.

5.   οἱ Ἕλληνες τὰ τῆς θαλάττης ἐπιστάμενοι ἐδύναντο τοὺς βαρβάρους νῑκῆσαι,
   καίπερ ἐλάττους ἔχοντες ναῦς.

6.   τὰ τοῦ πολέμου οὐκ ἔχοντες μόλις δυνάμεθα πολεμίοις ἀντέχειν.

7.   αἱ τῶν βαρβάρων νῆες μείζους ἦσαν καὶ βραδύτεραι ἢ αἱ τῶν Ἑλλήνων.

8.   οἱ ναῦται οἱ ἐν ἐκείνῃ τῇ νηὶ ἀγνοοῦσι πόσος χειμὼν γενήσεται.

9.   ἆρα ἐνέτυχες τῷ ποιμένι τῷ τὰ μῆλα ἀνὰ τὴν ὁδὸν ἐλαύνοντι;

10.   χαλεπὸν τὸ καλόν· οὕτω λέγουσιν οἱ σοφοὶ καὶ οὐχ ἁμαρτάνουσιν.

11.   καλὴ αὕτη ἡ παρθένος. ἆρ' οὐ θαυμάζεις τὸ καλὸν αὐτῆς;

12.   οἱ ἀγαθοὶ τοὺς μὲν φίλους ὠφελοῦσιν, τοὺς δὲ ἐχθροὺς βλάπτουσιν.

13.   ἆρα τὸ ἀληθὲς/τὰ ἀληθῆ λέγεις, ὦ παῖ; οἱ τὰ ψευδῆ λέγοντες κακῶς πράττουσιν.

14.   ὁ τοῦ βασιλέως οὐκ ἠπίστατο τὰ τῆς τύχης.

15.   τὸ ἄστυ ἔρημον ηὕρομεν καὶ νεκροὺς ἐν ταῖς ὁδοῖς κειμένους.

16.   ὁ πατὴρ τὸν παῖδα κελεύει ἐν τῇ οἰκίᾳ μένειν, ὁ δὲ οὐ πείθεται αὐτῷ.

17.   αὗται αἱ παρθένοι ἀνδρειότεραι ἦσαν ἐκείνων τῶν νεανιῶν.

18.   ὁ ἄγγελος πάντα ἐξηγήσατο πᾶσι τοῖς πολίταις.

19.   αὐτὸς ὁ βασιλεὺς εἰς τὴν ἀγορὰν εἶσιν ὡς ταῦτα τοῖς πολίταις ἀγγελῶν.

20.   ὁ βασιλεὺς πολλὰ στενάζων τὸν ἑαυτοῦ παῖδα ἔθαψεν (*buried*).

Uses of the Cases

Nominative

1. Subject of a finite verb, e.g.:

    ὁ ἄνθρωπος γεωργεῖ τὸν κλῆρον.
    The man cultivates the farm.

2. Complement with the linking verb εἰμί and verbs of becoming such as γίγνομαι, e.g.:

    ὁ κλῆρός ἐστι μῑκρός.
    The farm is small.

    οἱ δὲ εὐθὺς σύες γίγνονται.
    And immediately they become pigs.

Genitive

1. Genitive of possession, e.g.:

    ὁ τοῦ παιδὸς κύων
    the boy's dog or *the dog of the boy*
    Note that the word in the genitive case is here in the attributive position between the article and the noun. It may also be placed after the repeated article, e.g.: ὁ κύων ὁ τοῦ παιδός

    The genitive often simply links one noun to another without any notion of possession, e.g.:
    ὕβρις . . . ἐκφέρει καρπὸν ἄτης.
    Insolence produces fruit of ruin.

2. Genitive with certain adjectives, such as αἴτιος, *responsible (for)*, and ἄξιος, *worthy (of)*, e.g.:

    δεῖ γάρ σε ἄξιον γίγνεσθαι τῶν πατέρων.
    You must become worthy of your fathers.

3. Genitive of the whole or partitive genitive, e.g.:

    τῶν παρόντων πολλοί
    many of those present

    ὁ Λεωνίδης πάντων τῶν στρατιωτῶν ἄριστος ἦν.
    Leonidas was the best of all the soldiers.

    Note that this genitive often comes first in its phrase, e.g.:
    τῶν πολῑτῶν οἱ μὲν ἔμενον, οἱ δὲ ἀπῆλθον.
    Some of the citizens were staying, others went away.

4. Genitive of time within which, e.g.:

    πέντε ἡμερῶν, *within five days*
    νυκτός, *at / by night*

5. Genitive of comparison, e.g.:

    ὁ ἀνὴρ μείζων ἐστὶ τοῦ παιδός.
    The man is bigger than the boy.

6. Genitive of separation or origin, e.g.:

    τὸ ἄστυ πολὺ ἀπέχει τῆς θαλάττης.
    The city is far from the sea.

    οἱ δοῦλοι ἐπαύσαντο ἔργου.
    The slaves stopped from work / stopped working.

δύο παῖδες **Κροίσου** ἐγένοντο.
*Two sons were born **from** Croesus* (we say *to Croesus*).

7. Genitive with certain prepositions, often expressing ideas of place from which, e.g.: ἀπὸ τοῦ ἄστεως, *from **the city***.

8. Genitive with certain verbs, e.g.:

The genitive is used after verbs that mean *to hold onto* (ἔχομαι, λαμβάνομαι), *to rule* (ἄρχω, κρατέω, βασιλεύω), *to hit* (τυγχάνω), *to miss* (ἁμαρτάνω), *to perceive* (ἀκούω, αἰσθάνομαι), and *to share in* (μετέχω), e.g.:

ὁ Θησεὺς τῇ ἀριστερᾷ <u>λαμβάνεται</u> **τῆς** τοῦ θηρίου **κεφαλῆς**.
*Theseus <u>takes hold of</u> **the head** of the beast with his left hand.*

Verbs of perceiving take the genitive of the person but the accusative of the thing perceived, e.g., **σοῦ** <u>ἀκούω</u>, *I hear **you***, but **ταῦτα** <u>ἀκούω</u>, *I hear **these things.***

Verbs of remembering and forgetting take the genitive, e.g.:

τῶν φίλων <u>μέμνησο</u>. *<u>Remember</u> **your friends**.*

τῶν φίλων οὐκ <u>ἐπελάθοντο</u>. *They did not <u>forget</u> **their friends**.*

The following verbs in the vocabulary lists are used with the genitive case:
ἀκούω, *I hear* (a person talking; the accusative is used for the thing heard)
ἔχομαι, *I hold onto*
λαμβάνομαι, *I seize, take hold of*
παύομαι, *I cease from*

9. Genitive absolute

The genitive of a participle and a noun or pronoun form a phrase that is independent of the grammatical construction in the rest of the sentence, e.g.:

θάλποντος τοῦ ἡλίου, ὑπὸ ἐλάᾳ ἐκάθηντο.
Since the sun was hot, *they were sitting under an olive tree.*

Dative

1. Indirect object with verbs of giving, showing, telling, etc., e.g.:

οὕτω **τῷ Μῑνωταύρῳ** σῖτον παρέχουσιν.
*In this way they supply food **to the Minotaur**.*
*In this way they supply **the Minotaur** with food.*

2. The dative of the person concerned or interested, *e.g.:*

πᾶς ἀνὴρ **ἑαυτῷ** πονεῖ.
*Every man labors **for himself**.*

ὁ Σόλων Ἀθηναίοις νόμους ἔθηκεν.
*Solon made laws **for the Athenians**.*

Sometimes this use of the dative may be rendered in English by a possessive adjective (= possessive dative), e.g.:

οὐ πρὸς ἄνδρας **ἡμῖν** γίγνεται ἡ μάχη.
*The battle **for us** (= **our battle)** is not against men.*

3. Dative of the possessor, e.g.:

ἔστιν **αὐτῷ** παῖς τις ὀνόματι Θησεύς.
literally: *There is **for him** a child, Theseus by name.*
He has a child named Theseus.

4. Dative of respect, e.g.:

ὀνόματι Θησεύς
Theseus by name

5. Dative of means or instrument, e.g.:

τῇ ἀριστερᾷ λαμβάνεται τῆς τοῦ θηρίου κεφαλῆς.
He takes hold of the head of the beast with his left hand.

6. Dative of accompaniment (without a preposition), e.g.:

ταῖς ναυσὶ πλευσόμεθα.
We will sail with our ships.

ἡ ναῦς διεφθάρη αὐτοῖς τοῖς ἀνδράσιν.
The ship was destroyed, crew and all.

7. Dative of time when, e.g.:

τῇ τρίτῃ ἡμέρᾳ ἀφῑκόμεθα.
We arrived on the third day.

8. Dative of degree of difference with comparatives and superlatives, e.g.:

ὁ ἀνὴρ πολλῷ μείζων ἐστὶ τοῦ παιδός.
The man is much bigger (bigger by much) than the boy.

9. Dative with certain prepositions, especially those that indicate the place where someone or something is or something happens, e.g.:

πρὸς τῇ κρήνῃ
by the spring

10. Dative with certain verbs, e.g.:

ἕπεσθέ μοι ἀνδρείως.
Follow me bravely.

The following verbs in the vocabulary lists are used with the dative case:

ἀντέχω, *I resist*

βοηθέω, *I come to X's aid; I come to rescue/aid X*

διαλέγομαι, *I talk to, converse with*

δοκεῖ, impersonal, *it seems (good)*, e.g., δοκεῖ μοι, *it seems good to me; I think it best;* + dat. and infin., e.g., δοκεῖ αὐτοῖς σπεύδειν, *it seems good to them to hurry, they decide to hurry*

εἴκω, *I yield*

ἐμπῑ́πτω, *I fall into; I fall upon; I attack*

ἔξεστι(ν), impersonal + dat. and infin., *it is allowed/possible*

ἐπιπλέω, *I sail against*

ἕπομαι, *I follow*

εὔχομαι, *I pray to*

ἡγέομαι, *I lead*

μάχομαι, *I fight against*

ὀργίζομαι *I grow angry at; I am angry at*

πείθομαι, *I obey*

πιστεύω, *I trust, am confident (in); I believe*

προσβάλλω, *I attack*

προσέρχομαι, *I approach*

προσχωρέω, *I go toward, approach*

συλλαμβάνω, *I help*
συμβάλλω, *I join battle with*
συμπίπτω, *I clash with*
τέρπομαι, *I enjoy*
χράομαι, *I use; I enjoy*

Accusative

1. Direct object of many verbs, e.g.:

    ὁ ἄνθρωπος γεωργεῖ **τὸν κλῆρον**.
    *The man cultivates **the/his farm**.*

    A few verbs can take two accusative objects (*double accusative*), e.g.:

    τοῦτό σε ἐρωτῶ.   τοῦτό σε αἰτῶ.
    *I ask **you this**.*   *I ask **you for this**.*

    ὁ γραμματιστὴς **τοὺς παῖδας τὰ γράμματα** διδάσκει.
    *The schoolmaster **teaches the boys writing**.*

2. Accusative used as the subject of an infinitive, e.g.:

    δεῖ **ἡμᾶς** <u>παρεῖναι</u>.
    literally, **(For) us** <u>to be there</u> *is necessary*.
    We must be there.

3. Adverbial accusative

    The neuter accusative of adjectives and of some pronouns is often used
    adverbially, e.g., the comparative adverb is the neuter accusative singular of the
    comparative adjective; thus, θᾶσσον = *more quickly*. The superlative adverb is
    the neuter accusative plural of the superlative adjective; thus, τάχιστα = *very
    quickly*, *most quickly*.

    The words μέγα, πολύ, ὀλίγον, οὐδέν, and τί are commonly used
    adverbially, e.g.:

    μέγα βοᾷ. *He / she shouts **loudly**.*
    οὐδέν σε φοβεῖται. *He / she does **not** fear you **at all**.*
    τί τοῦτο ποιεῖς; **Why** *are you doing this?*

    Another kind of adverbial accusative is the accusative of respect, e.g.:

    ὁ Κροῖσος Λυδὸς ἦν **τὸ γένος**.
    *Croesus was Lydian **with respect to his race**, i.e., **by birth**.*

    ἀνήρ τις ἀφίκετο οὐ καθαρὸς **τὰς χεῖρας**.
    *A man arrived not clean **with respect to/in respect to his hands**.*

    Another kind of adverbial accusative is the accusative of duration of time or
    extent of space, e.g.:

    ἐμείναμεν **πέντε ἡμέρᾱς**.
    *We stayed **five days**.*

    τὸ ἄστυ **πολλοὺς σταδίους** ἀπέχει.
    *The city is **many stades** distant.*

    Another kind of adverbial accusative is the accusative absolute, used with
    participles of impersonal verbs instead of the genitive absolute, e.g.:

    δόξαν τὸν παῖδα ἐς τὴν ἄγρᾱν πέμψαι, ὁ Κροῖσος μάλιστα ἐφοβεῖτο.
    When he had decided *to send his son to the hunt, Croesus was very
    afraid.*
    (The word δόξαν is the accusative neuter of the aorist participle of δοκεῖ = *it
    having seemed best* =*it having been decided*.)

ἐξὸν ἐς τὴν ἄγραν ἰέναι, ὁ Ἄτυς εὐθὺς ὁρμᾶται.
Being allowed to go to the hunt, Atys sets out at once.
(The word ἐξόν is the accusative neuter of the participle of ἔξεστι(ν) = *it being possible, it being allowed*.)

δέον τὸ θηρίον αἱρεῖν, ἐς τὸ ὄρος ἔσπευδον.
Since it was necessary to take the beast, they hurried to the mountain.
(The word δέον is the accusative neuter of the participle of δεῖ = *it being necessary*.)

4. The accusative is used in oaths after νή (positive) and μά (negative), e.g.:

νὴ τοὺς θεούς. . . .   μὰ τὸν Δία. . . .
By the gods, I will....   ***By*** Zeus, I won't. ...

5. Accusative with certain prepositions, especially with those expressing motion toward someone or something, e.g.:

πρὸς **τὸν οἶκον** βαδίζει.
He/she walks toward ***his/her house***.

Supplementary Grammar Exercise 3 (after Chapter 26)

Identify the uses of the cases in the underlined phrases:

1. ὁ Κροῖσος φοβούμενος μὴ δόρατι βληθείη ὁ παῖς, ἐκέλευσεν αὐτὸν μάχης ἀπέχειν.

     ὁ Κροῖσος _____

     δόρατι _____

     μάχης _____

2. ἀνήρ τις, Φρύγιος τὸ γένος, ἐς τὰς Σάρδῑς ἀφικόμενος, τὸν Κροῖσον κάθαρσιν ᾔτησεν.

     τὸ γένος _____

     τὸν Κροῖσον κάθαρσιν _____

3. δόξαν καθῆραι αὐτόν, ὁ Κροῖσος ἐπυνθάνετο πόθεν ἥκει καὶ τίνος πατρὸς ἐγένετο.

     δόξαν _____

     τίνος πατρὸς _____

4. δέον τὸ ἀληθὲς εἰπεῖν, ὁ ξένος ἀπεκρίνατο· "Γορδίου μὲν ἐγενόμην, ὄνομα δὲ μοί ἐστιν Ἄδρηστος, φονεύσᾱς δὲ τὸν ἐμαυτοῦ ἀδελφὸν ἄκων πάρειμι."

     δέον _____

     Γορδίου _____

     Ἄδρηστος _____

     ἐμαυτοῦ _____

5. ὁ δὲ Κροῖσος δεξάμενος αὐτόν, "ἥκεις ἐς φίλους," ἔφη. "μένε οὖν ἐν τοῖς ἡμετέροις οἰκίοις ὅσον ἂν χρόνον βούλῃ."

     τοῖς ἡμετέροις οἰκίοις _____

     ὅσον . . . χρόνον _____

6. ἄγγελοί τινες, Μῦσοὶ <u>τὸ γένος</u>, ἐς <u>Σάρδῑς</u> ἀφικόμενοι, "πέμψον <u>ἡμῖν</u>, ὦ βασιλεῦ," ἔφασαν, "<u>τὸν σὸν παῖδα</u> ἵνα μέγα θηρίον <u>τῆς χώρᾱς</u> ἐξέλωμεν."

    τὸ γένος _____

    Σάρδῑς _____

    ἡμῖν _____

    τὸν σὸν παῖδα _____

    τῆς χώρᾱς _____

7. ὁ δὲ Κροῖσος, "δύο μὲν παῖδές εἰσί <u>μοι</u>, ὧν οὗτος, Ἄτυς <u>ὀνόματι</u>, <u>πολλῷ</u> φιλαίτερος ἐστί μοι <u>τοῦ ἑτέρου</u>."

    μοι _____

    ὀνόματι _____

    πολλῷ _____

    τοῦ ἑτέρου _____

8. "οὐ μὰ <u>Δία</u> πέμψω αὐτὸν <u>ὑμῖν</u>, τὸν δὲ Ἄδρηστον πέμψω <u>νεᾱνίαις</u> τε καὶ <u>κυσίν</u>."

    Δία _____

    ὑμῖν _____

    νεᾱνίαις . . . κυσίν _____

9. ὁ δὲ παῖς, <u>οὐδὲν</u> φοβούμενος τὴν ἄγρᾱν, τὸν πατέρα ἔπεισεν ἑαυτὸν πέμψαι· "οὐ γάρ," φησίν, "πρὸς ἄνδρας <u>ἡμῖν</u> γίγνεται ἡ μάχη."

    οὐδὲν _____

    ἡμῖν _____

10. <u>ἐξὸν</u> οὖν ἐς τὴν ἄγρᾱν ἰέναι, ὁ Ἄτῡς <u>τριῶν ἡμερῶν</u> ὡρμήθη μετὰ τῶν λογάδων νεᾱνιῶν.

    ἐξὸν _____

    τριῶν ἡμερῶν _____

11. <u>μακρὰν</u> οὖν <u>ὁδὸν</u> πορευθέντες καὶ τὸ θηρίον εὑρόντες, <u>τῶν νεᾱνιῶν</u> οἱ μὲν αὐτὸ ἐδίωκον, οἱ δὲ περιστάντες κύκλῳ ἐσηκόντιζον.

    μακρὰν . . . ὁδὸν _____

    τῶν νεᾱνιῶν _____

12. ὁ δὲ Ἄδρηστος ἀκοντίζων <u>τοῦ ὑός</u>, <u>τοῦ</u> μὲν ἁμαρτάνει, τυγχάνει δὲ <u>τοῦ</u> Κροίσου <u>παιδός</u>.

    τοῦ ὑός _____

    τοῦ _____

    τοῦ . . . παιδός _____

13. <u>τοῦ</u> δὲ <u>κακοῦ</u> οὐκ Ἄδρηστος αἴτιος ἦν ἀλλὰ θεῶν τις.

    τοῦ . . . κακοῦ _____

Correlatives: Interrogative, Indefinite, Demonstrative, and Relative Pronouns and Adjectives

Interrogative	Indefinite	Demonstrative	Relative

1. PERSONAL PRONOUNS AND ADJECTIVES

Pronouns	**Pronouns**	**Adjectives**	**Definite Pronouns**
τίς; τί; *who?* *what?*	τις, τι, *someone,* *anyone;* *something,* *anything*	οὗτος, αὕτη, τοῦτο, *this* ὅδε, ἥδε, τόδε, *this* ἐκεῖνος, -η, -ο, *that*	ὅς, ἥ, ὅ or ὅσπερ, ἥπερ, ὅπερ, *who, whose,* *whom, which,* *that*
Adjectives	**Adjectives**	*that*	**Indefinite Pronouns**
τίς; τί; *which?* *what?*	τις, τι, *a certain; a;* *some; any*		ὅστις, ἥτις, ὅ τι, *anyone who,* *whoever;* *anything that,* *whatever*

2. EXPLANATORY ADVERBS

πῶς; *how?*	πως, *somehow*	οὕτω(ς), ὧδε, ὥς, *thus, like this*	ὡς, ὥσπερ, ὅπως, *as; just as; how*

3. LOCATIONAL ADVERBS

ποῦ; *where?*	που, *somewhere*	ἔνθα, ἐκεῖ, *there* ἐνθάδε, ἐνταῦθα, *here; there*	οὗ, οὗπερ, ὅπου, *where*
ποῖ; *whither?* *to where?* *where?*	ποι, *to some place*	δεῦρο, *hither* ἔνθα, ἐκεῖσε, *thither* ἐνθάδε, ἐνταῦθα, *hither, thither*	οἷ, ὅποι, *to what place*
πόθεν; *whence?* *from where?*	ποθέν, *from some place*	ἐντεῦθεν, *from this place* ἐκεῖθεν, *from that place*	ὅθεν, ὁπόθεν, *whence,* *from where*

4. TEMPORAL ADVERBS

πότε; *when?*	ποτέ, *at some time; once; ever*	τότε, *then*	ὅτε, ὁπότε, *when*

Interrogative	Indefinite	Demonstrative	Relative

5. QUALITATIVE ADJECTIVES

ποῖος, ποία, ποῖον, *(of) what kind?*	ποιός, ποιά, ποιόν *of some kind*	τοιοῦτος, τοιαύτη, τοιοῦτο, *such; of this kind* τοιόσδε, τοιάδε, τοιόνδε, *such; of this kind; such as the following*	οἷος, -ᾱ, -ον or ὁποῖος, ὁποία, ὁποῖον, *(such) as*

6. QUANTITATIVE ADJECTIVES

πόσος, -η, -ον; *how much?* pl., *how many?*	ποσός, ή, -όν, *of some size*	τοσοῦτος, τοσαύτη, τοσοῦτο, *so large, so great; pl., so many*	ὅσος, -η, -ον ὁπόσος, -η, -ον, *as large as; as much as; as; how much; pl., as many as; as; how many*

7. ALTERNATIVE ADJECTIVES

πότερος, -ᾱ, -ον; *which (of two)?*		ἕτερος, -ᾱ, -ον, *one or the other (of two)*	ὁπότερος, -ᾱ, -ον, *which of two*

The words ὅστις, ὅπως, ὅπου, and so forth, are often used to introduce indirect questions instead of the ordinary form of the interrogative, e.g.:

εἰπέ μοι **ποῦ/ὅπου** ἐστὶν ὁ πατήρ.

*Tell me **where** father is.*

Supplementary Grammar Exercise 4

Translate into English. Identify each correlative word and locate each in the chart above:

1. "πῶς τοῦτο ἐποίησας;" "τοῦτο ὧδε ἐποίησα, ὥσπερ παρήνεσεν ὁ πατήρ."

2. "πόθεν ἥκεις;" "οὐκ οἶδα ὁπόθεν· τῆς γὰρ ὁδοῦ ἥμαρτον."

3. "ποῦ οἰκεῖ ὁ γέρων;" "ἐκεῖ οἰκεῖ ὁ γέρων ἐγγὺς τοῦ ποταμοῦ, ὅπου εἶδον αὐτὸν νεωστί (*recently*)."

4. "ἐν ποίᾳ νηὶ δεῦρο ἔπλευσας;" "ἐν τοιαύτῃ νηὶ ἔπλευσα οἵᾱ σῖτον ἀπὸ τῆς Αἰγύπτου φέρει."

5. τοσοῦτον χρόνον ἐν τῇ ἀγορᾷ ἐμένομεν ὅσον ἐκέλευσας.

6. ἡ παρθένος τὸν πατέρα ἤρετο ποῖ ἔρχεται· ὁ δὲ οὐκ ἤθελεν ἀποκρίνεσθαι.

7. "πότε οἴκαδε ἐπάνεισιν ἡ μήτηρ;" "ἡ μήτηρ οἴκαδε ἐπάνεισιν ὅταν τὸν πατέρα εὕρῃ."

8. "πόσᾱς ναῦς ἔχουσιν οἱ πολέμιοι;" "οὐκ οἶδα ἔγωγε ὁπόσᾱς ναῦς ἔχουσιν."

9. ὁ ὁπλίτης τῇ μὲν ἑτέρᾳ χειρὶ δόρυ ἔφερε, τῇ δὲ ἑτέρᾳ ξίφος.

10. ὁ στρατηγὸς δύο ἀγγέλους ἔπεμψεν, οἱ δὲ οὐ λέγουσι τὰ αὐτά· ποτέρῳ πιστεύωμεν;

Uses of πρίν

The conjunction πρίν may mean *until* or *before*.

a. After a negative main clause πρίν means *until*, and the usual rules for temporal conjunctions apply, i.e., like ἕως it is followed by the indicative in past time and the indefinite construction (ἄν + subjunctive, usually aorist) in future time, e.g.:

αἱ γυναῖκες <u>οὐκ ἀπῆλθον</u> **πρὶν ἀφίκετο** ὁ ἱερεύς.
*The women <u>did not go away</u> **until** the priest **arrived**.*

αἱ γυναῖκες <u>οὐκ ἀπίασι</u> **πρὶν ἂν ἀφίκηται** ὁ ἱερεύς.
*The women <u>will not go away</u> **until** the priest **arrives**.*

b. After a positive main clause πρίν usually means *before*, and it is followed by an infinitive. As in indirect statements, if the subject of the infinitive is the same as that of the leading verb, it is not expressed (but may be intensified with αὐτός); if the subject of the infinitive is different from that of the leading verb, it is in the accusative, e.g.:

<u>ἀποπέμπουσιν</u> αὐτὸν **πρὶν ἀκοῦσαι**.
*<u>They send</u> him <u>away</u> **before they hear** him.*

<u>ἐδείπνησα</u> **πρὶν ἰέναι** εἰς τὴν ἐκκλησίᾱν.
*<u>I dined</u> **before I went** or **before going** to the Assembly.*

οἱ πολῖται <u>συνῆλθον</u> **πρὶν εἰσιέναι** τοὺς πρυτάνεις.
*The citizens <u>gathered</u> **before** the Prytaneis **came in**.*

Supplementary Grammar Exercise 5 (after Chapter 27)

Translate into English. Show how the rules stated above are illustrated in these sentences:

1. ὁ νεᾱνίᾱς εἰς τὸ ἄστυ ἀφίκετο πρὶν γενέσθαι ἡμέρᾱν.

2. πρὶν ἀπιέναι, ὁ πατὴρ τοὺς παῖδας ἐκέλευσε τῇ μητρὶ πάντα πείθεσθαι.

3. οὐ πειρᾱσόμεν εἰς τὴν ναῦν εἰσβῆναι πρὶν ἂν κελεύσῃ ὁ ναύκληρος.

4. οἱ ἄγγελοι οὐκ ἀπῆλθον ἀπὸ τῶν Δελφῶν πρὶν ἐθέσπισεν ἡ Πῡθίᾱ.

5. πρὶν ἄρξαι τῆς μάχης, ὁ Κῦρος τοὺς στρατιώτᾱς ἐκέλευσε τοῦ Κροίσου φείδεσθαι.

Uses of ὡς

1. The word ὡς may be used as a conjunction meaning "as" with a verb in the indicative, e.g.:

    σώφρων ἐστὶν ὁ νεᾱνίᾱς, **ὡς ἐμοὶ δοκεῖ/ ὡς ἔοικε/ ὡς λέγεται.**
    *The young man is sensible, **as it seems to me/as it seems/as it is said.***

2. As a conjunction used with the indicative, ὡς may also mean "when," e.g.:

    ὡς ἀφίκοντο, τὸν δοῦλον ἐκάλεσαν.
    When they arrived, *they called the slave.*

3. As a conjunction used with the subjunctive in primary sequence or the optative in secondary sequence, ὡς may introduce a purpose clause (negative ὡς μή), e.g.:

    ἀνδρείως μαχόμεθα **ὡς** τὴν πατρίδα **σώσωμεν.**
    *We are fighting bravely **so that we may save** our fatherland (= **to save** our fatherland).*

    ἀνδρείως ἐμαχεσάμεθα **ὡς** τὴν πατρίδα **σώσοιμεν.**
    *We fought bravely **so that we might save** our fatherland (= **to save** our fatherland).*

    σπεύδουσιν **ὡς μὴ** ὀψὲ **ἀφίκωνται.**
    *They are hurrying **so that they may not arrive** late (= **lest they arrive** late = **so as not to arrive** late).*

4. When introducing an indirect statement, ὡς is a conjunction meaning "that," e.g.:

    εἶπεν ὁ ἄγγελος **ὡς** πάρεισιν οἱ πρέσβεις.
    *The messenger said **that** the ambassadors were present.*

    It differs from ὅτι in that it often introduces a statement that the speaker regards as an opinion or as untrue, e.g.:

    λέγει **ὡς** ὑβριστής εἰμι καὶ βίαιος.
    *He says **that** I am insolent and violent.*
    He alleges that I am insolent and violent.

5. As an adverb, ὡς may modify an adjective, another adverb, or a verb and mean "how," e.g.:

    ὡς τρέχουσιν οἱ παῖδες.
    How *the boys run!*

    ὡς ταχέως τρέχουσιν οἱ παῖδες.
    How quickly *the boys run!*

    ἐθαύμαζον **ὡς ταχέως** τρέχουσιν οἱ παῖδες.
    *I was surprised **how quickly** the boys were running.*

6. Prepositional phrases may be used with ὡς to express purpose, e.g.:

    ὁ Ἀρχίδᾱμος περὶ τὰς Ἀχαρνὰς **ὡς ἐς μάχην** ταξάμενος ἔμεινε.
    *Archidamus was staying around Acharnae drawn up **as for battle** (i.e., **for the purpose of fighting**).*

7. A future participle with or without ὡς may express purpose, e.g.:

    παρεσκευάζοντο **ὡς πολεμήσοντες.**
    *They were preparing themselves **to make war** (lit., **as being about to make war**).*

8. A participle may also be used with ὡς to express alleged cause, e.g.:

> τὸν νεᾱνίᾱν ἐκόλασαν **ὡς ἀδικήσαντα**.
> They punished the young man **for having done wrong**.

> τὸν γέροντα οἰκτίρουσιν **ὡς μαινόμενον**.
> They pity the old man **as being mad**.

9. With a superlative adjective or adverb, ὡς means *as . . . as possible*, e.g.:

> **ὡς πλεῖστοι, as many as possible**
> **ὡς τάχιστα, as quickly as possible**

The verb δύναμαι is sometimes added, e.g.:

> ἤρεσσον **ὡς τάχιστα ἐδύναντο**.
> They rowed **as quickly as they could**.

Supplementary Grammar Exercise 6 (after Chapter 28)

Translate into English. Show how the rules stated above are illustrated in these sentences:

1. ὡς εἰς τὸν Πειραιᾶ ἀφῑκόμεθα, εὐθὺς ἐσπεύσαμεν πρὸς τὴν ἀγορᾱ́ν.

2. ἐκεῖ δὲ ἠκούσαμέν τινος λέγοντος ὡς αἱ νῆες ἤδη εἰς τὸν λιμένα πεπλευκυῖαι εἶεν. ἀλλὰ ἐψεύδετο (*he was lying*)· αἱ γὰρ νῆες οὔπω (*not yet*) ἀφιγμέναι ἦσαν.

3. ὅταν αἱ νῆες ἀφικῶνται, ἴμεν πρὸς τὸν λιμένα ὡς αὐτὰς θεᾱσόμενοι.

4. ἴωμεν οὖν δι᾽ ὀλίγου πρὸς τὸν λιμένα ὡς τὰς ναῦς θεᾱσώμεθα.

5. ὡς καλαί εἰσιν αἱ νῆες· ὡς ταχέως εἰσπλέουσιν.

6. ἤδη τὰς ναῦς ἔξεστιν ἰδεῖν πρὸς τὴν Σαλαμῖνα ὡς τάχιστα πλεούσᾱς.

7. ἄκουε δή· εἰς ὀργὴν καθέστηκεν ὁ ναύαρχος, ὡς ἔοικε, καὶ τοὺς ἐρέτᾱς (*rowers*) μέμφεται ὡς βραδέως ἐρέσσοντας.

8. ὁ Δικαιόπολις καὶ οἱ οἰκεῖοι ὡς εἰς ἀνάστασιν παρεσκευασμένοι εἰσίν.

Uses of the Negative

The negative οὐ is used:

1. in all independent clauses with the indicative and with the potential optative
2. in indirect statements and questions, where the negatives of the direct words are retained
3. in causal clauses, definite relative and temporal clauses, and in ὥστε clauses with the indicative
4. in negative clauses of fearing, e.g.:

> ἐφοβούμην μὴ ἐν καιρῷ **οὐκ** ἀφίκωμαι/ἀφικοίμην.
> *I was afraid that I would (might) **not** arrive in time.*

The negative μή is used:

1. with imperatives and with subjunctives (hortatory, deliberative, prohibitions) in independent clauses
2. in wishes for the future with the optative
3. With the infinitive in *all* constructions *except* indirect statement (where the negatives of the direct words are used)
4. in purpose clauses (ἵνα, ὅπως, ὡς + subjunctive or optative), in conditional clauses, in indefinite (or general) clauses (relative and temporal), in generic relative clauses or with generic participles (i.e., relative clauses or participles describing not particular persons or things but types), and in relative clauses with future indicative expressing purpose
5. in positive clauses of fearing, e.g.:

> φοβοῦμαι **μὴ** δι' ὀλίγου εἰς πόλεμον καταστῶμεν.
> *I am afraid **that** we will (may) soon get into war.*

N.B.:

1. The negative with the participle is οὐ unless the participle has a conditional force, e.g.:

> οὐ μαθήσῃ κιθαρίζειν **μὴ** μελετῶν.
> *You won't learn to play the lyre, **unless** you practice.*

or the phrase is generic, e.g.:

> οἱ **μὴ** τὴν πόλιν φιλοῦντες οὐκ ἄξιοί εἰσι τῑμῆς.
> *The sort of people who do **not** love the city are not worthy of honor.*

2. Verbs expressing hope or threat or promise sometimes have μή with the future infinitive, e.g.:

> οἱ Ἀθηναῖοι ἤλπιζον τοὺς Πελοποννησίους **μὴ** ἐς τὸ ἐγγυτέρω προϊέναι.
> *The Athenians hoped the Peloponnesians would **not** advance nearer.*

3. In indirect questions μή is sometimes found instead of the usual οὐ.
4. Note the following compound negatives:

οὐδέ, *nor, and not, not even*	μηδέ
οὔτε ... οὔτε, *neither ... nor*	μήτε ... μήτε
οὐδείς, οὐδεμία, οὐδέν, *no one, nothing*	μηδείς, μηδεμία, μηδέν
οὐδέποτε, *never*	μηδέποτε
οὐκέτι, *no longer*	μηκέτι
οὔπω, *not yet*	μήπω
οὐδέτερος, -ᾱ, -ον, *neither* (of two)	μηδέτερος, -ᾱ, -ον

5.   Repeated negatives normally reinforce each other, e.g.,

οὐκ ἔπραξε τοιοῦτο **οὐδεὶς οὐδέποτε**.
No one ever did such a thing.

But if the compound negative precedes the simple negative, they cancel each other, making an emphatic positive, e.g.,

οὐδεὶς οὐχ ὁρᾷ τὴν ναῦν.
No one doesn't see (= *everyone* sees) the ship.

Supplementary Grammar Exercise 7 (after Chapter 30)

Translate into English. Show how the rules above are illustrated in these sentences:

1.   οὐδέποτε οὕτως ἐδήχθην ὡς νῦν, ἅτε (*because*) τῶν πολῑτῶν οὐ παρόντων ἐς τὴν ἐκκλησίᾱν.

2.   μηκέτι ἐν Πυκνὶ μένωμεν· οὐ γὰρ ἥκουσιν οὐδὲ οἱ πρυτάνεις.

3.   ἐὰν μὴ δι' ὀλίγου ἀφίκωνται οἱ πρυτάνεις, οἱ πολῖται οὐκέτι μενοῦσιν.

4.   εἰ μὴ περὶ εἰρήνης λέγοιτε, οὐκ ἂν σῑγῴην ἐγώ.

5.   ὁ κῆρυξ τὸν Δικαιόπολιν ἐκέλευσε μὴ λοιδορεῖν τοὺς ῥήτορας μηδὲ ὑποκρούειν.

6.   οἱ βάρβαροι ἄνδρας οὐχ ἡγοῦνται τοὺς μὴ δυναμένους πλεῖστα πιεῖν.

7.   ὁ Δικαιόπολις σαφῶς ᾔδει τὸν βασιλέᾱ οὐκ οὐδέποτε χρῡσίον πέμψοντα.

8.   εἴθε μηκέτι ψεύδοιντο (*lie*) οἱ πρέσβεις.

9.   οὐ γὰρ οἷός τ' ἐστὶν οὐδέτερος τὸν δῆμον ἐξαπατᾶν (*to deceive*).

10.   οὐδεὶς γὰρ οὐκ οἶδεν αὐτοὺς οὐδὲν ἀληθὲς λέγοντας.

11.   οὐκ ἐθελόντων οὔτε τῶν πρυτανέων οὔτε τοῦ δήμου σπονδὰς ποιεῖσθαι, τῷ Δικαιοπόλιδι ἔδοξε μὴ ἀθῡμεῖν (*to despair*) ἀλλὰ ἔγρον μέγα ἐργάσασθαι.

12.   φοβούμενος γὰρ μὴ ἄλλως (*any other way*) οὐδέποτε γένοιτο εἰρήνη, τὸν Ἀμφίθεον ἐς Λακεδαίμονα ἔπεμψεν.

13. ἤλπιζε γὰρ τοὺς Λακεδαιμονίους μὴ ἐκβαλεῖν τὸν Ἀμφίθεον, ἀθάνατον ὄντα,
ἀλλὰ σπονδὰς ποιήσειν.

_____

_____

14. ὅστις γὰρ ἂν ἀθανάτου μὴ ἀκούῃ, δι’ ὀλίγου κακῶς πράττει.

_____

15. καίπερ οὔπω ἐπανελθόντος τοῦ Ἀμφιθέου, ὁ Δικαιόπολις χαίρει ὥσπερ οὐκέτι
πολέμῳ χρώμενος.

_____

_____

Uses of the Participle

Aspect and Time

The present participle represents the action as a process (simultaneous with the time of the main verb), the aorist as an event (simultaneous with or prior to the time of the main verb), and the perfect as a state; the future participle is used when the action of the participle is subsequent to that of the main verb (often expressing purpose, with or without ὡς), e.g.:

ἐξῆλθον **βοῶντες**. (present; simultaneous process)
*They went out **shouting**.*

βοήσᾱς εἶπεν. (aorist; simultaneous event)
*He said **with a shout**.*

τὴν γῆν **καταλιπόντες** ταχέως ἔπλευσαν. (aorist; prior event)
***After leaving** the land, they sailed quickly.*

κεῖνται **τεθνηκότες**. (perfect; state)
*They lie **dead**.*

ἥκουσιν ὑμῖν (**ὡς**) **ἀγγελοῦντες**. (future; subsequent)
*They have come **to tell** you.*

Substantive Use of Participles

With definite articles, participles may form phrases that function as nouns or noun phrases, e.g.:

οἱ τεθνηκότες = *the dead*   οἱ θεώμενοι = *the spectators*
οἱ τὴν πατρίδα φιλοῦντες = *those who love their country*

Participles Taking the Place of Clauses

Participles may be used in Greek to represent most of the relationships between verbs for which English uses clauses, e.g.:

1. Temporal, e.g.:

    οἴκαδε **ἐπανελθόντες** τὸν πατέρα ἐζήτουν.
    ***When they had returned home**, they looked for their father.*

    ἐν τοῖς ἀγροῖς **μένοντες** πολλὰ καὶ κακὰ ἔπασχον.
    ***While they were staying** in the country, they suffered many terrible things.*

2. Concessive, usually with καί or καίπερ, e.g.:

    καί/καίπερ πολλὰ καὶ κακὰ **πάσχοντες**, οὐκ εἶξαν.
    ***Although they were suffering** many hardships, they did not yield.*

3. Causal, often with ἅτε (real cause) or ὡς (alleged cause), e.g.:

    ἅτε πολλὰ καὶ κακὰ **παθόντες**, τοῖς πολεμίοις ἑαυτοὺς παρέδοσαν.
    ***Because they had suffered** many hardships, they surrendered to the enemy.*

    τὸν Περικλέᾱ ἐν αἰτίᾳ εἶχον **ὡς πείσαντα** σφᾶς πολεμεῖν.
    *They blamed Pericles **on the grounds that he had persuaded** them to go to war.*

4. Purpose, with future participle with or without ὡς, e.g.:

    ἥκουσιν (**ὡς**) ὑμῖν τὰ γενόμενα **ἀγγελοῦντες**.
    *They have come **to tell** you what happened.*

5. With ὥσπερ = *as if*, e.g.:

   ὥσπερ ἤδη σαφῶς **εἰδότες** ὃ δεῖ πράττειν, οὐκ ἐθέλετε ἀκούειν.
   *You do not wish to listen, **as if you** clearly **knew (as if** clearly **knowing)**
   what has to be done.*

6. Conditional, negative μή, e.g.:

   οὐδέποτε μαθήσεται κιθαρίζειν **μὴ μελετῶν**.
   *He will never learn to play the lyre, **if he does not practice**.*

7. Indirect statement after verbs of knowing, seeing, and hearing, e.g.:

   οἶδά σε σώφρονα **ὄντα**.
   *I know that you **are** wise.*

   ᾐσθόμην εἰς κίνδυνον **καταστάς**.
   *I perceived **that I had got** into danger.*

   So also sometimes after other verbs, e.g., ἀγγέλλω:

   Κῦρον **ἐπιστρατεύοντα** ἤγγειλεν.
   *He announced that Cyrus **was marching against** (them).*

Supplementary Participles

λανθάνω	ῥᾷον <u>ἔλαθον</u> **εἰσελθόντες**. *They entered more easily without being seen.*
	<u>ἔλαθεν</u> ἑαυτὸν τοῦτο **ποιήσας**. *He did this unawares.*
τυγχάνω	<u>ἔτυχον</u> **παρόντες** οἱ πρέσβεις. *The ambassadors happened to be present.*
	<u>ἔτυχον</u> ἐπὶ τοὺς Πέρσας **στρατευόμενοι**. *They were just then campaigning against the Persians.*
φθάνω	<u>ἔφθασαν</u> πολλῷ τοὺς Πέρσας **ἀφικόμενοι**. *They, arriving, anticipated the Persians by much.* *They arrived long before the Persians.*
φαίνομαι	<u>φαίνεται</u> σοφὸς **ὤν**. *He is shown to be wise.* Compare: <u>φαίνεται</u> σοφὸς **εἶναι**. *He seems to be wise.*
δῆλός ἐστιν	<u>δῆλοί εἰσιν</u> ἡμῖν **ἐπιβουλεύοντες**. *They are clearly plotting against us.* *It is clear that they are plotting against us.*

Genitive Absolute and Accusative Absolute

See pages 167 and 169–170 of this Workbook.

Supplementary Grammar Exercise 8 (after Chapter 30)

Translate into English. Show how the rules above are illustrated in these sentences:

1. ὁ Δικαιόπολις πάντας τοὺς πολίτας ἔφθασεν ἐς τὴν Πύκνα ἀφικόμενος.

2. μόνος ὤν, στένει, εἰρήνης ἐρῶν, στυγῶν μὲν ἄστυ, τὸν δ' ἑαυτοῦ δῆμον ποθῶν.

3. ἥκει παρεσκευασμένος τοὺς ῥήτορας λοιδορεῖν, μὴ λέγοντας περὶ τῆς εἰρήνης.

---

4. ὁ Δικαιόπολις τοὺς πρυτάνεις ἐν ὀργῇ εἶχεν ὡς οὐ τῑμῶντας τὴν εἰρήνην.

---

5. ἔτυχον παρόντες οἱ παρὰ βασιλέως πρέσβεις, ἀπὸ τῆς Ἀσίᾱς ἀφικόμενοι.

---

6. ὁ Δικαιόπολις τοὺς τῶν Ἀθηναίων πρέσβεις στυγεῖ, ὡς ἀλάζονας ὄντας.

---

7. ὠργίζετο αὐτοῖς ἅτε δύο δραχμὰς τῆς ἡμέρᾱς δεξαμένοις.

---

8. δῆλοί εἰσιν οἱ πρέσβεις ψευδῆ λέγοντες.

---

9. πάντες ἴσμεν τὸν βασιλέᾱ οὐδὲν χρῡσίον ἡμῖν πέμψοντα.

---

10. οἱ βάρβαροι ἄνδρας ἡγοῦνται μόνους τοὺς πλεῖστα δυναμένους πιεῖν.

---

11. ὁ Δικαιόπολις φησὶν ἀνοήτους εἶναι τοὺς Ἀθηναίους, προσδοκῶντας χρῡσίον ἐκ τῶν βαρβάρων.

---

12. ὁ Ἀμφίθεος ἔλαθε τοὺς τοξότᾱς ἐς τὴν ἐκκλησίᾱν ἐσδραμών.

---

13. καίπερ θεὸς ὤν, οὐ δύναμαι πρὸς τὴν Λακεδαίμονα πορεύεσθαι, μὴ διδόντων μοι ἐφόδια (*journey money*) τῶν πρυτάνεων.

---

14. ὁ Δικαιοπόλις τὸν Ἀμφίθεον ἔπεμψεν ὡς σπονδὰς ποιησόμενον πρὸς τοὺς Λακεδαιμονίους.

---

15. χαίρει ὥσπερ ἤδη πεποιημένων τῶν σπονδῶν.

Third Person Imperatives

Greek verbs have 3rd person imperatives, e.g.:

οἱ δ' οὖν βοώντων.
*So **let them shout!***

The complete sets of present and aorist imperatives of λύω are:

Present Active
Singular

2	λῦ-ε	*Be loosening!*
3	λῡ-έτω	*Let him/her be loosening!*

Plural

2	λύ-ετε	*Be loosening!*
3	λῡ-όντων	*Let them be loosening!*

Present Middle
Singular

2	λύ-ου	*Be ransoming!*
3	λῡ-έσθω	*Let him/her be ransoming!*

Plural

2	λύ-εσθε	*Be ransoming!*
3	λῡ-έσθων	*Let them be ransoming!*

Present Passive
Singular

2	λύ-ου	*Be in the process of being loosened!*
3	λῡ-έσθω	*Let him/her be in the process of being loosened!*

Plural

2	λύ-εσθε	*Be in the process of being loosened!*
3	λῡ-έσθων	*Let them be in the process of being loosened!*

Aorist Active
Singular

2	λῦ-σον	*Loosen!*
3	λῡ-σάτω	*Let him/her loosen!*

Plural

2	λύ-σατε	*Loosen!*
3	λῡ-σάντων	*Let them loosen!*

Aorist Middle
Singular

2	λῦ-σαι	*Ransom!*
3	λῡ-σάσθω	*Let him/her ransom!*

Plural

2	λύ-σασθε	*Ransom!*
3	λῡ-σάσθων	*Let them ransom!*

Aorist Passive
Singular

2	λύ-θητι	*Be loosened!*
3	λυ-θήτω	*Let him/her be loosened!*

Plural

2	λύ-θητε	*Be loosened!*
3	λυ-θέντων	*Let them be loosened!*

Supplementary Grammar Exercise 9

Translate into English.   Identify all 3rd person imperatives:

1. οἱ μὲν δοῦλοι τοὺς βοῦς λῡσάντων καὶ οἴκαδε ἐπανελθόντων, ὁ δὲ παῖς μετ' ἐμοῦ σπευδέτω.

2. μὴ φοβείσθων αἱ παρθένοι ἀλλ' ἐν τῇ οἰκίᾳ ἥσυχοι (*quietly*) μενόντων.

3. πάντες οἱ παρόντες σῑγώντων καὶ τὴν πομπὴν θεᾱσθων.

4. μὴ ὀργισθήτω ὁ δεσπότης ἀλλὰ τοὺς τοῦ δούλου λόγους ἀκουσάτω.

5. μὴ μαχέσθων οἱ νεᾱνίαι ἀλλὰ καθήσθων ἐν τῇ ἀγορᾷ.

Review of Prepositions

The following list includes all of the prepositions that have occurred in the α and β stories and the tail readings in Books I and II. Prepositions generally have a range of meanings that must be learned by observation of their use in context. The number and Greek letter after the entry for a preposition indicate the chapter in which the preposition occurs in a vocabulary list; e.g., the entry "**ἀνά** + acc. (5α)" indicates that this preposition occurs in Vocabulary 5α. The absence of a number and Greek letter after an entry means that the preposition does not occur in any vocabulary list; these prepositions are used in the stories and glossed when they occur. The phrases given as examples usually contain the first occurrences of the prepositions in the stories; a preposition often occurs in a story before it is formally introduced in a vocabulary list.

ἅμα + dat. (29δ)
  together with: ἅμα τῷ παιδί
    (5α:21)
ἀνά + acc. (5α)
  up: ἀνὰ τὴν ὁδόν (5α:4)
ἀντί + gen. (28β)
  instead of: ἀντὶ φίλου (28β:25–26)
ἀντίον + gen.
  opposite: ἀντίον τῆς ἵππου
    (27β:18)
ἀπό + gen. (4α)
  from: ἀπὸ τοῦ ἄστεως (4α:20)
διά + gen. (9α)
  through: δι' ὀλίγου, *through little
    (time) = soon* (5α:8)
διά + acc. (18β)
  because of: διὰ τοῦτο (18β:46)
ἐγγύς + gen. (13β)
  near: ἐγγὺς τῆς οἰκίας (9 tail
    reading:8)
εἰς + acc. (2β)
  into: εἰς τὸν ἀγρόν (2β:3)
  to: εἰς τὴν κρήνην (4 tail
    reading:1)
  at (with verbs such as ἀφικνέομαι):
    εἰς τὴν νῆσον (6α:14)
  for: εἰς πολλὰς ἡμέρας (6β:5–6)
  for (of purpose): εἰς τὸ λέγειν τε
    καὶ πράττειν (24β:16)
  against: ἐς αὐτόν (23 tail
    reading:1)
ἐκ, ἐξ + gen. (3α)
  out of: ἐκ τοῦ ἀγροῦ (1β:2), ἐξ
    ἔργων (8α:23)
ἐκτός + gen. (22β)
  outside: ἐκτὸς ὁρίων (22β:30)

ἐν + dat. (3β)
  in: ἐν ταῖς Ἀθήναις (1α:1–2)
  on: ἐν τῇ ὁδῷ (4β:9)
  among: ἐν τοῖς δούλοις (11 tail:5)
ἕνεκα + preceding gen. (21α)
  for the sake of; because of: τίνος
    ἕνεκα (21α:5–6)
ἐντός + gen. (20γ)
  within: λιμένος πολυβενθέος ἐντός
    (16β:29)
  inside: ἐντὸς τῶν τειχῶν (20γ:12)
ἐξόπισθε(ν) + gen. (30δ)
  behind: ἐξόπισθε τῆς κανηφόρου
    (30δ:148)
ἔξω + gen. (20δ)
  outside: ἔξω τῶν τειχῶν (20δ:31–
    32)
ἐπί + gen. (20δ and 24β)
  toward, in the direction of: ἐπὶ τῆς
    Κορίνθου (20δ:12)
  on: ἐπὶ τῶν βάθρων (24β:6)
ἐπί + dat. (5β and 18β)
  upon, on: ἐπὶ τῇ γῇ (5β:16)
  for (of price): ἐπὶ μιᾷ δραχμῇ
    (18β:12–13)
  for (of purpose): ἐπὶ ναυμαχίᾳ
    (29α:10)
ἐπί + acc. (5β, 9α, 26α, and 29α)
  at; against: ἐπ' αὐτόν (5β:8)
  onto (with ἀναβαίνω): ἐπὶ ἄκρᾱν
    τὴν ἀκτήν (7 tail reading:4)
  upon: ἐπὶ τὸν ὄχθον (15 tail
    reading:3)
  to or *for* (of direction or purpose):
    ἐπὶ πόλεμον (26α:8–9)
  for (of time): ἐπὶ δύο ἔτεα (27α:1)

at (of time): ἐπὶ τὴν ἔω (29α:26)

κατά + acc. (5α, 11β, 17β, 21β, 24α, 25α, 26α, and 28α)

down: κατὰ τὴν ὁδόν (5 tail reading:5)

distributive: κατ᾽ ἔτος, *each year* (6α:5) and καθ᾽ ἡμέρᾱν, *every day* (24α:2)

by: κατὰ θάλατταν (11β:38)

on: κατὰ τοῦτο τοῦ ὄρους (14 tail reading:6)

according to: κατὰ νόμον (17β:46)

at (of time): κατ᾽ ἐκεῖνον τὸν χρόνον (21β:1–2)

through: κατὰ τοὺς θησαυρούς (25α:13–14)

with regard to: κατὰ τὸν παῖδα (26α:4)

after: κατ᾽ αὐτόν (28α:11)

μετά + gen. (6α)

with: μετὰ τῶν ἑταίρων (6α:11)

μετά + acc. (of time and place) (6α)

after (of time): μετὰ τὸ δεῖπνον (3β:7)

after (of place): μετ᾽ αὐτούς (5α:9)

ὄπισθε(ν) + gen. (27β)

behind: ὄπισθεν τοῦ ἱεροῦ (9α:35)

παρά + gen. (30β)

from: παρὰ σοῦ (26 tail reading:11)

παρά + dat.

at the house of: παρ᾽ ἑαυτῷ (24α:9)

παρά + acc. (11α and 29δ)

to (of persons only): παρὰ ἰᾱτρόν τινα (11α:4)

along, past: παρὰ τὴν Σικελίᾱν (10 tail reading:2)

in respect of each = distributive: παρ᾽ ἕκαστον ἔργον καὶ λόγον (24α:21–22)

περί + gen. (7α and 18α)

about, concerning: περὶ ἀνδρὸς πολυτρόπου (7α:6)

around: περὶ ἧς (18α:3)

περί + dat. (29δ)

concerning: περὶ τῷ χωρίῳ (29δ:9–10)

περί + acc. (7α)

around: περὶ Τροίᾱν (7α:8)

πλήν + gen. (29ε)

except, except for: πλὴν ἑνός (8 tail reading:7)

πρό + gen. (10β)

before (of time or place): πρὸ τῆς νυκτός (10β:9–10)

in preference to: πρὸ εἰρήνης (28β:29)

πρός + gen. (26β)

from, at the hand of: πρὸς αὐτοῦ (26β:5)

πρός + dat. (4α and 24β)

at: πρὸς τῇ κρήνῃ (4: title)

near, by: πρὸς τῇ ὁδῷ (5 tail reading:9)

in addition to: πρὸς τούτοις (24β:11)

πρός + acc. (1β, 11β, and 27α)

to, toward: πρὸς τὸ ἕρμα (1β:3)

upon, onto: πρὸς τὸν τοῦ Δικαιοπόλιδος πόδα (3α:18)

against: πρὸς τοὺς λίθους (11β:3–4)

toward (of time): πρὸς ἑσπέρᾱν (17α:25)

with (i.e., in relation to): πρὸς ῎Αμᾱσιν (27α:45)

σύν + dat. (17α)

with: σὺν θεῷ (12β:30–31)

ὑπέρ + gen. (8β)

on behalf of, for: ὑπὲρ σοῦ (7 tail reading:2)

over, above: ὑπὲρ Θερμοπυλῶν (14 tail reading: title)

ὑπέρ + acc. (18α)

over, above: ὑπὲρ τὸ ὄρος (14 tail reading:1)

ὑπό + gen. (16α)

under: ὑπὸ τῶν προβάτων (7β:33)

by (of agent): ὑφ᾽ ἡμῶν (16α:16) (22α:23)

because of: ὑπὸ τῆς παρεούσης συμφορῆς (28α:17)

ὑπό + dat. (5β)

under: ὑπὸ τῷ δένδρῳ (1β:5)

ὑπό + acc. (5β and 29ε)

under (with verbs of motion): ὑπὸ τὸ ζυγόν (2β:7–8)

at (of time): ὑπὸ νύκτα (29ε:29)

Supplementary Grammar Exercise 10

Translate the underlined English phrases into Greek using the nouns and prepositions supplied:

1. He came <u>together with the woman</u>. ἡ γυνή: ἅμα _____

2. She chose me <u>instead of her friend</u>. ἡ φίλη: ἀντί _____

3. She left <u>because of the trouble</u>. τὸ πρᾶγμα: διά _____

4. He bought the sacrifice <u>for two drachmas</u>.
   δύο δραχμαί: ἐπί _____

5. The dog waited <u>outside the sheepfold</u>.
   τὸ αὔλιον: ἐκτός _____

6. The sheep slept <u>inside the sheepfold</u>.
   τὸ αὔλιον: ἐντός _____

7. The men are fighting <u>for the sake of honor</u>.
   ἡ τῑμή: ἕνεκα _____

8. He is marching <u>behind the general</u>.
   ὁ στρατηγός: ἐξόπισθε(ν) _____

9. They camped <u>outside the gates</u>. αἱ πύλαι: ἔξω _____

10. They traveled <u>in the direction of Athens</u>.
    αἱ Ἀθῆναι: ἐπί _____

11. We were delayed <u>for three days</u>. τρεῖς ἡμέραι: ἐπί _____

12. He tried to do it <u>at the right time</u>. ὁ καιρός: κατά _____

13. Dicaeoplis was a farmer <u>at this time</u>.
    οὗτος ὁ χρόνος: κατά _____

14. We marched <u>through Greece</u>. ἡ Ἑλλάς: κατά _____

15. It was hidden <u>behind the walls</u>. τὸ τεῖχος: ὄπισθε(ν) _____

16. Messengers just arrived <u>from the king</u>.
    ὁ βασιλεύς: παρά _____

17. They sailed <u>along the island</u>. ἡ νῆσος: παρά _____

18. We worried greatly <u>concerning the empty house</u>.
    ἡ κενὴ οἰκίᾱ: περί _____

19. They all surrendered <u>except for the general</u>.
    ὁ στρατηγός: πλήν _____

20. We suffered hardship <u>from the king</u>.
    ὁ βασιλεύς: πρός _____

21. <u>In addition to harmony</u>, they are taught rhythm.
    ἡ ἁρμονίᾱ: πρός _____

22. They made a treaty <u>with the enemy</u>.
    οἱ πολέμιοι: πρός _____

23. The girls walked <u>with their friends</u>. ἡ φίλη: σύν _____

24. They journeyed <u>over the rough land</u>.
    ἡ τρᾱχεῖα γῆ: ὑπέρ _____

25. They prospered <u>at the time of peace</u>.
    ἡ εἰρήνη: ὑπό _____

ANSWER KEY

ANSWERS: CHAPTER 17

Exercise 17α
1. ἐλήφθη, ληφθήσεται. 2. ἐλήφθημεν, ληφθησόμεθα. 3. ἐλήφθησαν, ληφθήσονται. 4. ἐφιλήθης, φιληθήσει or φιληθήσῃ. 5. ἐφιλήθημεν, φιληθησόμεθα. 6. ἐφιλήθητε, φιληθήσεσθε. 7. ἐτῑμήθησαν, τῑμηθήσονται. 8. ἐτῑμήθη, τῑμηθήσεται. 9. ἐτῑμήθην, τῑμηθήσομαι. 10. ἐδηλώθην, δηλωθήσομαι. 11. ἐδηλώθης, δηλωθήσει or δηλωθήσῃ. 12. δηλωθῆναι, δηλωθήσεσθαι.

Exercise 17β
1. λυθεῖσα. 2. φιληθεῖσα. 3. ληφθὲν. 4. τῑμηθέντες. 5. δηλωθέν.

Exercise 17γ
1. ἐπέμφθη, πεμφθήσεται. 2. ἐφυλάχθης, φυλαχθήσει or φυλαχθήσῃ. 3. ἐψεύσθημεν, ψευσθησόμεθα. 4. πείσθητι. 5. ἐγνώσθησαν, γνωσθήσονται. 6. ἐκελεύσθητε, κελευσθήσεσθε. 7. ἐβλήθην, βληθήσομαι. 8. ἠλάθην, ἐλαθήσομαι. 9. εὑρέθης or ηὑρέθης, εὑρεθήσει or εὑρεθήσῃ. 10. ὤφθησαν, ὀφθήσονται.

Exercise 17δ
1. I arrive (at). 2. I sit. 3. formerly, before, earlier; first. 4. I follow. 5. I happen to be sitting. 6. I get to know, learn. 7. to where? whither? 8. I get up. 9. with.

Exercise 17ε
1. ἔγωγε. 2. ἀπέχω. 3. σὺν θεοῖς. 4. δέω. 5. πότερον . . . ἤ. 6. αἴρω. 7. οἶδα. 8. πλέω. 9. τυγχάνω.

Exercise 17ζ
1. ἀρῶ, ἦρα, ἦρκα, ἦρμαι, ἤρθην. 2. ἀφέξω, ἀπέσχον. 3. ἀφίξομαι, ἀφῑκόμην, ἀφῖγμαι. 4. γνώσομαι, ἔγνων, ἔγνωκα, ἔγνωσμαι, ἐγνώσθην. 5. δήσω, ἔδησα, δέδεκα, δέδεμαι, ἐδέθην. 6. ἕψομαι, ἑσπόμην. 7. πλεύσομαι, ἔπλευσα, πέπλευκα. 8. τεύξομαι, ἔτυχον, τετύχηκα. 9. λύσω, ἔλῡσα, λέλυκα, λέλυμαι, ἐλύθην. 10. δακρύσω, ἐδάκρῡσα, δεδάκρῡκα, δεδάκρῡμαι. 11. παύσω, ἔπαυσα, πέπαυκα, πέπαυμαι, ἐπαύθην.

Exercise 17η
The Tablet of Cebes I.

We were happening to be walking around in the sanctuary of Kronos, in which we were looking at many other temple offerings; and a certain tablet was set up in front of the temple, on which there was a certain picture, strange and having peculiar stories, which we were not able to figure out what in the world they were. For the representation seemed to us to be neither a city nor a military camp, but there was an enclosure, having within itself two other enclosures, one bigger, the other smaller. There was also a gate in the first enclosure. And at the gate a big crowd seemed to us to be standing, and also within, in the enclosure, a certain number/multitude of women were seen. And standing in the gateway, a certain old man was giving the appearance as [if] giving [= of giving] some orders to the entering crowd.

Exercise 17θ
1. ἐνεγράφημεν, ἐγγραφησόμεθα. 2. ἐνεγράφησαν, ἐγγραφήσονται. 3. ἐγγράφητι. 4. διεφθάρη, διαφθαρήσεται. 5. διαφθαρῆναι, διαφθαρήσεσθαι. 6. διεφθάρην, διαφθαρήσομαι. 7. διεφθάρητε, διαφθαρήσεσθε.

Exercise 17ι
1. ἐδυνήθην. 2. ἐχάρησαν. 3. ὠργίσθη. 4. ἐπορεύθητε. 5. ἐβουλήθης. 6. ἐπιστηθείς. 7. ἐπιστηθῆναι. 8. διελεξάμεθα or διελέχθημεν.

Exercise 17κ

1. Cheer up! Don't be afraid! 2. suppliant. 3. holy, pious. 4. sacred precinct. 5. not much later, soon. 6. somehow. 7. I think; I am minded. 8. servant; attendant. 9. I entrust.

Exercise 17λ

1. ὁ νόμος. 2. καθαρός, -ά, -όν. 3. ὀψέ. 4. ἀκέομαι. 5. ἡ ψυχή. 6. κατά. 7. χρή. 8. θαρρέω. 9. ἱερός or ὅσιος.

Exercise 17μ

1. ἀκοῦμαι, ἠκεσάμην. 2. ἐπιτρέψω, ἐπέτρεψα, ἐπιτέτροφα, ἐπιτέτραμμαι, ἐπετράπην. 3. πιστεύσω, ἐπίστευσα, πεπίστευκα, πεπίστευμαι, ἐπιστεύθην. 4. κελεύσω, ἐκέλευσα, κεκέλευκα, κεκέλευσμαι, ἐκελεύσθην. 5. πορεύσομαι, ἐπορευσάμην, πεπόρευμαι, ἐπορεύθην.

Exercise 17ν

The Tablet of Cebes II.

While we were puzzling among ourselves about the story-telling for a long time, an old man standing nearby said, "Strangers, you are experiencing nothing strange, being at a loss about this picture. For not even do many of the natives know what in the world this story-telling means; for it is not a local dedication; but a certain stranger once long ago arrived here, an intelligent man and one skilled with regard to wisdom, one pursuing in word and deed a Pythagorean and Parmenidean life-style, who dedicated to Kronos both this sanctuary and the picture."

Stranger "Then," I said," do you know even the man himself, [from] having seen [him]?"

Old Man "[Yes,] and I admired him," he said, "[since he was] a very old man, being rather young [myself]. For he was discussing many serious things. And at that very time I heard him explaining also about this story-telling many times."

ANSWERS: CHAPTER 18

Exercise 18α

1. δίδως. 2. ἐδίδοσαν. 3. ἐδίδοτε. 4. ἔδωκε(ν). 5. δώσουσι(ν). 6. ἔδοτε. 7. ἐδίδουν. 8. διδόᾱσι(ν). 9. διδόναι. 10. δώσεις. 11. δίδου. 12. διδοῦσα. 13. δούς. 14. δότε. 15. δοῦναι.

Exercise 18β

1. δώσομαι. 2. δίδοται. 3. δομένῳ. 4. δίδοσθαι. 5. ἔδου. 6. δόσθαι. 7. διδομένου. 8. δίδοσαι. 9. ἐδόμην. 10. ἐδίδοτο. 11. ἐδίδοντο. 12. ἐδιδόμην. 13. δώσεσθαι. 14. ἐδιδόμεθα. 15. δόσθε. 16. δίδοσθε.

Exercise 18γ

1. ἐδόθη. 2. δοθήσεται. 3. δοθήσονται. 4. ἐδόθησαν.

Exercise 18δ

1. it is clear. 2. I put, place. 3. thanks; gratitude. 4. holy; august. 5. over, above. 6. about, concerning; around. 7. I laugh.

Exercise 18ε

1. χάριν ἀποδίδωμι. 2. εὐμενής, -ές. 3. δίδωμι. 4. ὁ ὕπνος. 5. κῑνέω. 6. δῆλος, -η, -ον. 7. ὑπέρ.

Exercise 18ζ

1. γελάσομαι, ἐγέλασα, ἐγελάσθην. 2. δώσω, ἔδωκα, δέδωκα, δέδομαι, ἐδόθην. 3. θήσω, ἔθηκα, τέθηκα, ἐτέθην. 4. φιλήσω, ἐφίλησα, πεφίληκα, πεφίλημαι, ἐφιλήθην. 5. δόξω, ἔδοξα, δέδογμαι, ἐδόχθην. 6. καλῶ, ἐκάλεσα, κέκληκα, κέκλημαι, ἐκλήθην. 7. πλεύσομαι or πλευσοῦμαι, ἔπλευσα, πέπλευκα. 8. σκέψομαι, ἐσκεψάμην, ἔσκεμμαι. 9. κῑνήσω, ἐκίνησα, κεκίνηκα, κεκίνημαι, ἐκῑνήθην.

Exercise 18η

The Tablet of Cebes III.

    Stranger "Well then, by Zeus," I said, "if there does not happen to be any pressing [great] business for you, explain [it] to us; for we very much desire to hear what in the world the story is."

    Old Man "No problem, strangers," he said. "But first it is necessary for you to hear *this*, that the explanation has something dangerous [in it]."

    Stranger "Such as what?" I said.

    Old Man "[Just this,] that, if you (will) pay attention," he said, "and if you (will) understand the things said, you will be wise and happy, but if not, being [becoming] foolish and unhappy and spiteful and stupid, you will live badly. The explanation is like the riddle of the Sphinx, which that one used to propose to humans. If a person understood it, he was saved, if he did not understand, he perished at the hands of the Sphinx.

Exercise 18θ

1. τίθεμεν. 2. θήσουσι(ν). 3. τίθησι(ν). 4. ἔθηκα. 5. ἔθεμεν. 6. τιθέναι. 7. θήσειν 8. ἐτίθεσαν. 9. τιθέᾱσι(ν). 10. ἐτίθην. 11. θεῖναι 12. τίθετε. 13. τιθεῖσα. 14. θείς. 15. θές.

Exercise 18ι

1. τίθεσο. 2. ἐτίθετο. 3. θησόμεθα. 4. τίθεσθαι. 5. τιθεμένῃ. 6. ἔθετο. 7. τίθενται. 8. ἐθέμην. 9. τίθεται 10. ἐτιθέμην. 11. ἐτίθεσο. 12. θέσθε. 13. θεμένης. 14. θήσεσθαι. 15. ἐτίθεσθε. 16. θέσθαι.

Exercise 18κ

1. ἐτέθη. 2. τεθήσεται. 3. τεθήσονται. 4. ἐτέθησαν.

Exercise 18λ

1. I march against, attack. 2. rather than. 3. certainly; however. 4. matter; trouble. 5. they have been for a long time now. 6. I set up; I dedicate. 7. enemy. 8. How are things? 9. sacrifice. 10. because of. 11. I miss; I make a mistake, am mistaken. 12. I run toward. 13. certainly not. 14. at; of price, for. 15. I am right.

Exercise 18μ

1. τὰ χρήματα. 2. φιλαίτερος, -ᾱ, -ον. 3. κρατέω. 4. παραδίδωμι. 5. διά + acc. 6. πάλαι. 7. διότι. 8. τίνα γνώμην ἔχεις; 9. ἐχθρός, -ά, -όν. 10. τρέχω. 11. μᾶλλον. 12. τὸ κράτος. 13. ὑγιής, -ές. 14. ἐπί + dat. 15. ἡ γνώμη.

Exercise 18ν

The Tablet of Cebes III.

"It's the same thing in the case of this explanation. Mindlessness/Foolishness is a Sphinx for humankind. It poses these things as riddles, what [is] good, what [is] bad, what [is] neither good nor bad in life. If someone does not understand these things, he perishes at its hands, not at once, as the one eaten up by the Sphinx died, but little by little he is destroyed in his whole life, just as those [who are] handed over for retribution. But if someone does learn, his mindlessness/foolishness perishes instead, and he himself is saved and becomes blessed and happy in his entire life. So you pay attention, and do not be heedless!"

Exercise 18ξ

1. ἁμαρτήσομαι, ἥμαρτον, ἡμάρτηκα, ἡμάρτημαι, ἡμαρτήθην. 2. δραμοῦμαι, ἔδραμον, δεδράμηκα. 3. τῑμήσω, ἐτίμησα, τετίμηκα, τετίμημαι, ἐτῑμήθην. 4. πειράσω, ἐπείρᾱσα, πεπείρᾱκα, πεπείρᾱμαι, ἐπειράθην. 5. κρατήσω, ἐκράτησα, κεκράτηκα, κεκράτημαι, ἐκρατήθην. 6. θεάσομαι, ἐθεᾱσάμην, τεθέᾱμαι. 7. χρήσομαι, ἐχρησάμην, κέχρημαι, ἐχρήσθην. 8. γελάσομαι, ἐγέλασα, γεγέλασμαι, ἐγελάσθην. 9. δηλώσω, ἐδήλωσα, δεδήλωκα, δεδήλωμαι, ἐδηλώθην. 10. τολμήσω, ἐτόλμησα, τετόλμηκα, τετόλμημαι, ἐτολμήθην.

ANSWERS: CHAPTER 19

Exercise 19α

1. βαίνοντος; the farmer walking to Athens, as the farmer is walking to Athens, etc.
2. γυναικὸς; the woman being present, since the woman is present, etc. 3. γενομένης; day having come about, at daybreak. 4. ἐκφευγόντων; as the slaves are fleeing out of the field, since the slaves are escaping from the field, etc. 5. τοῦ; the man coming into the house, as the man is coming into the house, etc. 6. ποιησαμένου; the priest having made the sacrifice, when the priest had made the sacrifice, etc. 7. παίδων; the children (boys) being present, since the children (boys) are present, etc. 8. πλευσάσης; the ship having sailed, although the ship had sailed, etc.

Exercise 19β

a = 4. b = 10. c = 7. d = 6. e = 7. f = 3. g = 9. h = 8. i = 5. j = 8. k = 9. l = 2. m = 8. n = 5. o = 12. p = 11. q = 1. r = 7.

Exercise 19γ

1. I stood. 2. olive; olive tree. 3. I return home. 4. I collect, gather. 5. I stand.

Exercise 19δ

1. ὁ νόστος. 2. ἵστημι. 3. τὸ πεδίον. 4. ἐσθίω. 5. ἐστάθην. 6. ἀνίστημι.

Exercise 19ε

1. ἔδομαι, ἔφαγον, ἐδήδοκα. 2. στήσω, ἔστησα, ἔστην, ἔστηκα, ἐστάθην. 3. συλλέξω, συνέλεξα, συνείλοχα, συνείλεγμαι, συνελέγην. 4. βλάψω, ἔβλαψα, βέβλαφα, βέβλαμμαι, ἐβλάφθην or ἐβλάβην. 5. λείψω, ἔλιπον, λέλοιπα, λέλειμμαι, ἐλείφθην. 6. πέμψω, ἔπεμψα, πέπομφα, πέπεμμαι, ἐπέμφθην.

Exercise 19ζ

The Tablet of Cebes IV.

Stranger "O Heracles, how you have put us into [a state of] great desire, if these things are so."

Old Man "But," he said, "these things are so."

Stranger "Well then, you could not be too quick in describing these things, since we will pay attention in no careless way, since indeed the penalty is such."

Old Man Then taking up a certain staff and extending [it] toward the picture, he said, "Do you see this enclosure?"

Stranger "We see [it]."

Old Man "It is necessary first for you to know this, that this place is called Life. And the large crowd standing near the gate—these are the people about to enter into Life. The old man standing up there having a certain scroll in one hand and as if showing something with his other hand, he is called Daemon; and he is giving orders to the ones entering [as to] what it is necessary for them to do, as they enter into Life; and he is showing them what sort of road it is necessary for them to walk [on], if they are to be saved in Life."

Exercise 19η

1. ἵστησι(ν). 2. ἵστατε. 3. ἵστασαν. 4. ἵστην. 5. ἵστημι. 6. ἔστησαν. 7. ἱστάναι. 8. στῆσον. 9. ἵστης. 10. ἱστάντες. 11. ἔστησε(ν). 12. ἔστην. 13. στήσεις. 14. στήσουσα. 15. ἔστη. 16. στάς. 17. στήσειν. 18. στήσᾱς. 19. στῆναι. 20. στᾶσα.

Exercise 19θ

Part I: a = 9. b = 1. c = 4. d = 7. e = 6. f = 8. g = 3. h = 2. i = 10. j = 5.
Part II: a = 8. b = 5. c = 9. d = 10. e = 1. f = 4. g = 6. h = 2. i = 7. j = 3.

Exercise 19ι

1. They revolt/are revolting from the king. 2. They made/appointed the man general.
3. The woman got/fell into a state of fear = became afraid. 4. We got into a state of flight

= We fled. 5. You appointed/made Theseus king. 6. We revolted from our masters.
7. Today I was appointed/was made priest of Dionysus.   8. Who set up/established the
laws? 9. We put the enemy (in)to flight. 10. Why did you make/appoint this man
general?

Exercise 19κ

1. I stand away from; I revolt from. 2. deserted. 3. fear; panic. 4. I signal; I sign; I show.
5. he/she fell into perplexity, became perplexed. 6. most sweetly; most pleasantly; most
gladly. 7. I meet. 8. terrible; clever; skilled. 9. woods, forest.

Exercise 19λ

1. ὁ ποιμήν. 2. καθίστημι. 3. τρᾱχύς, -εῖα, -ύ. 4. παραινέω. 5. ἀγνοέω. 6. βαθύς,
-εῖα, -ύ. 7. ἀναπαύομαι. 8. ὁ ὦμος.

Exercise 19μ

1. ἀναπαύσομαι, ἀνεπαυσάμην, ἀναπέπαυμαι. 2. παραινέσω or παραινέσομαι,
παρῄνεσα, παρῄνεκα, παρῄνημαι, παρῃνέθην. 3. σημανῶ, ἐσήμηνα, σεσήμασμαι,
ἐσημάνθην. 4. κόψω, ἔκοψα, κέκοφα, κέκομμαι, ἐκόπην. 5. τυπτήσω. 6. γράψω,
ἔγραψα, γέγραφα, γέγραμμαι, ἐγράφην. 7. ἀποστήσομαι, ἀπέστην.

Exercise 19ν

The Tablet of Cebes V.

    Stranger "So what sort of road does he order them to walk (on), or how?" I said.

    Old Man "Do you see then," he said, "by the gate a certain throne situated [lit.,
lying] at the place at which the crowd is entering, [a throne] on which sits a woman
counterfeit in character and appearing alluring, who holds a certain cup in her hand?"

    Stranger "I see [her]. But who is she?" I said.

    Old Man "She is called Deceit," he says, "the one who leads all humans astray."

    Stranger "Then what does she do?"

    Old Man "She makes those entering into life drink of her own power."

    Stranger "What is this drink?"

    Old Man "Error," he said, "and ignorance."

    Stranger "Then what?"

    Old Man "After drinking this, they journey into Life."

    Stranger "So do all people drink error or not?"

ANSWERS: CHAPTER 20

Exercise 20α

1. δείκνῦσι(ν). 2. δείκνυτε. 3. ἐδείκνῡν. 4. δείκνυμεν. 5. δεικνύναι. 6. δείξετε.
7. ἐδείκνῡ. 8. ἔδειξε(ν). 9. δείξατε. 10. δείξομεν.

Exercise 20β

1. ἔζευξας. 2. ἐζεύξατε. 3. ζεύξεις. 4. ζεύγνυτε. 5. ἐζεύγνυτε. 6. ζευγνῦᾱσι(ν).
7. ζεύξειν. 8. ζευγνύς. 9. ζεύξᾱς. 10. ζεῦξαι.

Exercise 20γ

a= 5. b = 7. c = 1. d = 10. e = 6. f = 8. g = 2. h = 3. i = 9. j = 4.

Exercise 20δ

1. suddenly. 2. size. 3. within, inside. 4. I look down on. 5. place. 6. down; below. 7. it is
pleasing. 8. safe.

Exercise 20ε

1. δείκνῡμι. 2. ἄνω. 3. τὸ αἷμα. 4. λίθινος, -η, -ον. 5. δήπου. 6. τὸ τέκνον.
7. ὁ λέων. 8. αἱ Ἐρῑνύες.

Exercise 20ζ

The Tablet of Cebes VI.

Old Man "All people drink," he said, "but some [drink] more, others less. But still don't you see within the gate a certain number of other women, having various shapes?"

Stranger "I see."

Old Man "They, then, are called Opinions and Desires and Pleasures. When(ever) the crowd enters, they leap up and embrace each one, then they lead [them] away."

Stranger "Where do they lead them away?"

Old Man "Some [lead them] to salvation," he said, "others to perdition through/because of deceit."

Stranger "O sir, how dangerous you say the drink [to be]!"

Old Man "And indeed," he said, "all [the women] promise that they will lead [them] to the best things and to a happy and profitable life. But they, on account of the ignorance and error that they have drunk from Deceit, do not find of what sort the true road in Life is, but they wander at random, as you see also the ones going in earlier how they are led around to wherever it happens/at random."

Exercise 20η

1. ἀρέσει, ἤρεσε. 2. δείξω, ἔδειξα, δέδειχα, δέδειγμαι, ἐδείχθην. 3. κατόψομαι, κατεῖδον. 4. φεύξομαι, ἔφυγον, πέφευγα. 5. ἄξω, ἤγαγον, ἦχα, ἦγμαι, ἤχθην. 6. πρᾱ́ξω, ἔπρᾱξα, πέπρᾱγα, πέπρᾱγμαι, ἐπρᾱ́χθην.

Exercise 20θ

1. εἷσαν. 2. ἥσουσι(ν). 3. εἷτε. 4. ἷεσαν. 5. ἵην. 6. ἕτε. 7. ἵησι(ν). 8. ἥσεις. 9. ἥσει. 10. ἱέντες. 11. ἵετε. 12. ἱέναι. 13. εἷναι. 14. ἷεμεν. 15. ἥσειν.

Exercise 20ι

1. ἵεντο. 2. ἵεμαι. 3. ἵεσθαι. 4. ἱέμην. 5. ἵεσθε. 6. ἱεμένη. 7. ἵενται.

Exercise 20κ

a = 2. b = 4. c = 6. d = 1. e = 5. f = 3.

Exercise 20λ

a = 5. b = 1. c = 4. d = 3. e = 2. f = 6.

Exercise 20μ

1. The men were escaping our notice sleeping. / The men were sleeping without our noticing it. 2. The men happened to be sleeping. / The men, as it chanced, were sleeping. 3. The slave appears/seems to be working. 4. The slaves are shown to be/are clearly working. 5. We anticipated our friends in returning home. / We returned home before our friends did. 6. I escaped my master's notice coming into the house. / I came into the house without my master noticing. 7. The girl anticipates you in bringing the water. / The girl brings the water before you do. 8. You happen to be here at the right time. / By chance you are here at the right time.

Exercise 20ν

1. I let go, release; I send; I throw. 2. some. 3. I escape someone's notice. 4. far, by far. 5. anger. 6. I pity. 7. I throw (at). 8. toward, in the direction of. 9. I go past; I pass in, enter; I come forward (to speak).

Exercise 20ξ

1. κρύπτω. 2. τήμερον. 3. ἵημι or ἀφίημι. 4. δειπνέω. 5. μή. 6. ἐπί (+ acc.). 7. συνίημι. 8. προέρχομαι. 9. ἔξω.

Exercise 20ο

1. ἥσω, ἧκα, εἷκα, εἷμαι, εἵθην. 2. κρύψω, ἔκρυψα, κέκρυμμαι, ἐκρύφθην. 3. λήσω, ἔλαθον, λέληθα. 4. διώξω or διώξομαι, ἐδίωξα, δεδίωχα, ἐδιώχθην. 5. φυλάξω, ἐφύλαξα, πεφύλαχα, πεφύλαγμαι, ἐφυλάχθην. 6. δόξω, ἔδοξα, δέδογμαι, ἐδόχθην. 7. εὔξομαι, ηὐξάμην, ηὗγμαι. 8. οἰκτιρῶ, ᾤκτιρα.

Exercise 20π

The Tablet of Cebes VII.

Stranger "I see these [men]," I said. "And that woman—who is [she], the one like a blind [person] and seeming to be someone insane and standing on a certain round rock?"

Old Man "She is called Fortune," he said; "and she is not only blind and insane, but also deaf."

Stranger "What task [work] does she have?"

Old Man "She goes around everywhere," he said; "and from some [people] she seizes their possessions and gives them to others; but from the same people she again takes away right away [those things] that she has given and gives [them] to others at random and with no security. Therefore, even her sign well reveals her nature."

Stranger "Of what sort [is] this [sign]?" I said.

Old Man "[The sign is] that she stands on a round rock."

Stranger "Then what does this show?"

Old Man "[It shows that] neither safe nor firm/secure is the gift from her. For there are great and bitter disappointments, whenever anyone trusts her."

ANSWERS: CHAPTER 21

Exercise 21α

1. λύωσι(ν) 2. δηλοῖ. 3. φιλῶμεν. 4. τῑμᾶτε. 5. δηλῶσι(ν). 6. φιλῶ. 7. τῑμᾶται.
8. λύωμαι. 9. φιλῆσθε. 10. λύῃς. 11. φιλώμεθα. 12. δηλῶμεν. 13. φιλῇ. 14. τῑμᾷ.
15. λύηται. 16. δηλῶσθε. 17. λύωμεν. 18. δηλῶμαι. 19. φιλῆτε. 20. τῑμῶσι(ν).
21. λύητε. 22. δηλῶται. 23. τῑμῶ. 24. λύωνται. 25. φιλῶνται.

Exercise 21β

1. ἄρητε. 2. βῶ. 3. λῡσώμεθα. 4. ποιήσηται. 5. γραφῆτε. 6. λύσητε. 7. βῶσι(ν).
8. γνῶτε. 9. ποιήσῃς. 10. γένωνται. 11. μείνω. 12. γραφῇς. 13. μείνωμεν. 14. γένηται.
15. λίπῃ. 16. γένωμαι. 17. ποιήσωμεν. 18. βουληθῶ. 19. μείνωνται. 20. λυθῇς.
21. ποιηθῶσι(ν). 22. γραφῶ. 23. ἀρώμεθα. 24. ποιήσωνται. 25. λίπητε.

Exercise 21γ

1. B; What am I to do? / What should I do? 2. E; If you do this, . . . 3. C; Don't go/come into the field! 4. A; Let's hurry home! 5. D; . . . . so that you may save the men. 6. C; Don't do this! 7. A; Now let's see the Parthenon. 8. B; Should we sleep or not? 9. D; . . . so that we may go/walk home. 10. E; If we arrive before night, . . .

Exercise 21δ

1. I sacrifice. 2. 10,000. 3. if. 4. old man; ambassador. 5. I vote. 6. beginning; rule; empire. 7. for the sake of; because of. 8. I read.

Exercise 21ε

1. ἡ ἐκκλησίᾱ. 2. πολεμέω. 3. ἵνα. 4. ἀγορεύω. 5. ὁ ῥήτωρ. 6. νέος, -ᾱ, -ον.
7. βουλεύω. 8. πρόκειμαι.

Exercise 21ζ

1. ἀναγνώσομαι, ἀνέγνων. 2. βουλεύσω, ἐβούλευσα, βεβούλευκα, βεβούλευμαι, ἐβουλεύθην. 3. θύσω, ἔθῡσα, τέθυκα, τέθυμαι, ἐτύθην. 4. πολεμήσω, ἐπολέμησα, πεπολέμηκα, πεπολέμημαι, ἐπολεμήθην. 5. προκείσομαι. 6. ψηφιοῦμαι, ἐψηφισάμην, ἐψήφισμαι. 7. σπεύσω, ἔσπευσα, ἔσπευκα, ἔσπευσμαι. 8. πείσω, ἔπεισα, πέπεικα or πέποιθα, πέπεισμαι, ἐπείσθην.

Exercise 21η

The Tablet of Cebes VIII.

Stranger "This large crowd standing around her, what does it mean and what are they called?"

Old Man "They are called improvident; and they ask, each of them, for [those things] that she throws."

Stranger "So why do they not have a similar appearance, but some of them seem to rejoice, and others are disheartened, having stretched out their hands?"

Old Man "The ones of them who seem to be rejoicing and laughing," he said, "are the ones who have taken something from her; and these also call her Good Fortune. And the ones who seem to be weeping are those from whom she took away [those things] that she has given them before. And they in turn call her Bad Fortune."

Stranger "So what are [those things] that she gives them, that those who take them rejoice like that, and those who lose them weep?"

Old Man "These things," he said, "that to many people seem to be good."

Stranger "So what are these things?"

Old Man "Quite clearly wealth and good reputation and high birth and children and tyrannies and kingdoms and the other things as many as [are] similar to these things."

Stranger "So how are these things not good?"

Old Man "Concerning these things," he said, "it will suffice to discourse even again [i.e., later], but now let us be concerned with the story-telling."

Stranger "Let it be so!"

Exercise 21θ

1. ἴωμεν. 2. ἰῶμαι. 3. ἴωμεν. 4. δεικνύωμεν. 5. δεικνύηται. 6. παρῆτε. 7. παρῶσι(ν). 8. διδῶμεν. 9. διδῶνται. 10. ἴῃς. 11. ἴωμεν. 12. τιθῇ. 13. τιθώμεθα. 14. τιθῶμεν. 15. ἱστῶμεν. 16. ἱστῆσθε. 17. ἱστῶσι(ν).

Exercise 21ι

1. ὦμεν. 2. ᾖς. 3. ὦσι(ν). 4. δείξῃ. 5. δείξητε. 6. δειχθῇ. 7. δείξωμεν. 8. δῷς. 9. δῶμεν. 10. δῷ. 11. θῶ. 12. θῶσι(ν). 13. θῆτε. 14. σταθῶμεν. 15. στήσητε. 16. στήσωμεν.

Exercise 21κ

a = 4. b = 1. c = 7. d = 3. e = 9. f = 5. g = 2. h = 6. i = 8.

Exercise 21λ

1. I fill. 2. private person. 3. each (of two). 4. land. 5. on foot. 6. such. 7. I plot against. 8. power; strength; forces (military). 9. impossible; incapable. 10. I think. 11. last. 12. it is necessary.

Exercise 21μ

The Tablet of Cebes IX.

Old Man "Then do you see, when you go past this gate, another enclosure higher up and women standing outside the enclosure, adorned just as courtesans are accustomed [to be]?"

Stranger "Yes."

Old Man "Well then they are called Intemperance, Profligacy, Covetousness, and Flattery."

Stranger "So why are they standing here?"

Old Man "They are watching closely," he said, "the ones who have taken something from Fortune."

Stranger "Then what?"

Old Man "They leap up and embrace them and flatter [them] and ask [them] to stay with them, saying that they will have a life both sweet and painless and having no bad experience [in it] at all. If someone is persuaded by them to enter into Luxury, up to a certain point the pastime [i.e., his spending time there] seems to be sweet, so long as it titillates the man, [but] then no longer. For when he sobers up, he realizes that he was not eating, but he was being eaten up by her/it [i.e., Luxury] and was being treated insolently. And therefore when he squanders all the things, as many as he took from Fortune, he is forced to be a slave to these women and to endure all things and to behave in an unseemly manner and to do for their sake all things as many as are injurious, such as stealing, robbing temples, swearing falsely, betraying, plundering and all things as many as are similar to these. Then when everything runs out for them, they are handed over to Retribution."

Exercise 21ν

1. ἄρχω. 2. ἰδίᾳ. 3. ἡ στρατιά. 4. ὅμοιος, -ᾱ, -ον. 5. ὁ τρόπος. 6. δυνατός, -ή, -όν. 7. κατά + acc. 8. προάγω. 9. χρόνιος, -ᾱ, -ον. 10. ἡ τῑμή. 11. ἡ δίκη. 12. τοιόσδε, τοιάδε, τοιόνδε.

Exercise 21ξ

1. ἄρξω, ἦρξα, ἦργμαι, ἤρχθην. 2. νομιῶ, ἐνόμισα, νενόμικα, νενόμισμαι, ἐνομίσθην. 3. πληρώσω, ἐπλήρωσα, πεπλήρωκα, πεπλήρωμαι, ἐπληρώθην. 4. ὀργιοῦμαι or ὀργισθήσομαι, ὤργισμαι, ὠργίσθην. 5. θαυμάσομαι, ἐθαύμασα, τεθαύμακα, τεθαύμασμαι, ἐθαυμάσθην. 6. φράσω, ἔφρασα, πέφρακα, πέφρασμαι, ἐφράσθην. 7. κομιῶ, ἐκόμισα, κεκόμικα, κεκόμισμαι, ἐκομίσθην.

ANSWERS: CHAPTER 22

Exercise 22α

1. μὴ ἔλθῃ 2. μὴ οὐ γένηται. 3. μὴ οἱ πολέμιοι ἔλθωσιν. 4. ἰδεῖν. 5. μὴ ἀκούῃ. 6. εἰσβαλεῖν. 7. μὴ οὐ γένηται. 8. ποιεῖν.

Exercise 22β

1. ἐπεὶ ἦλθε: T; D. 2. ἐπειδὰν ἔλθῃ: T; I. 3. ὅστις ἂν τοῦτο ἴδῃ: R; I. 4. ὃς τοῦτο εἶδε(ν): R; D. 5. ἕως ἂν ὁ ἄγγελος ἀφίκηται: T; I. 6. ἐπεὶ ὁ ἄγγελος ἀφίκετο: T; D. 7. ὃ λέγει: R; D. 8. ὅ τι ἂν λέγῃ: R; I. 9. εἰ τοῦτο ποιεῖς: C; D. 10. ἐὰν τοῦτο ποιῇς: C; I. 11. ἐπειδὰν Ἀθήνᾱζε ἐπανέλθωμεν: T; I. 12. ἐπεὶ Ἀθήνᾱζε ἐπανήλθομεν: T; D. 13. ὅστις ἂν μένῃ: R; I. 14. εἰ μενεῖς: C; D.

Exercise 22γ

1. I stand up; I am forced to move; I move; I evacuate. 2. dwelling. 3. when; since. 4. all that, whoever. 5. until; before. 6. I wash. 7. anyone who, whoever. 8. when (ever).

Exercise 22δ

1. εἰσβάλλω. 2. ἡ ἀνάστασις. 3. ἡ φυλακή. 4. λούομαι. 5. ἐπειδή. 6. ὅσος, -η, -ον. 7. ὑπάρχω. 8. ἀνθίσταμαι.

Exercise 22ε

1. ἀντιστήσομαι, ἀντέστην, ἀνθέστηκα. 2. ἀναστήσομαι, ἀνέστην, ἀνέστηκα. 3. λούσομαι, ἔλουσα, λέλουμαι. 4. φανῶ or φανοῦμαι, ἔφηνα, πέφασμαι. 5. ἀγγελῶ, ἤγγειλα, ἤγγελκα, ἤγγελμαι, ἠγγέλθην. 6. βαλῶ, ἔβαλον, βέβληκα, βέβλημαι, ἐβλήθην. 7. φανήσομαι or φανοῦμαι, πέφηνα, ἐφάνην.

Exercise 22ζ

The Tablet of Cebes X.

Stranger "Of what sort is she?"

Old Man "Do you see a little behind them," he said, "up there a small little door, as it were, and a certain place, narrow and dark?"

Stranger "Yes."

Old Man "Then also do women ugly and dirty and clothed in rags seem to be together?"

Stranger "Yes."

Old Man "Well then, they [are as follows]," he said, "the one holding the whip is

called Retribution, the one holding her head on her knees [is called] Grief, the one pulling
out her hair [is called] Distress."

    Stranger "This other man standing near them, someone deformed and gaunt and
naked, and with him some other [a female] like him, ugly and gaunt, who is he?"

    Old Man "The one is called Lamentation," he said, "and the other [is called]
Despair, and she is his sister. So he is handed over to them and lives with them while
being punished; then from there again he is thrown into the other house, into
Unhappiness, and thus he brings to an end [his] remaining life in total unhappiness,
unless Repentance meets up with him, encountering [him] of [her own] choice."

Exercise 22η

1. ὅτι ὁ φίλος/ἡ φίλη πάρεσται. 2. ὅτι ἐπάνεισιν. 3. ὅτι ἡ κόρη/ἡ παρθένος ἀπῆλθε
πρὸς τὴν κρήνην. 4. ὅτι τὸ ὕδωρ κομιεῖ. 5. ὅτι οἱ πολέμιοι προέρχονται. 6. ὅτι ἐγγύς
εἰσιν. 7. ὅτι ὁ δοῦλος οὐκ ἐπόνησεν. 8. ὅτι κάμνει. 9. ὅτι ὁ κύων ἀπέδραμεν. 10. ὅτι
ὁ κύων ἐν τῷ ἀγρῷ μένει.

Exercise 22θ

1. ὅστις ἐστίν/τίς ἐστιν. 2. ὅπου/ποῖ ἐρχόμεθα; 3. τί ὁ πατὴρ ἀπῆλθεν. 4. ὁπόσον
χρόνον/πόσον χρόνον ἡ θυγάτηρ ἀπέσται. 5. ὁπότε/πότε ἐργαζόμενος παύσεται.
6. ὅ τι/τί ὁ ξένος ἐκόμισεν. 7. ὅπου/ποῦ οἱ παῖδές εἰσιν. 8. ὅστις/τίς κόπτει.
9. ὁπόθεν/πόθεν ὁ κύων ἐπανῆλθεν. 10. ὁπόσον ὕδωρ/πόσον ὕδωρ ἡ κόρη/ἡ παρθένος
ἐκόμισεν.

Exercise 22ι

1. wagon. 2. so great. 3. I grieve. 4. spring. 5. never. 6. I give in, yield. 7. so that, in order
to.

Exercise 22κ

1. ἐκτός. 2. ὁ πύργος. 3. ζεύγνῡμι. 4. τὸ στρατόπεδον. 5. προσδέχομαι. 6. οἱ οἰκεῖοι.
7. ἡ βουλή.

Exercise 22λ

The Tablet of Cebes XI.

    Stranger "Then what happens, if Repentance encounters him?"

    Old Man "She takes him away from his troubles and introduces another Opinion to
him, the one leading to True Education, and at the same time also the one [leading] to the
so-called False Education."

    Stranger "Then what happens?"

    Old Man "If he accepts," he says, "this Opinion, the one about to lead him to True
Education, after being cleansed by her he is saved and becomes blessed and happy in his
life; but if not, he is again led astray by False Opinion."

Exercise 22μ

1. ζεύξω, ἔζευξα, ἔζευγμαι, ἐζεύχθην or ἐζύγην. 2. ἀποκτενῶ, ἀπέκτεινα, ἀπέκτονα.
3. μενῶ, ἔμεινα, μεμένηκα. 4. κρινῶ, ἔκρῑνα, κέκρικα, κέκριμαι, ἐκρίθην. 5. ἀποκρι-
νοῦμαι, ἀπεκρῑνάμην, ἀποκέκριμαι, ἀπεκρίθην.

ANSWERS: CHAPTER 23

Exercise 23α

1. τὴν θυγατέρα πρὸς τὴν κρήνην βαίνειν. 2. τὴν θυγατέρα πρὸς τὴν κρήνην
βήσεσθαι. 3. τὴν θυγατέρα πρὸς τὴν κρήνην βῆναι. 4. πρὸς τὴν κρήνην βήσεσθαι.
5. τοὺς παῖδας ἐκ τοῦ ἀγροῦ ἐπανελθεῖν. 6. αὐτὸς πρὸς τὸν ἀγρὸν βαίνειν. 7. τοὺς
παῖδας ἰδεῖν. 8. μὴ βήσεσθαι πρὸς τὸν ἀγρόν. 9. τὰς φίλᾱς ὄψεσθαι. 10. ἡ παρθένος
οὐκ ἔφη τὰς φίλᾱς οἴκοι/κατ' οἶκον μένειν.

Exercise 23β

1. τὴν θυγατέρα πρὸς τὴν κρήνην βαίνουσαν. 2. τὴν θυγατέρα πρὸς τὴν κρήνην βησομένην. 3. τὴν θυγατέρα πρὸς τὴν κρήνην βᾶσαν. 4. πρὸς τὴν κρήνην βησομένη. 5. τοὺς παῖδας ἐκ τοῦ ἀγροῦ ἐπανελθόντας. 6. αὐτὸς πρὸς τὸν ἀγρὸν βαίνων. 7. τοὺς παῖδας ἰδών. 8. οὐ βησόμενοι πρὸς τὸν ἀγρόν. 9. τὰς φίλᾱς ὀψομένη. 10. τὰς φίλᾱς οἴκοι/κατ᾽ οἶκον οὐ μενούσᾱς.

Exercise 23γ

1. I marshal, draw up in battle array; I station, post. 2. garrison. 3. when. 4. I march out against, attack. 5. place. 6. invasion. 7. I sit down; I encamp. 8. where.

Exercise 23δ

The Tablet of Cebes XII.

Stranger "O Heracles, how great [is] this other danger! But False Education, of what sort is it?" I said.

Old Man "Do you not see that other enclosure?"

Stranger "Yes," I said.

Old Man "Then outside the enclosure beside the entrance does some woman stand, who seems to be very cleanly and well-behaved?"

Stranger "Yes."

Old Man "Well then, many purposeless men call this [woman] Education; but she is not, but [she is] False Education," he said. "Those indeed who are being saved, when they wish to go to True Education, they arrive here first."

Stranger "So is there not another road leading to True Education?"

Old Man "There is not," he said.

Exercise 23ε

1. ἡ προσβολή. 2. ἐπιτήδειος, -ᾱ, -ον. 3. περιοράω. 4. τὸ χωρίον. 5. ἡ αἰτίᾱ. 6. τέμνω. 7. ὁ δῆμος. 8. ἡ πεῖρα.

Exercise 23ζ

1. καθεδοῦμαι. 2. τάξω, ἔταξα, τέταχα, τέταγμαι, ἐτάχθην. 3. τεμῶ, ἔτεμον, τέτμηκα, τέτμημαι, ἐτμήθην. 4. ἀρῶ, ἦρα, ἦρκα, ἦρμαι, ἤρθην. 5. διαφθερῶ, διέφθειρα, διέφθαρκα or διέφθορα, διέφθαρμαι, διεφθάρην. 6. ἐγερῶ, ἤγειρα, ἠγρόμην, ἐγρήγορα, ἐγήγερμαι, ἠγέρθην.

Exercise 23η

1. εἶναι. 2. ἰούσᾱς. 3. εἰσβήσεσθαι. 4. παρέσεσθαι. 5. ποιήσειν. 6. δείξαντας or δειξάσᾱς. 7. ἐπανιέναι. 8. ἀφικέσθαι. 9. εἰσιόντας. 10. εὑρήσειν. 11. ὄντα. 12. ἰέναι.

Exercise 23θ

1 = B. 2 = A. 3 = C. 4 = C. 5 = A.

Exercise 23ι

1. ἧς. 2. ὧν. 3. οὗ. 4. οἷς. 5. αἷς.

Exercise 23κ

1. ἐγκρύπτω. 2. συμμένω. 3. συμφέρω. 4. ἐλλείπω. 5. συγγίγνομαι. 6. ἐμβαίνω.

Exercise 23λ

1. going out; marching forth; military expedition. 2. I think. 3. each. 4. I disband; I disperse. 5. stade. 6. I miss; I fail; I make a mistake.

Exercise 23μ

1. ἐμμένω. 2. οἱ Βοιωτοί. 3. ἐάω. 4. ἡ ἐλπίς.

Exercise 23ν

1. ἐάσω, εἴᾱσα, εἴᾱκα, εἴᾱμαι, εἰάθην. 2. οἰήσομαι, ᾠήθην. 3. αὐξήσω, ηὔξησα, ηὔξηκα, ηὔξημαι, ηὐξήθην. 4. λήψομαι, ἔλαβον, εἴληφα, εἴλημμαι, ἐλήφθην. 5. μαθήσομαι, ἔμαθον, μεμάθηκα.

Exercise 23 ξ
The Tablet of Cebes XIII.

Stranger "And these men walking back and forth inside the enclosure, who are they?"

Old Man "[They are] the lovers of False Education," he said, "having been deceived and thinking that they are associating with True Education."

Stranger "And what are they called?"

Old Man "Some [are called] poets," he said, "and others, orators, and others, logicians, and others, musicians, and others, mathematicians, and others, geometers, and others, astrologers, and others, grammarians, and others, epicureans, and others, peripatetics and as many others as are similar to these."

ANSWERS: CHAPTER 24

Exercise 24 α

1. ἀνδρεῖος. 2. σωφρονέστεραι. 3. ἀνδρειότατος 4. χαλεπώτερον. 5. σωφρονεστάτη.
6. ἀληθὴς. 7. ἀνδρειότεροι. 8. χαλεπωτάτη. 9. ἀνδρεῖαι. 10. σωφρονέστατοι.
11. ἀληθέστατος. 12. ἀνδρειοτέρᾱ. 13. σωφρονέστεροι. 14. ἀνδρειότατος.
15. ἀληθεστέρᾱ. 16. χαλεπώτεροι.

Exercise 24 β

1 = c. 2 = g. 3 = f. 4 = h. 5 = e. 6 = j. 7 = b. 8 = d. 9 = a. 10 = i.

Exercise 24 γ

1. education. 2. I study; I practice. 3. small. 4. schoolmaster. 5. I go; I visit. 6. I consider of great importance. 7. gymnastics. 8. glad(ly). 9. lyre player. 10. I live. 11. unjust.
12. so that, in order to.

Exercise 24 δ

1. αἰσχρός, -ά, -όν. 2. παιδεύω. 3. καθ' ἡμέρᾱν. 4. ἡ μουσική. 5. ὁ υἱός. 6. περὶ πλείστου ποιοῦμαι. 7. ὁ διδάσκαλος. 8. τὸ γράμμα. 9. ὁ σοφιστής. 10. διδάσκω. 11. ὁ τεκών.
12. δίκαιος, -ᾱ, -ον.

Exercise 24 ε
The Tablet of Cebes XIV.

Stranger "And those women seeming to be running around like [i.e., resembling] the first women, among whom you said was Intemperance, who are they?"

Old Man "Those are the same ones," he said.

Stranger "So do they come in even here?"

Old Man "By Zeus even here, but seldom and not as in the first enclosure."

Stranger "Then do the Opinions [come in] also?" I said.

Old Man "[Yes,] for the drink, which they drank from Deceit, stays even in these, and ignorance stays and with it indeed foolishness, and neither opinion nor the remaining evil will go away from them, until repudiating False Education they enter onto the true road and drink the powers purifying [them] of these things. Then when[ever] they are cleansed and throw out all the bad things as many as they have and the opinions and the ignorance and all the remaining evil, then indeed they will thus be saved. But remaining here with False Education they will never be released nor will any bad thing leave them because of these teachings."

Exercise 24 ζ

1. διδάξω, ἐδίδαξα, δεδίδαχα, δεδίδαγμαι, ἐδιδάχθην. 2. ζήσω or ζήσομαι.
3. παιδεύσω, ἐπαίδευσα, πεπαίδευκα, πεπαίδευμαι, ἐπαιδεύθην. 4. καμοῦμαι, ἔκαμον, κέκμηκα. 5. ἀφίξομαι, ἀφικόμην, ἀφῖγμαι. 6. δείξω, ἔδειξα, δέδειχα, δέδειγμαι, ἐδείχθην.

Exercise 24η

1 = i. 2 = e. 3 = g. 4 = j. 5 = a. 6 = h. 7 = c. 8 = d. 9 = b. 10 = f.

Exercise 24θ

1. κρείττονα or κρείττω. 2. ἡδίονα or ἡδίω. 3. θάττονα or θάττω. 4. ἐλάττονι. 5. μειζόνων. 6. πλείονες or πλείους. 7. ῥᾷον. 8. μείζονος. 9. καλλίοσι. 10. ἐλάττονας or ἐλάττους.

Exercise 24ι

1. rhythm. 2. I play the lyre. 3. old; of old. 4. intention; intellect. 5. at; near; by; in addition to. 6. soundness of mind, prudence; moderation, self-control. 7. deed. 8. again. 9. I take care for. 10. praise. 11. useful

Exercise 24κ

1. τὸ βιβλίον. 2. ὄλβιος, -ᾱ, -ον. 3. ἡ φωνή. 4. ἥδομαι. 5. ἐπί + gen. 6. τὸ σῶμα. 7. ἡ ἁρμονίᾱ. 8. χρηστός, -ή, -όν. 9. ἡ πονηρίᾱ. 10. ὁ μαθητής.

Exercise 24λ

1. ἐπιμελήσομαι, ἐπιμεμέλημαι, ἐπεμελήθην. 2. ἡσθήσομαι, ἥσθην. 3. κιθαριῶ, ἐκιθάρισα. 4. γνώσομαι, ἔγνων, ἔγνωκα, ἔγνωσμαι, ἐγνώσθην. 5. ἀποθανοῦμαι, ἀπέθανον, τέθνηκα. 6. εὑρήσω, ηὗρον or εὗρον, ηὕρηκα or εὕρηκα, ηὕρημαι or εὕρημαι, ηὑρέθην or εὑρέθην.

Exercise 24μ

The Tablet of Cebes XV.

    Stranger "So of what sort is this road leading to True Education?"

    Old Man "Do you see up there," he said, "that certain place, where no one lives, but it seems to be deserted?"

    Stranger "I see [it]."

    Old Man "Then [do you see] also a certain little door and a certain road before the door, which is not much frequented, but very few travel [on it] just as through some trackless waste seeming to be both rough and rocky?"

    Stranger "Yes," I said.

    Old Man "Surely then there seems also to be a certain high hill and an ascent very narrow and having high precipices on this side and on that."

    Stranger "I see [it]."

    Old Man "Well then this is the road," he said, "leading to True Education."

    Stranger "And it indeed looks very difficult."

    Old Man "Then also do you see up on the hill a certain great boulder both high and steep all around [lit., in a circle]?"

    Stranger "I see [it]," I said.

ANSWERS: CHAPTER 25

Exercise 25α

1. λύοιεν. 2. λῡοίμεθα. 3. λύσοιτο. 4. λύοισθε. 5. τῑμῷτε. 6. δηλοῖεν. 7. φιλοίην. 8. τῑμῷτο. 9. βούλοιντο. 10. τῑμηθήσοισθε. 11. δηλοίμην. 12. τῑμῷεν. 13. λύοιτο. 14. δηλώσοις. 15. γιγνοίμην. 16. φιλήσοιτο. 17. ἄροιην. 18. φιλοῖτε. 19. τῑμήσοιντο. 20. φιλοίη.

Exercise 25β

1. λύσαιμι. 2. λύσαιτο. 3. λυθείης. 4. τῑμήσειε(ν) or τῑμήσαι. 5. νῑκηθείην. 6. φιλήσειας or φιλήσαις. 7. λάβοιτε. 8. δηλωθείη. 9. λίποιτο. 10. τῑμήσαιντο. 11. γενοίμην. 12. βαῖμεν. 13. φιλήσαισθε. 14. μείναιμι. 15. ἄραιτε. 16. δηλώσειαν or δηλώσαιεν.

Exercise 25γ

1. εὕροις; OW. 2. ἂν παρασκευάσειεν or ἂν παρασκευάσαι; PO. 3. παρασκευάσειας or παρασκευάσαις; OW. 4. ὠφελοίη; OW. 5. ἂν ὠφελοίη; PO. 6. ὀργίζοιτο ἄν; PO.
7. ὀργίζοιτο; OW. 8. ἂν δέξαιτο; PO. 9. δέξαιτο; OW. 10. ἂν εὕροι; PO.

Exercise 25δ

1. εὕροιεν; P. 2. ὀργίζοιτο; F. 3. παρασκευάσειεν or παρασκευάσαι; P. 4. παράσχοι; IR.
5. πονήσειεν or πονήσαι; IT. 6. διαλέξαιτο; P. 7. εὕροι; IR. 8. προσβάλοιεν; F.

Exercise 25ε

1. kingdom. 2. I am able. 3. I overturn. 4. end. 5. I entertain. 6. viewing; sightseeing.
7. afterward; later. 8. I am abroad; I go abroad.

Exercise 25ζ

1. κατά. 2. ὁ θεράπων. 3. κρίνω. 4. τὰ βασίλεια. 5. ἡ σοφίᾱ. 6. θάπτω.
7. ὁ θησαυρός. 8. περιάγω.

Exercise 25η

1. θάψω, ἔθαψα, τέθαμμαι, ἐτάφην. 2. καταστρέψω, κατέστρεψα, κατέστραμμαι, κατεστράφην. 3. ἐπιστήσομαι, ἠπιστήθην. 4. κείσομαι. 5. ξενιῶ, ἐξένισα, ἐξενίσθην.
6. δυνήσομαι, δεδύνημαι, ἐδυνήθην. 7. κρινῶ, ἔκρῑνα, κέκρικα, κέκριμαι, ἐκρίθην.

Exercise 25θ

The Tablet of Cebes XVI.

Old Man "Then do you see also two women standing on the boulder, shining and in good bodily health, how they have stretched out their hands eagerly?"

Stranger "I see [them], but what are they called?" I said.

Old Man "One is called Self-Control," he said, "and the other Endurance; and they are sisters."

Stranger "So why have they stretched out their hands so eagerly?"

Old Man "They are encouraging," he said, "the ones arriving at the place to have courage and not to shrink back, saying that still for a short time it is necessary for them to endure, [and] then they will have come to a good [lit., beautiful] road."

Stranger "Then when they arrive at the boulder, how do they climb up? For I see no path leading to them [i.e., to Self-Control and to Endurance]."

Old Man "They go down from the precipice to meet [them] and drag them up to themselves, then they order them to rest a while. And after a short [time] they give [them] strength and courage and they promise that [they] will bring them to True Education and they show them the road, how it is both good [lit., beautiful] and smooth and easy to travel and pure of everything bad, just as you see."

Stranger "By Zeus it is plain."

Exercise 25ι

1. τιθεῖτο. 2. εἴη. 3. ἱσταῖεν. 4. δώσοιμι. 5. ἱεῖμεν. 6. ἴοιτε. 7. δεικνύοιο. 8. τιθεῖσθε.
9. ἐσοίμεθα. 10. ἱεῖτο. 11. στήσοις. 12. διδοῖντο.

Exercise 25κ

1. θεῖτο. 2. εἴην. 3. δοίμην. 4. εἶεν. 5. σταίης. 6. δοίη. 7. εἴην. 8. θεῖμεν.

Exercise 25λ

1. ἀπέλθοι. 2. ποιήσοι. 3. πράττοιεν. 4. ποιήσειεν or ποιήσαι.

Exercise 25μ

1. wealth. 2. sufficient; capable. 3. I despise. 4. happiness; prosperity; good luck.
5. prayer. 6. I drag. 7. strength. 8. both.

Exercise 25ν

1. ἕλξω, εἵλκυσα, εἵλκυκα, εἵλκυσμαι, εἱλκύσθην. 2. ἐάσω, εἴασα, εἴακα, εἴαμαι,
εἰάθην. 3. ἕψομαι, ἑσπόμην. 4. ἐργάσομαι, ἠργασάμην or εἰργασάμην, εἴργασμαι,
εἰργάσθην. 5. ἕξω or σχήσω, ἔσχον, ἔσχηκα, ἔσχημαι.

Exercise 25 ξ

The Tablet of Cebes XVII.

Old Man "Do you see then," he said, "also in front of that grove a certain place, which seems to be both beautiful and meadow-like and illuminated with much light?"

Stranger "Yes."

Old Man "Then do you see in the middle of the meadow another enclosure and another gate?"

Stranger "It is so. But what is this place called?"

Old Man "The dwelling-place of happy people," he said; "for here all the Virtues and Happiness spend their time."

Stranger "Very good," I said, "how beautiful you say the place to be!"

ANSWERS: CHAPTER 26

Exercise 26 α

1. εἰ νοστεῖ, ἔστιν. 2. ἐὰν νοστῇς or νοστήσῃς, ὄψει or ὄψῃ. 3. εἰ ἐνόστησεν, εἶδε. 4. ἐὰν νοστῇ or νοστήσῃ, ὄψεται. 5. ἐὰν νοστῇ or νοστήσῃ, ὁρᾷ. 6. εἰ ἀπεῖ, ὄψει or ὄψῃ. 7. εἰ νοστοίη or νοστήσειεν/νοστήσαι, ἑώρα.

Exercise 26 β

1. εἰ ἐπόνει, ἂν συνελάμβανε; Present CTF. 2. εἰ πονοίη or πονήσειε(ν)/πονῆσαι, ἂν συλλαμβάνοι or συλλάβοι; FR. 3. εἰ ἐπόνησε(ν), ἂν συνέλαβε(ν); Past CTF. 4. εἰ ἴοι or ἔλθοι, ἂν συνίοι or ἂν συνέλθοι; FR. 5. εἰ ἦλθε(ν), ἂν συνῆλθε; Past CTF. 6. εἰ ᾔειν or ᾔει, ἂν συνᾔειν or συνᾔει; Present CTF.

Exercise 26 γ

1. I purify. 2. house; palace. 3. spear. 4. I name; I call. 5. dream. 6. the one . . . the other. 7. unwilling(ly), involuntary(-ily). 8. I destroy; I ruin; I lose. 9. whence, from where. 10. I beg; I want. 11. to, for.

Exercise 26 δ

The Tablet of Cebes XVIII.

Old Man "Then do you see by the gate," he said, "that there is a certain woman beautiful and composed in her countenance, already in mature [lit., middle] and distinguished age, having a simple and unadorned robe? And she stands not on a round stone but on a square [one] safely placed. And with this woman are two other [women], seeming to be some daughters."

Stranger "It is plain that this is so."

Old Man "Well then of these, the one in the middle is Education, one [of the others is] Truth, the other [is] Persuasion."

Stranger "But why does she stand on a square stone?"

Old Man "[It is] a sign," he said, "that the road to her is both safe and secure for those who arrive and [that] the gift of the things that she gives is safe for those taking [them]."

Stranger "And what are they, [those things] that she gives?"

Old Man "Courage and Fearlessness," that [man] said.

Stranger "And what are these things?"

Old Man "Knowledge," he said, "[of the fact] that one would suffer nothing terrible in life."

Exercise 26 ε

1. φονεύω. 2. κατά + acc. 3. ὁ γάμος. 4. ἕτερος, -ᾱ, -ον. 5. φαίνω. 6. ἡ ἀλήθεια. 7. ἐφίσταμαι. 8. ἡ νέμεσις. 9. ἀπόλλυμαι. 10. πυνθάνομαι.

Exercise 26ζ

1. ἀπολῶ, ἀπώλεσα, ἀπόλλυμαι, ἀπολοῦμαι, ἀπωλόμην, ἀπολώλεκα, ἀπόλωλα.
2. δεήσομαι, ἐδεήθην. 3. ἐπέστην. 4. καθαρῶ, ἐκάθηρα, κεκάθαρμαι, ἐκαθάρθην.
5. ὀνομάσω, ὠνόμασα, ὠνόμακα, ὠνόμασμαι, ὠνομάσθην. 6. φονεύσω, ἐφόνευσα,
πεφόνευκα, πεφόνευμαι, ἐφονεύθην. 7. πεύσομαι, ἐπυθόμην, πέπευσμαι. 8. φανῶ or
φανοῦμαι, ἔφηνα, πέφασμαι. 9. γενήσομαι, ἐγενόμην, γέγονα, γεγένημαι.
10. γνώσομαι, ἔγνων, ἔγνωκα, ἔγνωσμαι, ἐγνώσθην. 11. διδάξω, ἐδίδαξα, δεδίδαχα,
δεδίδαγμαι, ἐδιδάχθην. 12. πεσοῦμαι, ἔπεσον, πέπτωκα.

Exercise 26η

1. the field; Direct Object. 2. very quickly, most quickly; Adverbial. 3. with respect to his
eyes; Respect. 4. for twenty days; Duration of Time. 5. It being allowed, Since it is
permitted; Absolute. 6. four stades; Extent of Space. 7. with respect to his race; Respect.
8. Why? Adverbial. 9. very much; Adverbial. 10. It being necessary, Since it was
necessary; Absolute.

Exercise 26θ

The Tablet of Cebes XIX.

    Stranger "O Heracles how beautiful [are] the gifts," I said. "But why [for the sake
of what] does she stand outside the enclosure like this?"
    Old Man "So that she may heal the ones arriving," he said, "and make [them] drink
her purifying power. Then when they are purified, she leads these [people] thus to the
Virtues."
    Stranger "How [is] this?" I said, "for I do not understand."
    Old Man "But you will understand," he said. "As if/As it were, if someone should
happen to be extremely ill, surely having gone [lit., having become] to a doctor he would
first throw out the things causing the illness with purgatives, then thus the doctor would
bring him into recovery and health, but if he were not to comply with [those things] that
[the doctor] was ordering, surely he would reasonably be rejected and would perish [lit.,
having been reasonably rejected, he would perish] with [lit., by] the disease."
    Stranger "I understand these things," I said.
    Old Man "Well then, in the same way," he said, "when someone arrives at
Education, she heals him and makes him drink of her own power, so that she may first
purify [him] and cast out all the bad things, as many as he had when he came [lit., as
many as he came having]."
    Stranger "Of what sort [are] these?"
    Old Man "Ignorance and error, which he had drunk from Deceit, and boastfulness
and desire and intemperance and wrath and greed and all the remaining things, with
which he was filled up in the first enclosure."

Exercise 26ι

1. The oxen must be yoked together. 2. Your friends must be called by you. / You must
call your friends. 3. It is necessary for us to run. / We must run. 4. It is necessary for you
to walk to the spring. / You must walk to the spring. 5. This must not be done by me. /
I must not do this.

Exercise 26κ

1. I send for. 2. cowardice. 3. what kind of? 4. murder. 5. X is a care to; there is a care to
X for Y. 6. when; since. 7. beast, wild beast. 8. I set loose; I let go.

Exercise 26λ

1. ὁ φύλαξ. 2. ἡ ἄγρα. 3. ἀποφαίνω. 4. ὁ κύκλος. 5. ἡ ἀθῡμίᾱ. 6. χαρίζομαι. 7. ἡ φήμη.
8. πρός.

Exercise 26μ

1. μελήσει, ἐμέλησε, μεμέληκε. 2. χαριοῦμαι, ἐχαρισάμην, κεχάρισμαι. 3. διαφθερῶ,

διέφθειρα, διέφθαρκα or διέφθορα, διέφθαρμαι, διεφθάρην. 4. γενήσομαι, ἐγενόμην, γέγονα, γεγένημαι. 5. ἐγερῶ, ἤγειρα, ἠγρόμην, ἐγρήγορα, ἐγήγερμαι, ἠγέρθην. 6. λείψω, ἔλιπον, λέλοιπα, λέλειμμαι, ἐλείφθην.

ANSWERS: CHAPTER 27

Exercise 27 α
1. λελυμένη. 2. πεφοβημένη. 3. πεφιλημένᾱς. 4. πεποιημένα. 5. τετῑμημένοι.
6. λελυμένος.

Exercise 27 β
1. Pf. λέλυται; Plpf. ἐλέλυτο. 2. Pf. λέλυσθε; Plpf. ἐλέλυσθε. 3. Pf. πεφίλημαι; Plpf. ἐπεφιλήμην. 4. Pf. πεφίληνται; Plpf. ἐπεφίληντο. 5. Pf. πεφιλήμεθα; Plpf. ἐπεφιλήμεθα. 6. Pf. τετίμησαι; Plpf. ἐτετίμησο. 7. Pf. τετίμηται; Plpf. ἐτετίμητο. 8. Pf. τετῑμημένη ὦ. 9. Pf. δεδηλωμένοι εἶεν/εἴησαν. 10. Pf. δεδηλῶσθαι. 11. Pf. δεδηλώμεθα; Plpf. ἐδεδηλώμεθα. 12. Pf. δεδήλωται; Plpf. ἐδεδήλωτο. 13. Pf. ἀφῑγμεθα; Plpf. ἀφῑγμεθα. 14. Pf. ἀφῑγμένη ᾖς. 15. Pf. ἀφῑγμέναι εἶμεν/εἴημεν. 16. Pf. βεβούλευνται; Plpf. ἐβεβούλευντο. 17. Pf. βεβούλευται; Plpf. ἐβεβούλευτο. 18. Pf. βεβουλεῦσθαι.

Exercise 27 γ
1. ὑπὸ τῶν ἀνδρῶν. 2. τοῖς ἀνδράσι(ν). 3. ὑπὸ τοῦ πατρός. 4. ὑπὸ τοῦ πατρός.
5. τῷ πατρί.

Exercise 27 δ
1. oracle. 2. straightway, at once. 3. I contend. 4. army. 5. neither. 6. I oppose. 7. oracle.
8. to, toward; upon, onto; against; with (i.e., in relation to). 9. I summon. 10. measure.
11. altogether; very; exceedingly. 12. temple offering. 13. I blame, find fault with.
14. some to some places . . . others to other places.

Exercise 27 ε
1. τὸ δῶρον. 2. τὸ ὅρκιον. 3. ἐπέρχομαι. 4. ἄλλοσε. 5. ἀγείρω. 6. ἡ Πῡθίᾱ. 7. καταλύω.
8. ἐπί + acc. 9. ὁ ἀριθμός. 10. διαβαίνω. 11. ἡ συμμαχίᾱ. 12. φωνέω. 13. καρτερός, -ά, -όν. 14. ὁ χρησμός.

Exercise 27 ζ
1. ἀγερῶ, ἤγειρα. 2. ἀγωνιοῦμαι, ἠγωνισάμην, ἠγώνισμαι. 3. ἀντιώσομαι, ἠντιώθην.
4. μέμψομαι, ἐμεμψάμην or ἐμέμφθην. 5. αἱρήσω, εἷλον, ᾕρηκα, ᾕρημαι, ᾑρέθην.
6. ἰέναι, ἰών, ᾖα, εἶμι, ἦλθον, ἐλήλυθα. 7. δραμοῦμαι, ἔδραμον, δεδράμηκα, δεδράμημαι.

Exercise 27 η
The Tablet of Cebes XX.

Stranger "Then when he is purified, where does she send him away?"

Old Man "Within," he said, "to Knowledge and to the other Virtues."

Stranger "Of what sort [are] these [Virtues]?" [lit., "Of what sort these?"]

Old Man "Do you not see," he said, "within the gate a chorus of women, how graceful and neat they seem to be and [how] they wear a plain and simple robe; and further [lit., still] how genuine they are and in no way beautified in their faces as the others [were]?"

Stranger "I see," I said. "But what are they called?"

Old Man "The first is called Knowledge," he said. "The others are sisters of this [woman], Bravery, Justice, Honorable Behavior, Prudence, Propriety, Freedom, Self-Control, Modesty."

Stranger "O most noble [of men]," I said, "how we are in great hope!"

Old Man "If you understand," he said, "and you acquire the habit of [those things] that you are hearing."

Stranger "But we will pay attention," I said, "as closely [lit., much] as possible."

Old Man "Therefore," he said, "you will be saved."

Exercise 27 θ

1. τέθαμμαι. 2. ἐξένισμαι. 3. ἤγγελμαι. 4. ἔψευσμαι. 5. ἔσκεμμαι. 6. γέγραμμαι.
7. ἔσπευσμαι. 8. ἀφῖγμαι.

Exercise 27 ι

1. Pf. λέλειπται; Plpf. ἐλέλειπτο. 2. Pf. λελεῖφθαι. 3. Pf. λελείμμεθα; Plpf. ἐλελείμμεθα.
4. Pf. κέκρισαι; Plpf. ἐκέκρισο. 5. Pf. κεκριμένος. 6. Pf. κεκριμένοι εἰσί(ν); Plpf. κεκριμένοι ἦσαν. 7. Pf. ἤγγελται; Plpf. ἤγγελτο. 8. Pf. ἠγγελμένα ἐστί(ν) Plpf. ἠγγελμένα ἦν.
9. Pf. πέπεισθε; Plpf. ἐπέπεισθε. 10. πεπεισμέναι εἶμεν/εἴημεν. 11. Pf. πέπεισμαι; Plpf.
ἐπεπείσμην. 12. Pf. πεφασμένοι εἰσί(ν); Plpf. πεφασμένοι ἦσαν. 13. Pf. πέφανται; Plpf.
ἐπέφαντο. 14. Pf. πεφασμένη. 15. Pf. δεδέγμεθα; Plpf. ἐδεδέγμεθα. 16. Pf. δεδεγμένη
ᾖς. 17. Pf. δεδέχθαι.

Exercise 27 κ

1. useless. 2. I kill. 3. cavalry. 4. behind. 5. quickly. 6. I endure, I am patient. 7. camel.
8. I spare. 9. cavalry.

Exercise 27 λ

1. προστάττω. 2. ἱππεύω. 3. τὸ ἔθνος. 4. ἀναστρέφω. 5. ὁ πεζός. 6. δειλός, -ή, -όν.
7. ὀπίσω. 8. ὁ ἵππος.

Exercise 27 μ

1. λέξω, ἔλεξα, λέλεγμαι, ἐλέχθην. 2. εἶπον. 3. ἐρῶ, εἴρηκα, εἴρημαι, ἐρρήθην.

Exercise 27 ν

The Tablet of Cebes XXI.

Stranger "When they receive him, where do they lead [him]?"

Old Man "To their mother," he said.

Stranger "But who is she?"

Old Man "Happiness," he said.

Stranger "And of what sort is she?"

Old Man "Do you see that road leading to that height, which is the acropolis of all
the enclosures?"

Stranger "I see [it]."

Old Man "Then stationed in/near the gateway does a certain graceful woman sit
on a high throne, adorned like a free woman and simply and crowned with a very
beautiful crown made of beautiful flowers?"

Stranger "It is plainly so."

Old Man "Well then, she is Happiness," he said.

ANSWERS: CHAPTER 28

Exercise 28 α

1. Pf. λελυκέναι. 2. Pf. λελύκαμεν; Plpf. ἐλελύκεμεν. 3. Pf. λελυκυῖα. 4. Pf. λελυκὼς ὦ.
5. Pf. λέλυκε(ν); Plpf. ἐλελύκει(ν). 6. Pf. λελυκυῖαι εἶτε/εἴητε. 7. Pf. πεπείκαμεν;
Plpf. ἐπεπείκεμεν. 8. Pf. πέπεικας; Plpf. ἐπεπείκης. 9. Pf. πεπεικότες εἶεν/εἴησαν.
10. Pf. πεπεικέναι. 11. Pf. πεπεικότες. 12. Pf. πεπεικυῖα ᾖ.

Exercise 28 β

1. Pf. τετίμηκε(ν); Plpf. ἐτετῑμήκει(ν). 2. Pf. πεφιληκυῖα. 3. Pf. δεδραμήκᾱσι(ν);
Plpf. ἐδεδραμήκεσαν. 4. Pf. βεβλήκαμεν; Plpf. ἐβεβλήκεμεν. 5. Pf. κεκρικέναι.
6. Pf. μεμαθηκὼς ὦ. 7. Pf. δεδηλώκᾱσι(ν); Plpf. ἐδεδηλώκεσαν. 8. Pf. νενομικέναι. 9. Pf.
μεμενηκυῖαι εἶμεν/εἴημεν or μεμενήκοιμεν. 10. Pf. κεκληκώς. 11. Pf. ηὑρήκαμεν or
εὑρήκαμεν; Plpf. ηὑρήκεμεν or εὑρήκεμεν. 12. Pf. τεθνηκέναι.

13. Pf. ἑστήκᾱσι(ν); Plpf. εἱστήκεσαν. 16. Pf. βέβηκα; Plpf. ἐβεβήκη.

Exercise 28γ

1 = F. 2 = E. 3 = A. 4 = I. 5 = H. 6 = K. 7 = C. 8 = B. 9 = D. 10 = G.

Exercise 28δ

1. Pf. γεγράφαμεν; Plpf. ἐγεγράφεμεν. 2. Pf. γέγραφας; Plpf. ἐγεγράφης. 3. Pf. γέγονα; Plpf. ἐγεγόνη. 4. Pf. ἥχᾱσι(ν); Plpf. ἥχεσαν. 5. Pf. ἀπεκτόναμεν; Plpf. ἀπεκτόνεμεν. 6. Pf. δεδείχατε; Plpf. ἐδεδείχετε. 7. Pf. ἐλήλυθε(ν); Plpf. εἰληλύθει(ν). 8. Pf. κέκρυφα; Plpf. ἐκεκρύφη. 9. Pf. τετάχατε; Plpf. ἐτετάχετε. 10. Pf. τετρόφαμεν; Plpf. ἐτετρόφεμεν. 11. Pf. λέλοιπα; Plpf. ἐλελοίπη. 2. Pf. ἐνηνόχᾱσι(ν); Plpf. ἠνηνόχεσαν. 13. Pf. πεπόμφαμεν; Plpf. ἐπεπόμφεμεν. 14. Pf. πέπομφας; Plpf. ἐπεπόμφης. 15. Pf. γεγόνᾱσι(ν); Plpf. ἐγεγόνεσαν. 16. Pf. λέλοιπα; Plpf. ἐλελοίπη.

Exercise 28ε

1. fear. 2. I take up; I pick up. 3. I sack. 4. either . . . or. 5. life. 6. I am caught; I am taken. 7. spirit; god; the power controlling one's destiny, fate, lot. 8. I burn completely.

Exercise 28ζ

1. ἐπιβαίνω. 2. ἡ πυρά. 3. κατά + acc. 4. καταπαύω. 5. ἡ ἀκρόπολις. 6. προλέγω. 7. ὁ ἱππεύς. 8. διαφέρει.

Exercise 28η

1. ἁλώσομαι, ἑάλων or ἥλων, ἑάλωκα or ἥλωκα. 2. κατακαύσω, κατέκαυσα, κατακέκαυκα, κατακέκαυμαι, κατεκαύθην. 3. οἴσω, ἤνεγκα or ἤνεγκον, ἐνήνοχα, ἐνήνεγμαι, ἠνέχθην.

Exercise 28θ

The Tablet of Cebes XXII.

Stranger "So when someone arrives here, what does she [i.e., Happiness] do?"

Old Man "She crowns him," he said, "with her own power, both she, Happiness, and all the other Virtues just as [someone crowns] those who have won the greatest contests."

Stranger "And what sort of contests has he himself won?" I said.

Old Man "The greatest ones," he said, "and [he has conquered] the greatest beasts, which were devouring him before and punishing him and making him a slave. He has conquered all these things and he threw them away from himself and he has overcome himself, so that those things are now a slave to him, just as he [was a slave] to them earlier."

Exercise 28ι

1 = D. 2 = F. 3 = A. 4 = H. 5 = G. 6 = C. 7 = B. 8 = E.

Exercise 28κ

1. οἶδε(ν). 2. ἴσμεν. 3. ἤδησθα or ἤδεις. 4. ἦσαν or ἤδεσαν. 5. εἴσομαι. 6. ἴστε. 7. ἴσᾱσι(ν). 8. ἤδει(ν). 9. ἦσμεν or ἤδεμεν. 10. εἴσονται.

Exercise 28λ

1. εἰδέναι. 2. εἰδυῖαι. 3. εἰδῶ. 4. εἰδεῖμεν. 5. εἰδώς. 6. ἴσθι. 7. εἰδότων. 8. ἴστε. 9. εἰδῶσι(ν). 10. εἰδεῖεν.

Exercise 28μ

1. I groan aloud. 2. instead of; against. 3. furthest; extreme. 4. I take to heart; I ponder. 5. cloud. 6. I have reminded myself = I remember. 7. happiness, bliss; prosperity. 8. I consider of no importance.

Exercise 28ν

1. ἀναμιμνῄσκω. 2. μεταγιγνώσκω. 3. ἡ σῑγή. 4. παρίσταμαι. 5. ἐπικαλέω. 6. ἡ ἡσυχίᾱ. 7. αἱρέομαι. 8. ἀνόητος, -ον.

Exercise 28 ξ

1. ἀναμνήσω, ἀνέμνησα, μέμνημαι, μνησθήσομαι, ἐμνήσθην. 2. ἐνθῡμήσομαι, ἐντεθύμημαι, ἐνεθῡμήθην. 3. παρέστην, παρέστηκα. 4. βουλήσομαι, βεβούλημαι, ἐβουλήθην. 5. ἐθελήσω, ἠθέλησα, ἠθέληκα. 6. μαχοῦμαι, ἐμαχεσάμην, μεμάχημαι. 7. χαιρήσω, κεχάρηκα, ἐχάρην.

Exercise 28 ο

The Tablet of Cebes XXIII.

    Stranger "Of what sort [are] these beasts [that] you are talking [about]? I very much desire to hear."

    Old Man "First," he said, "Ignorance and Error. Or do these not seem to you [to be] beasts?"

    Stranger "And indeed toilsome ones," I said.

    Old Man "Then Grief and Lamentation and Greed and Intemperance and every other Evil. He overcomes all these and is not overcome as before."

    Stranger "What beautiful deeds," I said, "and most beautiful victory! But still tell me that thing: what is the power of the crown, with which you said he is crowned?"

    Old Man "[A power] conferring happiness, young man. The one crowned with this power becomes happy and blessed and does not have his hopes for happiness in others, but in himself."

ANSWERS: CHAPTER 29

Exercise 29 α

The Tablet of Cebes XXIV.

    Stranger "How beautiful you say the victory [is]! When he is crowned, what does he do or where does he go?"

    Old Man "The Virtues, having taken him under their protection, lead him to that place from which he first came, and they show him those passing time there, how badly they pass their time and [how] wretchedly they live and how they are shipwrecked in life and wander and are led, overcome as if by enemies, some by Intemperance, some by Boastfulness, some by Greed, others by False Doctrine, and others by other Evils. From which terrible things, by which they have been bound, they are not able to free themselves, so as to be saved and to arrive here, but they are troubled throughout their whole life. They suffer this because of not being able to find the way here; for they forgot the command from the Daemon."

Exercise 29 β

1. lap; gulf. 2. I send; I equip; I take down (sails). 3. confusion. 4. neither. . . nor. 5. dawn. 6. I come after. 7. breeze. 8. I attack. 9. at dawn. 10. boat. 11. I blow out; I blow from. 12. naval battle.

Exercise 29 γ

1. ἡ πρύμνη. 2. κατὰ μέσον. 3. συνάγω. 4. ἡ πρῷρα. 5. φρουρέω. 6. ἡ ἤπειρος. 7. παραπλέω. 8. εἴσω. 9. ἐπιχειρέω. 10. ἡ τάξις.

Exercise 29 δ

1. ἐκπνευσοῦμαι and ἐκπνεύσομαι, ἐξέπνευσα, ἐκπέπνευκα. 2. ἐπιθήσομαι, ἐπεθέμην. 3. στελῶ, ἔστειλα, ἔσταλκα, ἔσταλμαι, ἐστάλην. 4. ὄψομαι, εἶδον, ἑόρᾱκα or ἑώρᾱκα, ἑώρᾱμαι or ὦμμαι, ὤφθην.

Exercise 29 ε

1. I go; I come. 2. I sink. 3. I send off. 4. preparation. 5. I fall against; I fall on. 6. I equip. 7. trophy. 8. I confuse.

Exercise 29ζ

1. ἐξαρτύσω, ἐξήρτῦσα, ἐξήρτῦκα, ἐξήρτῦμαι, ἐξηρτύθην. 2. καταδύσω, κατέδυσα, καταδέδυκα, καταδέδυμαι, κατεδύθην, κατέδῦν. 3. ταράξω, ἐτάραξα, τετάραγμαι, ἐταράχθην. 4. ἀκούσομαι, ἤκουσα, ἀκήκοα, ἠκούσθην. 5. ἐλῶ, ἤλασα, ἐλήλακα, ἐλήλαμαι, ἠλάθην. 6. ἔδομαι, ἔφαγον, ἐδήδοκα.

Exercise 29η

The Tablet of Cebes XXV.

Stranger "You seem to me to speak correctly. But I am also again at a loss about this, [as to] why the Virtues show him that place, from which he has come earlier."

Old Man "He was not aware/did not know accurately nor was he understanding," he said, "anything of the things there, but he was in doubt and because of ignorance and error, which he had drunk, he thought that things that were not good were good and things that were not bad were bad. Therefore also he was living badly, just as the others spending time there. But now having received knowledge/understanding of things that are beneficial he himself both lives well and sees these, [as to] how badly they fare."

Exercise 29θ

The Tablet of Cebes XXVI.

Stranger "When he sees everything, what does he do or where does he go hereafter?"

Old Man "Wherever he wants," he said. "For everywhere there is security for him just as for one possessing the Corycian cave, and everywhere, wherever he arrives, he will live well with respect to all things with complete safety. For all will receive him gladly just as those suffering [receive] the doctor."

Stranger "So he no longer fears even those women, who you said were beasts, lest he suffer something at their hands?"

Old Man "He will not be disturbed in any way either by Distress or by Grief or by Intemperance or by Greed or by Poverty or by any other Evil. For he is master of all things and is above all the things causing him pain before just as [are] those bitten by snakes. For surely those beasts [i.e., snakes] doing harm to all others up to [the point of] death do not pain those [i.e., those who have been bitten by snakes] because of their having [an] antidote. So also nothing any longer pains this man because of [his] having [an] antidote."

Exercise 29ι

1. experience; misfortune. 2. eager. 3. I encourage, exhort. 4. broad waters. 5. where. 6. I hold back. 7. defeat. 8. I bring (a ship) into harbor.

Exercise 29κ

1. I escape. 2. concerning. 3. wing (of a fleet or army). 4. I escape. 5. I come to X's aid. 6. sign. 7. at dawn. 8. I come to aid. 9. empty.

Exercise 29λ

The Tablet of Cebes XXVII.

Stranger "You seem to me to speak well. But still tell me this thing. Who are these people, the ones seeming to arrive from there, from the hill? Some of them, crowned, make an impression of a certain happiness, and some, uncrowned, [make an impression] of grief and confusion, and they seem to be worn out both in legs and heads, and they are being held back by some women."

Old Man "The crowned ones are those who have gotten through safely to Education, and they are happy at having met up with her. And the uncrowned ones— some, who have been rejected by Education, turn back being in a bad and wretched state; and others, who have been cowardly and who have not climbed up to Endurance, turn back again and wander in a trackless waste."

Stranger "The women following after them, who are they?"

Old Man "Griefs," he said, "and Distresses and Despairs and Disgraces and Ignorances."

Exercise 29 μ

1. ἐπιστρέφω. 2. τὰ ὅπλα. 3. ἀνάγομαι. 4. ὁρμέω. 5. ἐπεισβαίνω. 6. ἀφαιρέομαι. 7. ἀπολαμβάνω. 8. παρά + acc.

Exercise 29 ν

1. ἐπεστράφην. 2. ἀναμνήσω, ἀνέμνησα, μέμνημαι, μνησθήσομαι, ἐμνήσθην.

Exercise 29 ξ

1. opposed; opposite; hostile; the enemy. 2. I anticipate; I do something before someone else. 3. turn; turning; rout (of the enemy). 4. except, except for. 5. I flee for refuge. 6. oar. 7. in disorder. 8. I slay. 9. merchant ship. 10. I wait for.

Exercise 29 ο

The Tablet of Cebes XXVIII.

Stranger "You say that all evil things follow them."

Old Man "By Zeus," he said, "all [evil things] do follow after [them]. Whenever they arrive at the first enclosure to Luxury and Intemperance, they do not blame themselves, but they right away slander both Education and those going there, [about] how miserable and wretched and unhappy they are, those who, having abandoned the life with them [Luxury and Intemperance], live badly and do not enjoy the good things with them [Luxury and Intemperance]."

Stranger "What things do they say to be good?"

Old Man "Profligacy and intemperance, as one might say to be brief. For feasting in the manner of cattle they think is [the] enjoyment of [the] greatest good things."

Exercise 29 π

1. ἄτακτος, -ον. 2. ὑπομένω. 3. τὸ ναυάγιον. 4. ὅθεν. 5. ἐπιδιώκω. 6. ὑπό + acc. 7. ἡ βοήθεια. 8. ἡ ἀταξίᾱ.

Exercise 29 ρ

1. σφάξω, ἔσφαξα, ἔσφαγμαι, ἐσφάγην. 2. φθήσομαι, ἔφθασα or ἔφθην. 3. λήσω, ἔλαθον, λέληθα. 4. τεύξομαι, ἔτυχον, τετύχηκα.

Exercise 29 ς

A. 1. λέγω ὅτι ἡ Μέλιττα τὰς φίλᾱς εἶδεν, ἐπεὶ πρὸς τὴν κρήνην ἔβαινεν.
2. τὴν Μέλιττάν φημι τὰς φίλᾱς ἰδεῖν, ἐπεὶ πρὸς τὴν κρήνην ἔβαινεν.
3. οἶδα τὴν Μέλιτταν τὰς φίλᾱς ἰδοῦσαν, ἐπεὶ πρὸς τὴν κρήνην ἔβαινεν.

B. 1. λέγω ὅτι ὁ Φίλιππος τοὺς φίλους ἂν εἶδεν, εἰ πρὸς τὴν ἀγορὰν ἔβη.
2. τὸν Φίλιππόν φημι τοὺς φίλους ἂν ἰδεῖν, εἰ πρὸς τὴν ἀγορὰν ἔβη.
3. οἶδα τὸν Φίλιππον τοὺς φίλους ἂν ἰδόντα, εἰ πρὸς τὴν ἀγορὰν ἔβη.

ANSWERS: CHAPTER 30

Exercise 30 α

1. I long for. 2. heart. 3. having authority; legitimate; regular. 4. I talk; I chatter. 5. never yet. 6. I abuse. 7. prytaneis = presidents.

Exercise 30 β

1. ὀδυνάω. 2. ἀτεχνῶς. 3. στυγέω. 4. ἐράω. 5. εἶτα. 6. δάκνω.

Exercise 30 γ

1. δήξομαι, ἔδακον, δέδηγμαι, ἐδήχθην. 2. ὀδυνηθήσομαι, ὠδυνήθην.

Exercise 30 δ

The Tablet of Cebes XXIX.

Stranger "And the other women, the ones arriving from that place, both cheerful and laughing, what are they called?"

Old Man "Opinions," he said, "and, after leading to Education the ones having gone in toward the Virtues, they turn back so that they may lead others, and they report that [those] whom they led away then have already become happy."

Stranger "Do they [the Opinions] not," I said, "then go within to the Virtues?"

Old Man "[No,] for [it is] not right for Opinion to enter into Knowledge, but they hand them over to Education. Then, when Education receives [them], they [the Opinions] turn back again to lead others, just as ships having discharged their cargoes turn back again and are loaded with some other things."

Exercise 30ε

1. shield. 2. golden. 3. I perceive; I learn; I apprehend. 4. ever. 5. imposter, charlatan, quack. 6. from. 7. having an evil spirit; having bad luck. 8. I have gone, have departed. 9. yes, by Zeus! 10. whole, entire. 11. bird. 12. I am vexed (at); I am grieved (by).

Exercise 30ζ

The Tablet of Cebes XXX.

Stranger "You indeed seem to me," I said, "to explain these things well. But you have not yet shown us this thing, what the Daemon orders those entering into Life to do."

Old Man "To be confident," he said. "Therefore, you also be confident; for I will explain all things and will leave nothing out."

Stranger "You speak well," I said.

Old Man Then, after stretching out his hand again, he said, "Do you see that woman, who seems to be someone blind and to stand on a round rock, whom [better English, about whom] even just now I told you that she is called Fortune."

Stranger "We see [her]."

Exercise 30η

1. οἴμοι κακοδαίμων. 2. σαφῶς. 3. προσδοκάω. 4. ὁ μήν. 5. ἀθάνατος, -ον. 6. πρόσθε(ν). 7. ἡγέομαι. 8. ἡ βία. 9. ἀδικέω. 10. τὸ χρυσίον. 11. εἰς τὸ πρόσθεν.

Exercise 30θ

1. αἰσθήσομαι, ἠσθόμην, ἤσθημαι. 2. ἀχθέσομαι, ἠχθέσθην.

Exercise 30ι

The Tablet of Cebes XXXI.

Old Man "[The Daemon] orders [them, i.e., the people entering life]," he said, "not to trust this [woman] [Fortune] and to consider nothing secure or safe, whatever one receives from her and not to consider [these things] as one's own. For nothing prevents [her] from taking these things back again and giving them to another. For she is often accustomed to do this. So for this reason he orders [them] to be level-headed toward the gifts from her and not to rejoice when she gives nor to despair when she takes away and not to blame her nor praise her. For she does nothing with reason, but [she does] all things at random and as luck has it, just as I told you earlier. So because of this the Daemon orders [them] not to wonder, whatever she does, and not to be like the wicked bankers. For in fact they, whenever they take money [on deposit] from people, rejoice and think [it] to be their own, but whenever they are asked [for it] back, they are displeased and think that they have suffered terrible things, not remembering that they took the deposits on this condition that nothing prevents the depositor from taking it back. Accordingly the Daemon orders [them, i.e., the people entering life] to be in a similar state of mind also toward the gift from her [i.e., Fortune] and to remember that Fortune has such a nature as to take away the things she has given and quickly give them back many times over, and again to take away [the things] that she has given, but not only [those], but also the things in their possession beforehand. At all events he orders [them] to take from her [the things] that she gives and to go away speedily looking toward the secure and safe gift."

Exercise 30 κ

1. mouth. 2. I pour a libation. 3. defiled; foul; villainous. 4. grapevine. 5. I shout.

Exercise 30 λ

1. ἀνέκραγον. 2. σπείσω, ἔσπεισα, ἔσπεισμαι.

Exercise 30 μ

1. I inform. 2. call for holy silence. 3. blessed; happy. 4. I pour (X) over (Y). 5. truly, indeed. 6. I follow.

Exercise 30 ν

The Tablet of Cebes XXXII.

  Stranger "Of what sort [is] this [gift]?" [lit., "Of what sort this?"] I said.

  Old Man "[The gift] that they will take from Education, if they are brought safely through to there."

  Stranger "So what is this [gift]?"

  Old Man "True understanding of things that are beneficial," he said, "[is] a gift both safe and secure and never causing regret. So he orders [them, i.e., the people entering life] to flee speedily to this [i.e., Education], and when they come to those women, whom [better English—about whom] I said also before that they are called Intemperance and Luxury, he orders [them] to escape from there quickly and not to trust in these women in any way, until they arrive at False Education. Then he orders [them] to spend some time here and to take what they want from her as supplies for traveling, [and] then from there to go away toward True Education quickly. These are [the things] that the Daemon orders. Therefore anyone who does something contrary to them or takes no heed perishes [as] an evil person in an evil way.

Exercise 30 ξ

1. ᾄδω. 2. ἐξόπισθε(ν). 3. οἱ οἰκέται. 4. ἀπάρχομαι. 5. σφόδρα. 6. εὐφημέω.

Exercise 30 ο

1. ᾄσομαι, ᾖσα, ᾖσμαι, ᾔσθην. 2. καταχέω, κατέχεα, κατακέχυκα, κατακέχυμαι, κατεχύθην. 3. μηνύσω, ἐμήνῡσα, μεμήνῡκα, μεμήνῡμαι, ἐμηνύθην.

Exercise 30 π

1. δείξω, ἔδειξα, δέδειχα, δέδειγμαι, ἐδείχθην. 2. ζεύξω, ἔζευξα, ἔζευγμαι, ἐζεύχθην or ἐζύγην. 3. ἀνοίξω, ἀνέῳξα, ἀνέῳχα, ἀνέῳγμαι, ἀνεῴχθην. 4. ῥήξω, ἔρρηξα, ἔρρωγα, ἐρράγην. 5. σβέσω, ἔσβεσα, ἔσβηκα, ἐσβέσθην. 6. δώσω, ἔδωκα, δέδωκα, δέδομαι, ἐδόθην. 7. ἔσομαι. 8. ἥσω, ἧκα, εἷκα, εἷμαι, εἵθην. 9. στήσω, ἔστησα, ἔστην, ἕστηκα, ἐστάθην. 10. θήσω, ἔθηκα, τέθηκα, ἐτέθην.

Exercise 30 ρ

A. Present Particular Condition:

  1. εἶπεν ὅτι ἡ Μέλιττα μώρᾱ εἴη, εἰ πρὸς τὴν κρήνην τήμερον βαίνοι.

  2. ἔφη τὴν Μέλιτταν μώρᾱν εἶναι, εἰ πρὸς τὴν κρήνην τήμερον βαίνοι.

  3. ᾔδει τὴν Μέλιτταν μώρᾱν οὖσαν, εἰ πρὸς τὴν κρήνην τήμερον βαίνοι.

B. Past Contrary to Fact Condition:

  1. εἶπεν ὅτι ὁ Φίλιππος τοὺς φίλους ἂν εἶδεν, εἰ πρὸς τὴν ἀγορὰν ἔβη.

  2. ἔφη τὸν Φίλιππον τοὺς φίλους ἂν ἰδεῖν, εἰ πρὸς τὴν ἀγορὰν ἔβη.

  3. ᾔδει τὸν Φίλιππον τοὺς φίλους ἂν ἰδόντα, εἰ πρὸς τὴν ἀγορὰν ἔβη.

C. Future More Vivid Condition:

  1. εἶπεν ὅτι ἡ Μέλιττα τὰς φίλᾱς ὄψοιτο, εἰ πρὸς τὴν κρήνην βαίνοι.

  2. ἔφη τὴν Μέλιτταν τὰς φίλᾱς ὄψεσθαι, εἰ πρὸς τὴν κρήνην βαίνοι.

  3. ᾔδει τὴν Μέλιτταν τὰς φίλᾱς ὀψομένην, εἰ πρὸς τὴν κρήνην βαίνοι.

D. Future Less Vivid Condition:

  1. εἶπεν ὅτι ὁ Φίλιππος τοὺς φίλους ἂν ἴδοι, εἰ πρὸς τὴν ἀγορὰν βαίη.

2. ἔφη τὸν Φίλιππον τοὺς φίλους ἂν ἰδεῖν, εἰ πρὸς τὴν ἀγορὰν βαίη.
3. ᾔδει τὸν Φίλιππον τοὺς φίλους ἂν ἰδόντα, εἰ πρὸς τὴν ἀγορὰν βαίη.

Answers: Supplementary Grammar Exercise 1

1. βληθείς: AOR. PART. 2. ἐξέπλησε: AOR. IND. 3. ἔθεε: IMP. IND.—ONGOING.
4. ἀγγελέων: FUT. PART. 5. γεγονός: PERF. PART. 6. ἀφικόμενος: AOR. PART.
7. ἐσήμηνέ: AOR. IND. 8. συντεταραγμένος: PERF. PART. 9. ἐδεινολογέετο: IMP. IND.—
ONGOING. 10. ἀπέκτεινε: AOR. IND. 11. ἐκάθηρε: AOR. IND. 12. περιημεκτέων: PRES.
PART. 13. ἐκάλεε: IMP. IND.—ONGOING. 14. μαρτυρόμενος: PRES. PART.
15. πεπονθὼς εἴη: PERF. OPT. 16. παρῆσαν: IMP. IND.—ONGOING. 17. φέροντες:
PRES. PART. 18. εἵπετο: IMP. IND.—ONGOING. 19. στάς: AOR. PART. 20. παρεδίδου:
IMP. IND.—CON. 21. προτείνων: PRES. PART. 23. κελεύων: PRES. PART.
22. ἐπικατασφάξαι: AOR. INF. 24. λέγων: PRES. PART. 26 ἀπολωλεκὼς εἴη: PERF. OPT.
25. τὸν καθήραντα: AOR. PART. 27. ἀκούσάς: AOR. PART. 28. κατοικτίρει: HIST.
PRES. 29. λέγει: HIST. PRES.

Answers: Supplementary Grammar Exercise 2 (translations only)

1. Those on the island were suffering many bad things.
2. The old man is not prudent; for he does not understand the ways of fortune.
3. The men of today are no worse than their ancestors.
4. All wise men were honoring those who died in that battle.
5. The Greeks, understanding the ways of the sea, were able to defeat the barbarians although having fewer ships.
6. As we do not have the resources of war, we can scarcely stand up to our enemies.
7. The ships of the barbarians were bigger and slower than those of the Greeks.
8. The sailors in that ship don't know how great a storm there will be.
9. Did you meet the shepherd who was driving his flocks up the road?
10. Virtue is hard; so say the wise, and they are not wrong.
11. This girl is beautiful. Don't you admire her beauty?
12. Good men help [their] friends, and they harm [their] enemies.
13. Are you speaking the truth, boy? Those who tell lies fare badly.
14. The king's son was not understanding the ways of fortune.
15. We found the city deserted and corpses lying in the roads.
16. The father orders his son to stay in the house, but he does not obey him.
17. These girls were braver than those young men.
18. The messenger related everything to all the citizens.
19. The king himself will come into the agora to announce these things to the citizens.
20. The king groaning heavily [lit., many things] buried his own son.

Answers: Supplementary Grammar Exercise 3

1. ὁ <u>Κροῖσος</u> φοβούμενος μὴ <u>δόρατι</u> βληθείη ὁ παῖς, ἐκέλευσεν αὐτὸν <u>μάχης</u> ἀπέχειν.

    ὁ Κροῖσος: nominative subject

    δόρατι: dative of means or instrument

    μάχης: genitive of separation

2. ἀνήρ τις, Φρύγιος <u>τὸ γένος</u>, ἐς τὰς Σάρδῑς ἀφικόμενος, <u>τὸν Κροῖσον κάθαρσιν</u> ᾔτησεν.

    τὸ γένος: accusative of respect

    τὸν Κροῖσον κάθαρσιν: double accusative

3. δόξαν καθῆραι αὐτόν, ὁ Κροῖσος ἐπυνθάνετο πόθεν ἥκει καὶ <u>τίνος πατρὸς</u>
    ἐγένετο.

    δόξαν: accusative absolute

    τίνος πατρὸς: genitive of origin

4. <u>δέον</u> τὸ ἀληθὲς εἰπεῖν, ὁ ξένος ἀπεκρίνατο· "<u>Γορδίου</u> μὲν ἐγενόμην, ὄνομα δὲ <u>μοί</u>
    ἐστιν ˝Αδρηστος, φονεύσᾱς δὲ τὸν <u>ἐμαυτοῦ</u> ἀδελφὸν ἄκων πάρειμι."

    δέον: accusative absolute

    Γορδίου: genitive of origin

    μοι: dative of the possessor

    ˝Αδρηστος: nominative complement

    ἐμαυτοῦ: genitive of possession

5. ὁ δὲ Κροῖσος δεξάμενος αὐτόν, "ἥκεις ἐς φίλους," ἔφη. "μένε οὖν ἐν <u>τοῖς</u>
    <u>ἡμετέροις οἰκίοις</u> <u>ὅσον</u> ἂν χρόνον βούλῃ."

    τοῖς ἡμετέροις οἰκίοις: dative with preposition

    ὅσον . . . χρόνον: accusative of duration of time

6. ἄγγελοί τινες, Μῡσοὶ <u>τὸ γένος</u>, ἐς <u>Σάρδῑς</u> ἀφικόμενοι, "πέμψον <u>ἡμῖν</u>, ὦ βασιλεῦ,"
    ἔφασαν, "<u>τὸν σὸν παῖδα</u> ἵνα μέγα θηρίον <u>τῆς χώρᾱς</u> ἐξέλωμεν."

    τὸ γένος: accusative of respect

    Σάρδῑς: accusative with preposition

    ἡμῖν: dative of indirect object

    τὸν σὸν παῖδα: accusative of direct object

    τῆς χώρᾱς: genitive of separation

7. ὁ δὲ Κροῖσος, "δύο μὲν παῖδές εἰσί <u>μοι</u>, ὧν οὗτος, ˝Ατυς <u>ὀνόματι</u>, <u>πολλῷ</u>
    φιλαίτερος ἐστί μοι <u>τοῦ ἑτέρου</u>."

    μοι: dative of the possessor

    ὀνόματι: dative of respect

    πολλῷ: dative of degree of difference

    τοῦ ἑτέρου: genitive of comparison

8. "οὐ μὰ <u>Δία</u> πέμψω αὐτὸν <u>ὑμῖν</u>, τὸν δὲ ˝Αδρηστον πέμψω <u>νεᾱνίαις</u> τε καὶ <u>κυσίν.</u>"

    Δία: accusative in oath after μά

    ὑμῖν: dative of indirect object

    νεᾱνίαις . . . κυσίν: dative of accompaniment

9. ὁ δὲ παῖς, <u>οὐδὲν</u> φοβούμενος τὴν ἄγρᾱν, τὸν πατέρα ἔπεισεν ἑαυτὸν πέμψαι· "οὐ
    γάρ," φησίν, "πρὸς ἄνδρας <u>ἡμῖν</u> γίγνεται ἡ μάχη."

    οὐδὲν: adverbial accusative

    ἡμῖν: dative of the person concerned or interested (possessive)

10. <u>ἐξὸν</u> οὖν ἐς τὴν ἄγρᾱν ἰέναι, ὁ ˝Ατῡς <u>τριῶν ἡμερῶν</u> ὡρμήθη μετὰ τῶν λογάδων
    νεᾱνιῶν

    ἐξὸν: accusative absolute

    τριῶν ἡμερῶν: genitive of time within which

11. <u>μακρὰν</u> οὖν <u>ὁδὸν</u> πορευθέντες καὶ τὸ θηρίον εὑρόντες, <u>τῶν νεᾱνιῶν</u> οἱ μὲν αὐτὸ
    ἐδίωκον, οἱ δὲ περιστάντες κύκλῳ ἐσηκόντιζον.

    μακρὰν . . . ὁδὸν: accusative of extent of space

    τῶν νεᾱνιῶν: partitive genitive

12. ὁ δὲ Ἄδρηστος ἀκοντίζων <u>τοῦ ὑός</u>, <u>τοῦ</u> μὲν ἁμαρτάνει, τυγχάνει δὲ <u>τοῦ</u>
     Κροίσου <u>παιδός</u>.

> τοῦ ὑός: genitive with verb
>
> τοῦ: genitive with verb
>
> τοῦ . . . παιδός: genitive with verb

13. <u>τοῦ</u> δὲ <u>κακοῦ</u> οὐκ Ἄδρηστος αἴτιος ἦν ἀλλὰ θεῶν τις.

> τοῦ . . . κακοῦ: genitive with adjective

Answers: Supplementary Grammar Exercise 4 (translations only)

1. "How did you do this?" "I did it like this, as my father advised."
2. "Where have you come from?" "I don't know from where; for I missed the road."
3. "Where does the old man live?" "The old man lives there, near the river, where I saw him recently."
4. "In what kind of ship did you sail here?" "I sailed in the kind of ship that (such as) brings grain from Egypt."
5. We waited in the agora as long as [as much time as] you ordered.
6. The girl asked her father where he was going; but he was not wishing to answer.
7. "When will mother return home?" "Mother will return home when she finds father."
8. "How many ships do the enemy have?" "I don't know how many ships they have."
9. The hoplite carried a spear in one hand and a sword in the other.
10. The general sent two messengers, but they do not say the same things; which one are we to believe?

Answers: Supplementary Grammar Exercise 5 (translations only)

1. The young man reached the city before day broke.
2. Before going away, father told the children to obey their mother in all things.
3. We will not try to board the ship until the captain orders.
4. The messengers did not go away from Delphi until the Pythia had prophesied.
5. Before beginning battle, Cyrus told his soldiers to spare Croesus.

Answers: Supplementary Grammar Exercise 6 (translations only)

1. When we arrived at the Piraeus, we at once hurried to the agora.
2. There we heard someone saying/alleging that the ships had already sailed into the harbor. But he was lying; for the ships had not yet arrived.
3. When the ships arrive, we will go to the harbor to watch them.
4. So let us go soon to the harbor so that we may watch the ships.
5. How beautiful the ships are! How quickly they are sailing in!
6. Now it is possible to see the ships sailing as quickly as possible toward Salamis.
7. Listen: the admiral has got into a rage, as it seems, and blames the rowers for rowing [as rowing] slowly.
8. Dicaeopolis and his family have prepared themselves for evacuation.

Answers: Supplementary Grammar Exercise 7 (translations only)

1. I was never so stung as now, because the citizens are not here at the Assembly.
2. Let's not stay any longer on the Pnyx; for not even the prytaneis have come.
3. If the prytaneis don't arrive soon/unless the prytaneis arrive soon, the citizens will not wait any longer.
4. Unless you were to speak about peace, I wouldn't keep silent.
5. The herald ordered Dicaeopolis not to abuse the speakers and not to interrupt.
6. The barbarians do not consider the sort of people who cannot drink a lot [to be really] men.
7. Dicaeopolis was clearly aware that the King would never send gold.

8. I wish the ambassadors would stop lying. / May the ambassadors no longer lie.
9. For neither of them can deceive the people.
10. For everyone knows they are not saying a word of truth [are saying nothing true].
11. Since neither the prytaneis nor the people were willing to make a truce, Dicaeopolis decided not to despair but to do a great deed.
12. For fearing that peace would never happen any other way, he sent Amphitheus to Sparta.
13. For he was hoping that the Spartans would not throw Amphitheus out, as he was [lit., being] an immortal, but would make a truce.
14. For whoever does not listen to an immortal, soon fares badly.
15. Although Amphitheus has not yet returned, Dicaeopolis rejoices as if he were no longer involved in [lit., using, experiencing] war.

Answers: Supplementary Grammar Exercise 8 (translations only)
1. Dicaeopolis got to the Pnyx before all the citizens [anticipated all the citizens arriving].
2. When he's alone, he sighs, loving peace, hating the city and longing for his own deme.
3. He has come prepared to abuse the speakers, if they don't speak about peace.
4. Dicaeopolis was angry with the prytaneis for not honoring peace.
5. The ambassadors from the King happened to be present, having arrived from Asia.
6. Dicaeopolis loathes the Athenians' ambassadors, because he thinks they are imposters [as being imposters].
7. He was angry with them, because they had received two drachmas a day.
8. The ambassadors are clearly telling lies.
9. We all know that the King will send us no gold.
10. The barbarians consider only those who can drink the most [to be really] men.
11. Dicaeopolis says that the Athenians are fools, if they expect gold from the barbarians.
12. Amphitheus ran into the Assembly unseen by the archers.
13. Although I am a god, I cannot journey to Lacaedemon, unless the prytaneis give me journey money.
14. Dicaeopolis sent Amphitheus to make a truce with the Lacedaemonians.
15. He is rejoicing as if a peace treaty had already been made.

Answers: Supplementary Grammar Exercise 9 (translations only)
1. Let the slaves loosen the oxen and return home, but let the boy be hurrying with me.
2. Let the girls not be afraid but stay quietly in the house.
3. Let all those present be silent and watch the procession.
4. Let the master not be angry but listen to the words of the slave.
5. Let the young men not fight but sit in the marketplace.

Answers: Supplementary Grammar Exercise 10
1. ἅμα τῇ γυναικί. 2. ἀντὶ τῆς φίλης. 3. διὰ τὸ πρᾶγμα. 4. ἐπὶ δυοῖν δραχμαῖς. 5. ἐκτὸς τοῦ αὐλίου. 6. ἐντὸς τοῦ αὐλίου. 7. τῆς τῑμῆς ἕνεκα. 8. ἐξόπισθε τοῦ στρατηγοῦ. 9. ἔξω τῶν πυλῶν. 10. ἐπὶ τῶν Ἀθηνῶν. 11. ἐπὶ τρεῖς ἡμέρᾱς. 12. κατὰ τὸν καιρόν. 13. κατὰ τοῦτον τὸν χρόνον. 14. κατὰ τὴν Ἑλλάδα. 15. ὄπισθε τῶν τειχῶν. 16. παρὰ τοῦ βασιλέως. 17. παρὰ τὴν νῆσον. 18. περὶ τῇ κενῇ οἰκίᾳ. 19. πλὴν τοῦ στρατηγοῦ. 20. πρὸς τοῦ βασιλέως. 21. πρὸς τῇ ἁρμονίᾳ. 22. πρὸς τοὺς πολεμίους. 23. σὺν ταῖς φίλαις. 24. ὑπὲρ τὴν τρᾱχεῖαν γῆν. 25. ὑπὸ τὴν εἰρήνην.

XXXIII.

Old Man "Such is our story, strangers, on the tablet. If you need to inquire further concerning each of these things, there is no problem. For I will explain it to you."

Stranger "You speak well," I said. "But what does the Daemon order them to take from False Education?"

Old Man "Those things that seem to be useful."

Stranger "Then what are these things?"

Old Man "Literature," he said, "and those of the other scholarly disciplines that even Plato describes as having for young people the force of a bridle, as it were, so that they are not distracted to other things."

Stranger "Is it necessary to take these things, if one intends to go to True Education, or not?"

Old Man "There is no necessity," he said, "but they are useful for going more quickly. But these things contribute nothing toward becoming better people."

Stranger "Then," I said, "do you say that these things are not useful for becoming better men?"

Old Man "It is possible to become better men even without these things, but nevertheless, even these things are not useless. For, just as we sometimes understand things being said by foreigners through an interpreter, nevertheless it would not be useless for us to know the language ourselves, for then we would understand something more precisely; thus even without these scholarly disciplines nothing prevents us from becoming better men."

XXXIV.

Stranger "Do these learned men not surpass other people with regard to becoming better?"

Old Man "How will they surpass others, when they appear to have been deceived about good and bad things, just as the others, and to be still held fast by every evil? Nothing prevents a person from knowing literature and possessing all scholarly disciplines, but at the same time being drunken, intemperate, greedy, unjust, treacherous, and to sum up, foolish."

Stranger "Of course, it is possible to see many such people."

Old Man "How then do these people have an advantage from these scholarly disciplines with regard to becoming better people?"

XXXV.

Stranger "They do not, as it seems from this argument. But what is the reason," I said, "that they stay in the second enclosure as if drawing near to True Education?"

Old Man "And in what way does this help them," he said, "when often it is possible to see people arriving out of the first enclosure from Intemperance and the other Evil into the third enclosure to True Education—people who pass by those learned men? So, how do they still have any advantage if they are slower at moving than at learning?"

Stranger "How is this?" I said,

Old Man "Because those in the second enclosure, if nothing else, pretend to know things that they do not know. As long as they have this opinion, they are of necessity stuck and do not set out for True Education. Then do you not see the other thing, that even the Opinions from the first enclosure enter to them in the same way? As a result, these are no better than those, unless Repentance associates with them also and they are persuaded that they do not have Education, but rather False Education, by which they are being deceived. Being in the state of mind that they are in, they would never be saved. And you then, O strangers," he said, "act thus and spend time on what I'm saying, until you make it a habit. But concerning these same things you must pay attention often and not flag; you must consider other things as secondary. If not, there will be no advantage for you in what you hear now."

XXXVI.

Stranger "We will do this. But explain this, how are all the things that the people receive from Fortune not good—things such as living, being healthy, being rich, being well thought of, having children, being successful, and as many things as are similar to these things? Or again, how are their opposites not bad? For what you are saying seems to us very paradoxical and incredible."

Old Man "Come then," he said, "try to give the answer that seems right to each question I ask."

Stranger "I will do this," I said.

Old Man "Then, if someone lives badly, is living a good thing for that person?"

Stranger "It does not seem so to me, but rather a bad thing," I said.

Old Man "How then is living a good thing," he said, "if it is a bad thing for this person?"

Stranger "It seems to me that for people living badly living is a bad thing, and for people living well it is a good thing."

Old Man "Do you then say that living is both a bad thing and a good thing?"

Stranger "I do indeed."

XXXVII.

Old Man "Be sure what you are saying isn't implausible. For it is impossible for the same thing to be bad and good. For this same thing at any given time would be both helpful and harmful and something to be chosen and something to be avoided."

Stranger "It is indeed implausible. But how is living badly not something bad for the person for whom this condition exists? Then, if it is a bad thing for him, living itself is a bad thing."

Old Man "But living is not the same thing as living badly. Or does this not seem so to you?"

Stranger "Of course, it does not seem to me to be the same thing."

Old Man "Living badly, then, is a bad thing. But living is not a bad thing. Since, if it were a bad thing, it would be a bad thing for those living well, since living, which is a bad thing, would be their condition too."

Stranger "You seem to me to speak the truth."

XXXVIII.

Old Man "Then, since living fits both cases, both those living well and those living badly, living would be neither a good nor a bad thing. Just as cutting and burning do not produce sickness and health for those who are sick, but rather how the cutting is done does, so thus also with living: living itself is not a bad thing, but living badly is."

Stranger "This is so."

Old Man "If this is so, then consider whether you would wish to live badly or to die well and bravely?"

Stranger "I would prefer to die well."

Old Man "Then not even dying is a bad thing, if dying is often preferable to living."

Stranger "This is so."

Old Man "Then the same argument holds both concerning being healthy and being sick. For often it is not advantageous to be healthy, but the opposite, depending on the circumstances."

Stranger "You speak the truth."

XXXIX.

Old Man "Come now, let us consider also about being wealthy in this way, if it is possible to observe, as often it is possible to see, someone who is wealthy in some way, but this person is living badly and miserably."

Stranger "By Zeus, I know many people like this."

Old Man "Then wealth does not help them toward living well?"

Stranger "It does not seem to, for they themselves are worthless."

Old Man "Then wealth does not make them good, but Education does."

Stranger "Very likely."

Old Man "On the basis, then, of this argument, wealth is not a good thing, if it does not help those having it become better people."

Stranger "It seems so."

Old Man "Then, it is no advantage for some people to be wealthy, when they do not know how to use their wealth."

Stranger "It seems so to me."

Old Man "How then could anyone judge this thing to be a good thing—a thing that is often of no advantage to possess?"

Stranger "No one could."

Old Man "So if someone knows how to use wealth well and skillfully, he will live well, if not, badly."

Stranger "You seem to me to speak the absolute truth."

XL.

Old Man "So it boils down to this. It is possible to honor these things as being good, or to reject them as bad, but this is the thing disturbing and harming human beings: that, if they honor them and believe that being happy depends on these things alone, they then undertake to do all things on account of these things, and they do not avoid things that seem to be the most impious and shameful. They suffer these things because of their ignorance of the good. They do not know that a good thing does not arise from bad things. And it is possible to see many people who have acquired wealth from bad and shameful deeds; for example, from treachery and plunder and murder and flattery and robbery and from many other villainies also."

Stranger "Indeed it is."

XLI.

Old Man "Then if no good thing arises from a bad thing, as is likely, and if wealth arises from bad deeds, it is necessary that wealth is not a good thing."

Stranger "It follows thus from this argument."

Old Man "But it is possible to acquire neither wisdom nor just behavior from bad deeds, just as it is not possible to acquire unjust behavior and foolishness from good deeds, nor can all these exist at the same time in the same person. But nothing prevents wealth and glory and success and the rest—as many things as are similar to these—from existing at the same time in a person along with much wickedness. As a result these things would not be good things nor bad things, but being wise is alone a good thing, and being unwise is a bad thing."

Stranger "What you say seems sufficient to me," I said.